Advanced Praise for *Highway Robbery*

"A wake-up call from the front lines of transportation justice to mainstream environmentalists and transportation power brokers alike."

—Charles Komanoff,
Right Of Way (New York City)

"*Highway Robbery* is the aptly titled treatise-cum-outcry against one of the most ignored aspects of our racial inequity—our pricey, car-based policies. Highway subsidies have run roughshod over any notion of racial justice and these authors have laid out both the crime and correction for this discrimination in mobility, equity, and livability in a timely way."

—Jane Holtz Kay,
author of *Asphalt Nation*

"In spite of the 1965 Civil Rights Act, which was to eliminate policies and practices perpetuating racial inequalities, transit agencies have persisted in activities the authors contend must be driven by racism. [The authors] suggest that community groups and coalitions with social equity agendas have most effectively redressed the inequities inherent in transit plans. This book is a must read for urban planners, policy analysts, health planners, government officials, and community organizations interested in reducing racial inequalities, building strong healthy communities, and having transportation appropriately meet the needs of diverse populations."

—J. Eugene Grigsby III,
President and CEO, National Health Foundation

HIGHWAY ROBBERY

Transportation Racism & New Routes to Equity

Edited by
Robert D. Bullard
Glenn S. Johnson
Angel O. Torres

South End Press
Cambridge, Massachusetts

Cover design by Ellen P. Shapiro
Cover image by Digital Vision/Getty Images
Page design and production by the South End Press Collective
This book was designed using Adobe InDesign 2.0 using Arial and Times New Roman fonts.

Credits—Rosa Parks Riding the Bus, 1956 © Bettmann/CORBIS, reprinted with permission. Negro Expulsion from Railway Car, Philadelphia from the Library of Congress, LC-USZ62-45698. Images of the Bus Riders Union protest, MATEC protester, and BOSS organizer Malik Abdul used courtesy of the Labor/Community Strategy Center, the Environmental Justice Resource Center, and the Bay Area Transportation and Land Use Committee, respectively. TOLES, © 1998 The Buffalo News, reprinted with permission of Universal Press Syndicate. All rights reserved.

Library of Congress Cataloging-in-Publication Data

Highway robbery : transportation racism & new routes to equity / edited by Robert D. Bullard, Glenn S. Johnson, Angel O. Torres.
 p. cm.

 ISBN 0-89608-704-2 (pbk. : alk. paper)
 ISBN 0-89608-705-0 (cloth : alk. paper)

1. Transportation—Social aspects—United States. 2. Transportation and state—United States. 3. Local transit—United States—Case studies.
4. Race discrimination—United States. 5. United States—Race relations.
6. Social justice. I. Bullard, Robert D. (Robert Doyle), 1946- II. Johnson, Glenn S. (Glenn Steve) III. Torres, Angel O.

 HE206.2 .H54 2004
 388.4'089'00973--dc22
 2003021033

South End Press
7 Brookline Street, #1
Cambridge, MA 02139
http://www.southendpress.org
southend@southendpress.org

Printed in Canada on acid-free paper by union labor.
10 09 08 07 06 05 04   1 2 3 4 5

contents

Acknowledgments

Foreword by US Congressman John Lewis

Introduction   1
Robert D. Bullard

1   **The Anatomy of Transportation Racism**   15
Robert D. Bullard

2   **Los Angeles Bus Riders Derail the MTA**   33
Eric Mann

3   **Dismantling Transit Racism in Metro Atlanta**   49
Robert D. Bullard, Glenn S. Johnson, and Angel O. Torres

4   **Burying Robert Moses's Legacy in New York City**   75
Omar Freilla

5   **Transportation Choices in the San Francisco Bay Area**   99
Stuart Cohen and Jeff Hobson

6   **Transit Activism in Steel Town, USA**   121
Brian Nogrady and Ayanna King

7   **The Baltimore Transit Riders League**   145
Amy Menzer and Caroline Harmon

8   **Just Transportation**   161
Nancy Jakowitsch and Michelle Ernst

9   **Building Transportation Equity into Smart Growth**   179
Robert D. Bullard, Glenn S. Johnson, and Angel O. Torres

Appendix of Acronyms   199

Glossary of Terms   203

Principles of Environmental Justice   217

Selected Bibliography   221

Resource Organizations   225

Video Resources   231

About the Editors and Contributors   237

Index   241

Acknowledgments

There are a number of persons and organizations we wish to thank for making this book possible. We are especially grateful to Vernice Miller-Travis at the Ford Foundation, Michael Finley of the Turner Foundation, Hooper Brooks at the Surdna Foundation, Midge Taylor of the Public Welfare Foundation, and Melissa Crawford of the Heinz Endowments for supporting the transportation equity and smart growth work of the Environmental Justice Resource Center. We offer special thanks to the contributors who endured the constant nagging about deadlines. Finally, our hats go off to Joey Fox at South End Press for her patience and hard work in bringing this project to completion.

To Homer Plessy, Rosa Parks, and Freedom Riders worldwide

Foreword
US Congressman John Lewis

Four decades ago, I first went to Washington, DC, as a twenty-one-year-old student to begin a historic journey called the Freedom Rides. The Supreme Court had just issued a decision prohibiting discrimination in interstate travel. I was one of a group of young people who set out to test that decision by traveling from Washington through the Deep South, and into Louisiana by bus. The bus we rode symbolized freedom—freedom to travel as first-class American citizens.

Despite the new law, the barriers that had denied African Americans the freedom to travel were still in place. When we rode across the South, I saw the signs that divided the world into two classes of citizens: black and white. The signs read: White Men, Colored Men; White Women, Colored Women; White Waiting, Colored Waiting. As we traveled and challenged those signs, we were intimidated, attacked, and beaten.

Highway Robbery clearly illustrates that our struggle is not over. Today those physical signs are gone, but the legacy of Jim Crow transportation is still with us. Even today, some of our transportation policies and practices destroy stable neighborhoods, isolate and segregate our citizens in deteriorating neighborhoods, and fail to provide access to jobs and economic growth centers.

Neighborhoods in every major American city still post invisible signs that say: "Poor people and people of color are not welcome." The signs may be invisible, but the message is real. We must find ways to tear down these barriers and build bridges to an inclusive future. Sadly, even after passage of the Civil Rights Act of 1964, the Voting Rights Act of 1965, and the Fair Housing Act of 1968, the scars and stains of racism are still deeply embedded in American society.

Dear Universal Athenaeum Customer,

Universal Athenaeum provides online sales outlets for public and private libraries to resell their used media products. By assisting libraries with the sale of former institutional and donated media titles, Universal Athenaeum helps libraries fund collection development, reading programs, storytelling festivals, author visits, homework centers, writing seminars and other events in support of literacy and lifelong learning.

Most of the items we list are in good to very good condition, but items may include brand new copies of books, donations from library patrons, and items culled from circulation in the libraries' collections. Occasionally an item with excessive wear or damage escapes our inspection/screening process. We have found that most customers prefer the opportunity to inspect the item and decide for themselves if it meets their needs.

We want you to be fully satisfied with your purchase. If you find that the quality of this item is unacceptable, please

- contact us at info@universalathenaeum.us
- include your Order ID number in the subject line of your email

We will respond promptly to resolve the issue to your satisfaction.

Thanks for your business!
Universal Athenaeum Customer Service

TO REORDER YOUR UPS DIRECT THERMAL LABELS:

1. Contact your local UPS Customer Service Office.
2. Please refer to Label #02774006 when ordering.

We have come a great distance, but we are still a society deeply divided by race and class. From New York to Los Angeles, segregated housing, discriminatory land-use planning, and unjust transportation policies keep poor people and minorities separate and apart. Suburban road construction programs expand while urban transit systems are underfunded and fall into disrepair. Service jobs go unfilled in suburban malls and retail centers because public transit too often does not link urban job-seekers with suburban jobs.

Even in a city like Atlanta, Georgia—a vibrant city with a modern rail and public transit system—thousands of people have been left out and left behind because of discrimination. Like most other major cities, Atlanta's urban center is worlds apart from its suburbs. The gulf between rich and poor, minorities and whites, the "haves" and "have-nots" continues to widen.

We need to rededicate ourselves to providing necessary transportation services to all Americans. With the same discipline, moral urgency, and righteous indignation that empowered the civil rights movement during the 1960s, we must say "No!" to the new forms of segregation that permeate public transportation today.

In the same way that we fought for the right to vote, we must now battle against discrimination in transportation services. When we remove invisible race and class barriers that divide our society, only then will we have just transportation for all Americans.

Rosa Parks, 43, sits in the front of a city bus on December 21, 1956 in Montgomery, Alabama as a Supreme Court ruling that banned segregation on the city's public transit vehicles took effect. Mrs. Parks's arrest on December 1, 1955 for sitting in a bus forward of white passengers, touched off the historic Montgomery Bus Boycott.

Introduction
Robert D. Bullard

More than one hundred years ago, in the foreword to his classic book *The Souls of Black Folks*, W. E. B. DuBois declared that "the problem of the Twentieth Century is the problem of the color line." DuBois's diagnosis came seven years after the infamous *Plessy v. Ferguson* US Supreme Court decision codified "separate but equal" as the law of the land. Sadly, in the twenty-first century, the problem persists. *Highway Robbery* weighs in a half-century after the landmark US Supreme Court *Brown v. Board of Education* decision overturned *Plessy* and outlawed "separate but equal" in 1954. Unfortunately, decades of court rulings and civil rights laws have not eradicated the historic disparities between races or the discrimination that perpetuates them.[1] The United States remains a racially divided nation where extreme inequalities continue to persist in housing, schools, employment, income, environmental protection, and transportation.

The struggle against transportation racism has always been about civil rights, social justice, equity, and fair treatment. For more than a century, African Americans and other people of color have struggled to end transportation racism. Harbingers of the modern civil rights movement, Rosa Parks and the Montgomery Bus Boycott of the 1950s challenged transportation racism. Later, the Freedom Riders of the 1960s defied "Jim Crow" on interstate transportation. Despite the heroic efforts of many and the monumental human rights gains over the past five decades, transportation remains a civil rights and quality of life issue. Unfortunately, it appears that transportation–civil rights issues have dropped off the radar screens of many mainstream civil rights and social justice organizations at a time when racist political forces disguised as "conservatives" attempt to roll back and dismantle many hard-won civil rights gains. It is time to refocus attention on the role transportation plays in shaping human interaction, economic mobility, and sustainability. From New York City to Los Angeles, and a host of cities in between, people of color are banding together to challenge unfair, unjust, and illegal transportation policies and practices that relegate them to the back of the bus.

From Rosa Parks and the brave souls who risked their lives in the Montgomery Bus Boycott to John Lewis and the Freedom Riders, individual and organizational frontal assaults on racist transportation policies and practices represent attempts to literally dismantle the infrastructure of oppression. Natural heirs of the civil rights legacy, the Los Angeles Bus Riders Union in the 1990s and hundreds of grassroots groups in the early years of the new millennium have taken to our nation's buses, trains, streets, and highways and joined the battle against transportation racism. Transportation racism hurts people of color communities by depriving their residents of valuable resources, investments, and mobility. This book represents a small but significant part of the transportation equity movement—a movement that is redefining transportation as an environmental, economic, civil, and human right.

The need for transportation touches every aspect of our lives and daily routines. The course of one day could necessitate a range of activities: working, shopping, visiting friends, attending church, or going to the doctor. Furthermore, transportation provides access to opportunity and serves as a key component in addressing poverty, unemployment, and equal opportunity goals while ensuring equal access to education, employment, and other public services.

Lest anyone dismiss transportation as a tangential expense, consider that except for housing, Americans spend more on transportation than any other household disbursement, including food, education, and health care. The average American household spends one fifth of its income—or about $6,000 a year—for each car that it owns and operates.[2] It is not uncommon for many low-income, people of color households to spend up to one-third of their income on transportation. This book affirms that transportation is neither a marginal cost nor an irrelevant need, but a necessity.

Highway Robbery focuses on people of color because their struggles unite transportation and civil rights into one framework: transportation equity. Transportation equity is consistent with the goals of the larger environmental justice and civil rights movements. We emphasize issues of justice, fairness, and equity. We define transportation equity as a basic right, a right worth fighting for.

Transportation systems do not spring up out of thin air. They are planned—and, in many cases, planned poorly when it comes to people of color. Conscious decisions determine the location of freeways, bus stops, fueling stations, and train stations. Decisions to build highways, expressways, and beltways have far-reaching effects on land use, energy policies, and the environment. Decisions by county commissioners to bar the extension of public transit to job-rich economic activity centers in suburban counties and instead spend their transportation dollars on repairing and expanding the nation's roads have serious mobility implications for central city residents. Together, all these transportation decisions shape United States metropolitan areas, growth patterns, physical mobility, and economic opportunities.[3] These same transportation policies have also aided, and in some cases subsidized, racial, economic, and environmental inequities as evidenced by the segregated housing and spatial layout of our central cities and suburbs. It is not by chance that millions of Americans have been socially isolated and relegated to economically depressed and deteriorating central cities and that transportation apartheid has been created.

An Affair with the Automobile

Over the past 75 years, automobile production and highway construction have multiplied, while urban mass transit systems have been dismantled or allowed to fall into disrepair. The American automobile culture was spurred by massive government investments in roads (3 million miles) and interstate highways (45,000 miles). Automobiles account for 28 percent of our nation's energy consumption. Transportation consumes 67 percent of the petroleum used in the United States.[4] And over 75 percent of transportation energy is used by highway vehicles.

From 1998 to 1999, US gasoline consumption rose by 2.5 percent and vehicle miles traveled increased by 1.4 percent. More cars on the road has meant more pollution, traffic congestion, wasted energy, urban sprawl, residential segregation, and social disruption. Indeed, not all Americans have received the same benefits from the massive road and highway spending over the past several decades.

Generally, the benefits of highways are widely dispersed among the many travelers who drive them, while the burdens of those roads are more localized. Having a seven-lane freeway next door, for instance, is not a benefit to someone who does not even own a car. People of color are twice as likely to use nonautomotive modes of travel—public transit, walking, and biking—to get to work, as compared to their white counterparts. In urban areas, African Americans and Latinos comprise 54 percent of transit users (62 percent of bus riders, 35 percent of subway riders, and 29 percent of commuter riders).[5]

Many Americans have cars and the majority of American workers opt for private automobiles, which provide speed and convenience. Most drivers forego carpooling, with three-fourths of all commuting cars carrying only one person. Generally, people who commute using public transit spend twice as much time traveling as those who travel by car. Consider that the average commute takes about 20 minutes by car, 38 minutes by bus, and 45 minutes by train.

For millions of inner-city residents, public transportation is the only means of getting around. For them, there is no question that energy-efficient public transportation is needed for easy access to child-care services, shopping, job centers, and health care services.

Routes of Transportation Apartheid

The disparity of fruits borne by various transportation development projects is a grim story of a stolen harvest with disproportionate burdens and costs paid for in diminished health and life opportunities by poor people and people of color. Many federally subsidized transportation construction and infrastructure projects cut wide paths through low-income and people of color neighborhoods. They physically isolate residents from their institutions and businesses, disrupt once-stable communities, displace thriving businesses, contribute to urban sprawl, subsidize infrastructure decline, create traffic gridlock, and subject residents to elevated risks from accidents, spills, and explosions from vehicles carrying hazardous chemicals and other dangerous materials. Adding insult to injury, cutbacks in mass transit subsidies have the potential to further isolate the poor in inner-city neighborhoods from areas experiencing job growth—compromising what little they already have. So while some communities receive transportation benefits, others pay the costs. Some communities get roads, while others are stuck with the externalities such as exhaust fumes from other people's cars.

Public transit and roads are not created equal. Generally, public transit in the US is often equated with the poor and the less successful. On the other hand, roads are associated with private automobiles, affluence, and success. In reality, both transit and roads are subsidized and form the heart of our public transportation infrastructure. The lion's share of transportation dollars is spent on roads, while urban transit systems are often left in disrepair or are strapped for funds. Public transit has received roughly $50 billion since the creation of the Urban Mass Transit Administration over thirty years ago, while roadway projects have received over $205 billion since 1956.[6] Opaque transportation policy obscures the truth: transportation dollars are aiding and abetting the flight of people, jobs, and development to the suburban fringe.

The subsidies paid on behalf of suburban commuter transit riders, when compared with inner-city transit riders, illustrate the extreme lack of parity within transit project funding. Transit providers routinely respond differently to their urban, inner-city, transit-dependent riders and their suburban "choice" riders who have cars. Attempts to lure white suburban commuters out of their cars and onto transit often compete with providing quality services for urban transit-dependent people of color, handicapped, and elderly transit riders. There also appears to be an unwritten rule that the poor and people of color transit riders deserve fewer transit amenities than white suburbanites who own cars. Whether intended or unintended, some transit providers bend over backward to accommodate their mostly white suburban commuters with plush, air conditioned, clean-fuel and handicapped-accessible buses and trains, while inner-city transit riders are saddled with dilapidated, "dirty" diesel buses. Enticing suburban commuters out of their cars will relieve congestion and improve air quality for all and should be compatible with allocating equitable transportation dollars to urban transit needs.

Visions of Equitable Transportation

Much of transportation planning is about the flow of dollars—billions of dollars. Who gets what, when, where, why, and how much is not rocket science but political science. Why do some communities get transit while others are left out? Why do some communities get light rail while others get buses? Why are clean-fuel vehicles sent to one community and not another? Why are higher subsidies paid to one group of transit riders while other riders are shortchanged? What institutional changes are needed to build transportation equity into regional plans and programs? What progress have we made in eliminating racial discrimination in transportation decision-making? What community-organizing and legal strategies are effective in combating transportation racism? These and other transportation questions and issues are addressed in this book.

The Intermodal Surface Transportation Efficiency Act (ISTEA) and its iterations frame the context for understanding the government-imposed political and fiscal parameters within which transportation activists work. Congress passed ISTEA in 1991 to develop and improve public transportation in order "to achieve national goals for improved air quality, energy conservation, international competitiveness, and mobility for elderly persons, persons with disabilities, and economically disadvantaged persons in urban and rural areas of the country."[7] ISTEA also promised to build intermodal connections between people, jobs, goods and markets, and neighborhoods. ISTEA was written to expire in 1997, unless reviewed, updated, and reauthorized. In 1998, ISTEA was renewed as the Transportation Efficiency Act of the twenty-first century (TEA-21). TEA-21 was the largest infrastructure-funding bill ever passed. It included policy provisions for funding highways and transit programs through 2003.

ISTEA and TEA-21 changed the way federal transportation dollars are allocated, ensuring greater local control over what is funded and not funded. They also made advances toward the inclusion of the public into significant transportation decisions via input throughout the planning process. Despite the advances, transportation advocates continue to call for strong public support, public participation, and public accountability for transportation agencies in the development of transportation projects.

With the scheduled expiration of TEA-21 in September 2003, and the passing of TEA-3, the third incarnation of ISTEA was born.[8] Surface Transportation Policy Project (STPP) outlined the four challenges of the TEA-3: "Fix it first; create better transportation choices; build more livable communities; and learn to serve people."[9] Essentially, to be effective, TEA-3 must better involve stakeholders and the public.

Following the Money

The federal government funds most transportation projects in the United States, with most of the transportation funds being distributed through each state's department of transportation (DOT) and the local metropolitan planning organization (MPO) for each city. MPOs are the official planning bodies for regions with populations over 200,000 and have existed since the 1960s. The state DOTs have responsibility for all areas not contained within the jurisdiction of the MPOs; such areas are referred to as transportation management areas (TMAs).

Generally, MPOs are mandated to institute two types of plans before any type of transportation program can be funded: a regional transportation plan (RTP) and a transportation improvement program (TIP). By law, the RTP is a regional transportation blueprint extending for a minimum of 20 years into the future. The RTP must be updated every three years in areas that do not meet federal air-quality standards. The RTP includes a balanced mix of projects such as bridges, bicycle paths, sidewalks, transit services, new and upgraded roadways, safety improvements, transportation-demand management initiatives, and emission-reduction strategies.

The long-range RTP forms the basis upon which an annual short-range TIP is developed. The TIP is a list of projects that attempts to solve a region's transportation problems with short-term solutions. Each year hard choices must be made about which transportation system improvements to move forward and which ones to defer. TIPs must be consistent with the long-range RTP and must conform to various state and federal regulatory requirements, such as the Clean Air Act Amendments and the 1998 TEA-21. The TIP allocates federal funds for use in the construction of the highest priority transportation projects. TIPs must cover at least three years, but in many areas are developed with up to six years worth of projects. Only projects in the TIP may receive federal funding.[10]

The most successful community groups work the MPO's planning process and use the system to get what they want in terms of transportation investments, improvements, and services—from sidewalks to transit stations. People of color across the United States are fighting to get representation on transportation boards and commissions, and to get their fair share of transit services, bus shelters and other amenities, handicapped-accessible vehicles, and affordable fares. Some groups are waging grassroots campaigns to get "dirty" diesel buses and bus depots from being dumped in their neighborhoods. Groups are also struggling to get public transit systems linked to jobs and economic activity centers. They are challenging public transportation decisions as well as modernization and enhancement projects that shortchange poor people and people of color. This book examines some of the steps community-based organizations are taking to direct transportation dollars and services to their areas and at the same time dismantle institutional racism. It also explores some of the practical steps ordinary people and groups are taking to get the government to do the right thing by enforcing the laws that are on the books.

(In)visible Markers

In my fifty-five years as a black male, having grown up in the small town of Elba, Alabama, in the 1950s and 1960s, I can recall the double standards forced onto African Americans by Jim Crow laws. In the South, blacks and whites lived close to one another—though in separate neighborhoods. I remember walking on paved streets in the white neighborhoods that suddenly became dirt or gravel roads in the black community. Many of the roads in the black community did not have street signs, sidewalks, or streetlights. Blacks paid taxes just like whites, but black residents received few benefits.

In the 1960s, I remember the faded "Colored" and "White Only" signs in the bus stations in Troy, Montgomery, Birmingham, and Huntsville, as I made my three-hundred-mile journey from South Alabama to North Alabama to attend college at the predominately black A & M University. By the time I graduated in 1968, the signs were taken down. However, some blacks still would not enter the formerly "White Only" waiting rooms. In reality, "invisible" markers lingered, masking black denial and white privilege.

While most of the overt cases of transportation racism may have faded into history, the last vestiges of racial discrimination in transportation planning have not been totally eradicated. When I travel back to Montgomery and Birmingham, across the South, and to other regions of the country, it is clear that remnants of transportation racism linger. People of color still do not have equal access to transportation benefits, but receive more than their fair share of transportation externalities with "dirty" diesel buses, bus barns, refueling stations, railroad tracks, and highways disrupting and dividing their communities.

Since writing *Just Transportation: Dismantling Race and Class Barriers to Mobility* in 1997, not much has changed. Transportation equity issues continue to be major concerns among low-income and people of color groups around the country. Discrimination still places an extra "tax" on poor people and people of color who need safe, affordable, and accessible public transportation. Many root causes of this nation's transportation injustices have not evaporated in the past six years. Many of this nation's transportation-related disparities accumulated over a century. Even with sufficient resources and the coordinated commitment of the public in partnership with the corporations and the government, it will likely take years to dismantle the deeply ingrained legacy of transportation racism.

Organization of the Book

Conceptually, *Highway Robbery* extends and expands the analysis put forth in *Just Transportation*—using the same environmental-justice and transportation-equity lenses—but incorporating the changes and new developments that have taken place since 1997. One book could never tell the many transportation horror stories that exist in this nation, and this one only scratches the surface of this national tragedy. Of the hundreds of books that cover a wide range of transportation topics, few have dared to treat transportation racism as a central theme. Our analysis exposes the nation's dirty secret and forces transportation racism out of the closet. The authors assembled for this volume come from diverse racial, ethnic, and class backgrounds. Whether activist or academic, lawyer or client, planner or resident, personal transportation experience infuses each perspective.

In nine chapters, the authors present real case studies that call into question the fairness and legality of many US transportation policies, practices, and procedures. They also question the willingness of government to vigorously enforce existing transportation and civil rights laws with regard to race, color, or national origin. The authors clearly show that the nation is far from achieving colorblind transportation planning and spending in metropolitan regions coast to coast.

In Chapter 1, I provide a historical overview of the civil rights struggles embedded in transportation. The chapter defines transportation racism and uses challenges to unjust, unfair, and illegal transportation practices to place it in a historical and contemporary context. This chapter sets the framework for examining and understanding transportation racism.

Chapter 2, written by veteran activist Eric Mann, examines the historic transportation justice legal victory by the Labor/Community Strategy Center and the Bus Riders Union over the Los Angeles County Metropolitan Transportation Authority (MTA). The group's groundbreaking case challenged the MTA's funding allocation, which favored an expensive rail system that served a small and mostly white clientele, while diverting funds from the bus system that served mostly low-income people of color.

Chapter 3, coauthored by Robert D. Bullard, Glenn S. Johnson, and Angel O. Torres, examines transportation equity issues in the Atlanta metropolitan area. Their analysis outlines how racism contributed to housing segregation and blocked economic opportunities for African Americans.

In Chapter 4, Omar Freilla, program director for Sustainable South Bronx, chronicles the role Robert Moses played in creating over $27 billion worth of public works projects in New York City. His analysis details how the construction of highways, parkways, parks and playgrounds, bridges, and housing developments contributed to shaping the way New York City looks today, and the response by activists to reshape and reclaim their communities.

In Chapter 5, Bay Area activists Stuart Cohen and Jeff Hobson describe the development of the Bay Area Transportation and Land Use Coalition and the ways it has merged the environmental and equity agendas. The authors describe some of the successes and obstacles the coalition encountered in addressing environmental and equity issues in their region. They also discuss how various organizations can work together to build a coalition that focuses on a socially just and environmentally sustainable transportation system.

In Chapter 6, Brian Nogrady, the coordinator for the East Light Rail Transit Main Line Park Coalition, and Ayanna King, a native of Pittsburgh and director of the Pittsburgh Transportation Equity Project, describe how decades of government planning, funding, and administration of public transit facilities in Pittsburgh and East Allegheny County have discriminated against blacks and mixed-race communities—and isolated them from economic benefits that accrue from transit-oriented development.

In Chapter 7, Amy Menzer, housing director at Citizens Planning and Housing Association, and Caroline Harmon, an organizer for the Transit Riders League in Baltimore, examine two of the main tensions that surround their work: tension between the region's neighborhoods and the region's transit riders and tension between their dual roles as allies and adversaries of the MTA.

In Chapter 8, Nancy Jakowitsch, policy director at the Surface Transportation Policy Project (STPP) and Michelle Ernst, STPP senior analyst, discuss issues surrounding the TEA-3 spending priorities and its ability to advance transportation equity and environmental justice. The discussion also addresses changes in the legislation that could bring a greater scale of investment in transit, cleaner-fuel buses, affordable housing near transit stations, neighborhood planning grants, and traffic calming measures to make bicycling and walking safer around neighborhood schools.

Finally, Chapter 9, written by Robert D. Bullard, Glenn S. Johnson, and Angel O. Torres, examines the transportation equity and smart growth movement. The authors delineate a framework for incorporating social, environmental, economic, and transportation justice into a broad umbrella of "fair" and "smarter" growth. They see the need for a national strategy to develop and disseminate transportation equity and smart growth messages for people of color in various sectors in society. The authors conclude that more and more groups are challenging unjust, unfair, and unhealthy transportation policies and practices because safe, clean, efficient, affordable, and equitable transportation should be a right of all Americans.

notes

1. Robert D. Bullard and Glenn S. Johnson, eds., *Just Transportation: Dismantling Race and Class Barriers to Mobility* (Gabriola Island, British Columbia: New Society Publishers, 1997).

2. David Bollier, *How Smart Growth Can Stop Sprawl: A Fledgling Citizens Movement Expands* (Washington, DC: Essential Books, 1998), 8.

3. Bullard and Johnson, *Just Transportation*.

4. US Department of Transportation, "Strategic Goal: Human and Natural Environment," in *Transportation Indicators* (Washington, DC: Bureau of Transportation Statistics, December 2002), 120–125.

5. American Public Transit Association, *Americans in Transit: A Profile of Public Transportation Passengers* (Washington, DC: APTA, 1992).

6. Hank Dittmar and Don Chen, "Equity in Transportation Investments" (paper presented at the Transportation, Environmental Justice and Social Equity Conference in Chicago, IL, November 16–17, 1994), http://www.fta.dot.gov/library/policy/envir-just/backcf.htm.

7. http://www.tea3.org.

8. To learn more about TEA-3 and renewing the nation's surface transportation law, TEA-21, see http://www.tea3.org/about.htm.

9. Surface Transportation Policy Project, "STPP Release Position Statement for TEA-3: Coalition Focuses on Four Key Challenges," http://www.tea3/platform.asp.

10. For an in-depth discussion of TEA-21 and TEA-3, see http://www.tea3.org.

Transportation racism was not limited to southern Jim Crow laws passed in the nineteenth century, but also existed in northern states before the Civil War. This engraving from the *Illustrated London News*, September 27, 1856, shows a free black man being expelled from a white-only car in Philadelphia.

ONE

The Anatomy of Transportation Racism
Robert D. Bullard

In 1892, thirty-year-old black shoemaker Homer Plessy was arrested for sitting in a "white" car of the East Louisiana Railroad.[1] His refusal to sit in the "colored" car brought the weight of Louisiana's Separate Car Act—a 1890 act that provided separate railway carriages for white and black passengers—upon him. While Plessy contended that the Separate Car Act violated the Thirteenth and Fourteenth Amendments to the Constitution, he was found guilty. Plessy appealed the ruling to the Louisiana Supreme Court and lost. Determined to fight for his civil rights, Plessy appealed to the US Supreme Court, but lost once again.[2]

In May 1896, the US Supreme Court decision upheld the Separate Car Act of Louisiana that called for segregated "white" and "colored" seating on railroad cars. The *Plessy v. Ferguson* decision ushered in the infamous doctrine of "separate but equal." Reaching beyond the scope of transportation, the *Plessy* doctrine embraced many other areas of public life, such as rest rooms, theaters, and public schools, and provided legal basis for racial segregation in the United States. On behalf of a seven-person majority, US Supreme Court Justice Henry Brown wrote the following:

> That [the Separate Car Act] does not conflict with the Thirteenth Amendment, which abolished slavery...is too clear for argument...A statute which implies merely a legal distinction between the white and colored race—a distinction which is founded in the color of the two races, and which must always exist so long as white men are distinguished from the other race by color—has no tendency to destroy the legal equality of the two races....The object of the [Fourteenth Amendment] was undoubtedly to enforce the absolute equality of the two races before the law, but in the nature of things it could not have been intended to abolish distinctions based upon color, or to enforce social, as distinguished from political equality, or a commingling of the two races upon terms unsatisfactory to either.[3]

In 1953, a year before *Brown v. Board of Education of Topeka* struck down *Plessy's* "separate but equal" doctrine, African Americans in Baton Rouge, Louisiana, under the banner of the United Defense League (UDL), staged the nation's first successful bus boycott against transportation racism. African Americans accounted for the overwhelming majority of Baton Rouge bus riders and two-thirds of the bus company's revenue.[4] The UDL's economic boycott effectively disrupted the financial stability of the Baton Rouge bus company, costing it over $1,600 a day.

In December 1955, on the heels of the Baton Rouge bus boycott and the *Brown* decision, Rosa Parks, a forty-three-year-old black seamstress in Montgomery, Alabama, was arrested for refusing to give up her bus seat to a white man in defiance of local Jim Crow laws—igniting the modern civil rights movement. E. D. Nixon, the highly respected black labor leader who had organized the Black Brotherhood of Sleeping Car Porters Union in Montgomery, bailed Parks out of jail and gained her consent to use her case to challenge Jim Crow.[5]

Parks's action sparked new leadership around transportation and civil rights. Local black leaders met at Dexter Avenue Baptist Church and formed the Montgomery Improvement Association (MIA). They elected twenty-six-year-old Martin Luther King, Jr.—at the time, a little known minister at the Dexter Avenue Baptist Church—as their spokesperson. Though blacks were tired of seeing half-empty buses pass them up because the drivers were saving seats for whites, blacks were fighting for more than a seat on the front of the bus.[6] They were demanding black bus drivers, more stops in black neighborhoods, and the elimination of the practice of forcing black riders to pay at the front of the bus but enter through the back. The MIA, which led the bus boycott, inspired blacks not only to defy Jim Crow segregation on the buses, but to confront institutional racism that permeated all aspects of black life in America.

The MIA organized a volunteer car pool to transport boycott participants. The sophisticated transportation system devised by the MIA proved to be an effective weapon against the Montgomery bus company. In a matter of days, the MIA organized forty-eight dispatch and forty-two pick-up stations, creating car pools that operated with military precision. The Montgomery police quickly began arresting drivers and handing out tickets for overloading cars. Passengers waiting for rides were harassed and some were arrested for loitering. Still, no amount of police harassment managed to break the backbone of the 381-day bus boycott.[7]

In February 1956, the MIA filed suit in the US District Court challenging the legality of segregated buses. Shortly thereafter, King and some ninety other activists were arrested for conspiring to organize a boycott. King's trial made national news and exposed the ugly face of Jim Crow transportation. In June 1956, the US Supreme Court ruled in favor of the MIA.

Martin Luther King, Jr., recognized that racism in its many forms was holding blacks back economically and that blacks were being denied the basic rights that white Americans took for granted. In his speeches, he made it clear that the racism being fought in the Montgomery transit system was not an isolated occurrence, but that racism permeated every American institution.

> When you go beyond the relatively simple though serious problems such as police racism, however, you begin to get into all the complexities of the modern American economy. Urban transit systems in most American cities, for example, have become a genuine civil rights issue—and a valid one—because the layout of rapid-transit systems determines the accessibility of jobs to the black community. If transportation systems in American cities could be laid out so as to provide an opportunity for poor people to get to meaningful employment, then they could begin to move into the mainstream of American life. A good example of this problem is my home city of Atlanta, where the rapid-transit system has been laid out for the convenience of the white upper-middle-class suburbanites who commute to their jobs downtown. The system has virtually no consideration for connecting the poor people with their jobs. There is only one possible explanation for this situation, and that is the racist blindness of city planners.[8]

By linking the unequal treatment on and access to buses with the violation of constitutionally guaranteed civil rights, the MIA and their leaders built on the foundation laid by the UDL boycott in Baton Rouge. The Montgomery bus boycott was a turning point for many reasons. It introduced nonviolent direct action to the black South and demonstrated the collective power of a united black community. The basic organizing principles that came out of Montgomery were implemented in the nationwide civil rights movement and changed America forever.[9] The black masses would no longer be treated as second-class citizens, relegated to the back of the bus. They demanded to be treated as Americans.

The Freedom Riders of the early 1960s extended the attack on civil rights via transportation racism by challenging segregated seating on interstate buses. On May 4, 1961, an integrated group of thirteen Freedom Riders left Washington, DC, for New Orleans, Louisiana. When they reached Alabama, John Lewis and the young Freedom Riders were arrested and beaten and their buses fire-bombed.

In their attempt to test the reality of the *Brown* decision, the Freedom Riders never made it to New Orleans. Instead they were met by angry white mobs and racist police. Nevertheless, no amount of government-sanctioned violence could dampen the spirits and iron will of the freedom fighters. Suffering beatings and fire-bombings at the hands of mobs and police, more than four hundred Freedom Riders had been arrested by late summer 1961 for fighting transportation racism.[10]

The combined efforts of civil rights groups such as the Congress for Racial Equality (CORE), Student Nonviolent Coordinating Committee (SNCC), Southern Christian Leadership Conference (SCLC), Nashville Christian Leadership Conference (NCLC), Alabama Christian Movement for Human Rights, and National Association for the Advancement of Colored People (NAACP) prompted the Kennedy Administration to provide federal protection for the Freedom Riders and forced the Kennedy Administration to take a stand on civil rights. More importantly, the "Freedom Riders generated movement activity and music, helping educate and galvanize the black community for protest."[11]

Race Matters

Although the US has made tremendous strides in civil rights, race still matters in America.[12] In his classic book *Invisible Man*, Ralph Ellison illustrated that white racism not only harms individuals, but it also renders black people and their communities invisible.[13] By one definition, white racism is the "socially organized set of attitudes, ideas, and practices that deny African Americans and other people of color the dignity, opportunities, freedoms, and rewards that this nation offers white Americans."[14] Racism combines with public policies and industry practices to provide benefits for whites while shifting costs to people of color.[15] Many racist acts and practices are institutionalized informally—and in some cases become standard public policy. For decades, it was legal and common practice for transit agencies to operate separate and unequal systems for whites and blacks and for city, county, and state government officials to use tax dollars to provide transportation amenities for white communities while denying the same services to black communities.

American cities continue to be racially polarized. Residential apartheid is the dominant housing pattern for most African Americans—still the most segregated ethnic group in the country. Nowhere is this separate society contrast more apparent than in the nation's central cities and large metropolitan areas. Urban America typifies the costly legacy of slavery, Jim Crow, and institutionalized discrimination.[16]

America's dirty secret, institutionalized racism is part of our national heritage.[17] Racism is a potent tool for sorting people into their physical environment.[18] St. Claire Drake and Horace R. Cayton, in their 1945 groundbreaking *Black Metropolis*, documented the role racism played in creating Chicago's South Side ghetto.[19] In 1965, psychologist Kenneth Clark proclaimed that racism created our nation's "dark ghettos."[20] In 1968, the National Advisory Commission on Civil Disorders, the Kerner Commission, reported that "white society is deeply implicated in the ghetto" and that "white institutions created it, white institutions maintain it, and white society condones it."[21] The black ghetto is kept contained and isolated from the larger white society through well-defined institutional practices, private actions, and government policies.[22] Even when the laws change, some discriminatory practices remain.

Some contend that "racism is an integral, permanent, and indestructible component of this society."[23] Permanent or not, racism continues to be a central factor in explaining the social inequality, political exploitation, social isolation, and the poor health of people of color in the United States. Furthermore, contemporary race relations in America can no longer be viewed in the black-white paradigm. Racism makes the daily life experiences of most African Americans, Latino Americans, Native Americans, and Asian and Pacific Islander Americans very different from that of most white Americans. Modern racism must be understood as an everyday lived experience.[24]

Not having reliable public transportation can mean the difference between gainful employment and a life of poverty in the ghettos and barrios. Since most do not have cars, transportation is even more crucial for the vulnerable population that is moving from welfare to work. Training, skills, and jobs are meaningless if millions of Americans can't get to work. Of course, it would be ideal if job centers were closer to the homes of inner-city residents, but few urban core neighborhoods have experienced an economic revitalization that can rival the current jobs found in the suburbs. Transportation remains a major stumbling block for many to achieve self-sufficiency. It boils down to "no transportation, no job," and, more often than not, public transportation does not connect urban residents to jobs.

Transportation policies did not emerge in a race- and class-neutral society. Transportation-planning outcomes often reflected the biases of their originators with the losers comprised largely of the poor, powerless, and people of color. Transportation is about more than just land use. Beyond mapping out the paths of freeways and highways, transportation policies determine the allocation of funds and benefits, the enforcement of environmental regulations, and the siting of facilities. Transportation planning affects residential and commercial patterns, and infrastructure development.[25] White racism shapes transportation and transportation-related decisions, which have consequently created a national transportation infrastructure that denies many black Americans and other people of color the benefits, freedoms, opportunities, and rewards offered to white Americans. In the end, racist transportation policies can determine where people of color live, work, and play.[26]

Transportation planning has duplicated the discrimination used by other racist government institutions and private entities to maintain white privilege. The transportation options that are available to most Americans today were shaped largely by federal policies as well as individual and institutional discrimination. Transportation options are further restricted by both the geographic changes that have taken place in the nation's metropolitan regions and historical job discrimination dictating limited incomes.[27] Transportation decision-making is political. Building roads in the job-rich suburbs while at the same time blocking transit from entering these same suburbs are political decisions buttressed by race and class dynamics. In cities and metropolitan regions all across the country, inadequate or nonexistent suburban transit serves as invisible "Keep Out" signs directed against people of color and the poor.

Birth of a Movement

The environmental justice movement has its roots in the transport and illegal dumping of toxic waste along roadways in North Carolina. In 1978, over 30,000 gallons of oil laced with the highly toxic polychlorinated biphenyl (PCB) was illegally dumped along 210 miles of roadway in fourteen North Carolina counties—the largest PCB "spill" ever recorded in the United States. The contaminated oil was left on the roadways for four years.

In 1982, the State of North Carolina decided a disposal site was needed for 30,000 cubic yards of soil contaminated with highly toxic PCBs. Warren County, a poor and mostly African American county, was selected for the dumpsite. Over 500 protesters, the majority of them African American, were arrested for protesting "Hunt's Dump" (named for then governor James Hunt). This marked the first time Americans had been jailed protesting the siting of a waste facility.

The protesters were unsuccessful in blocking the PCB landfill. Nevertheless, they brought national attention to siting inequities and galvanized African American church leaders, civil rights organizers, and grassroots activists around environmental justice issues.[28]

The demonstrations against the PCB landfill prompted Walter Fauntroy, District of Columbia delegate and chairman of the Congressional Black Caucus, to request a US General Accounting Office (GAO) investigation of hazardous waste facility siting in Region IV of the Environmental Protection Agency (EPA), comprised of Alabama, Florida, Georgia, Kentucky, Mississippi, North Carolina, South Carolina, and Tennessee. African Americans made up about one-fifth of the population in EPA's Region IV, and the 1983 GAO report discovered that three of the four offsite hazardous waste landfills in the region were located in predominately African American communities. Today, all of the offsite commercial hazardous waste landfills in the region are located in predominately African American communities.

The events in Warren County also prompted the United Church of Christ (UCC) Commission for Racial Justice to produce its landmark Toxic Wastes and Race study.[29] The 1987 UCC commission study documented that three out of five African Americans lived in communities with abandoned toxic waste sites and that 60 percent of African Americans (fifteen million) lived in communities with one or more waste sites. The study found that three of the five largest commercial hazardous waste landfills were located in predominately African American or Latino communities and accounted for 40 percent of the nation's total hazardous waste landfill capacity in 1987.

In 1990, *Dumping in Dixie: Race, Class and Environmental Quality* chronicled environmental justice struggles of rural, urban, and suburban African American communities in the South. Meanwhile, *Confronting Environmental Racism* in 1993 and *Just Transportation* in 1997 continued to affirm that if a community happens to be poor, inner-city, or inhabited by people of color, chances are it will receive less environmental protection and fewer transportation amenities than an affluent, suburban, white community.[30]

In response to this initial activism and documentation, grassroots groups sprang up all over the country to combat these unequal, unjust, and illegal practices. Couched within social, economic, and environmental justice contexts, various child care and housing advocates, health providers, educators, environmentalists, members of organized labor, have in recent years reintroduced transportation equity into the larger political and civil rights agenda.

Global Environmental Justice

In 1991, the First National People of Color Environmental Leadership Summit advanced environmental justice beyond its antitoxics focus to embrace more global issues like public health, land rights, land use, community empowerment, sustainability, energy, transboundary waste trade, and transportation. The summit was held in Washington, DC, and attracted over 1,000 people from all fifty states, including Alaska and Hawaii. Summit delegates came from as far away as Puerto Rico, Mexico, the Marshall Islands, and several African nations. They adopted the Principles of Environmental Justice to take back to their respective communities and serve as a guide in grassroots organizing.

In October 2002, environmental justice leaders convened the Second National People of Color Environmental Leadership Summit (Summit II) in Washington, DC. Over 1,400 individuals representing grassroots and community-based organizations, faith-based groups, organized labor, civil rights, youth, and academic institutions made their way from nearly every state to the nation's capital to participate. The vast majority, over 75 percent, of Summit II attendees came from community-based organizations. The new faces, individuals who were not present at the first summit in 1991, outnumbered the veteran environmental justice leaders two to one.

In an effort to have substantive materials going in and coming out of Summit II, a nationwide call for resource policy papers was issued. Summit II commissioned two dozen policy papers on subjects ranging from childhood asthma, energy, transportation equity, TEA-3 and environmental justice, to smart growth, "dirty" power plants, climate justice, brownfields redevelopment, occupational health and safety, and human rights. The policy papers helped guide the workshops and hands-on training sessions. Women's strong presence in the movement was evidenced by their leading, moderating, or presenting in more than half of the eighty-six workshops.

Summit II brought three generations (elders, seasoned leaders, and youth activists) of the environmental justice movement together. Summit II delegates called for youth and students to be integrated into the leadership of the environmental justice movement. The challenges of building a multiethnic, multiracial, multi-issue, anti-racist movement was present at both summits. Language and cultural barriers still hinder communication across the various ethnic groups. Much work is still needed to build trust, mutual respect, and principled relationships across racial, ethnic, cultural, gender, and age lines. Nevertheless, the strength of the environmental justice movement is in the diversity of the organizations and their constituents working together for positive change.

Changes that occurred between the first and second summits showed that the environmental justice (EJ) movement had made tremendous strides in one decade. When the first summit was convened in 1991, there were no EJ networks, university-based environmental justice centers, or environmental justice legal clinics. Today, there are a dozen EJ networks, four EJ centers, and growing numbers of university-based legal clinics that have environmental justice as an emphasis. The University of Michigan offers both a masters and a doctoral degree in environmental justice—the only such program in the country.

The 1991 summit saw adoption of the Principles of Environmental Justice. At Summit II, there was general consensus among participants that environmental justice must be a top priority in the twenty-first century. Despite improvements in the way government carries out environmental protection, gaps persist. Community groups are faced with rollbacks and the steady chipping away at civil liberties, basic civil and human rights, and environmental protection. It is clear that environmental justice advocates have to continue making their voices heard.

The Government Responds

Getting the government to support the environmental justice agenda was not easy. In response to growing public concern and mounting scientific evidence, on February 11, 1994, President Clinton issued Executive Order 12898, "Federal Actions to Address Environmental Justice in Minority Populations and Low-Income Populations" (EO 12898). This order was not a new law but an attempt to address environmental injustice within already existing federal laws and regulations. It was an attempt to reinforce what had been law for three decades: Title VI of the Civil Rights Act of 1964, the National Environmental Policy Act of 1969 (NEPA), and the Federal-Aid Highway Act of 1970.

Title VI of the Civil Rights Act of 1964 prohibits discriminatory practices in programs receiving federal funds. It states "No person in the United States shall, on the ground of race, color, or national origin, be excluded from participation in, be denied the benefits of, or be subjected to discrimination under any program or activity receiving Federal financial assistance."[31]

The National Environmental Policy Act (NEPA) set policy goals for the protection, maintenance, and enhancement of the environment with the explicit agenda of assuring a safe, healthful, productive, and aesthetically and culturally pleasing environment for all Americans. NEPA requires federal agencies to prepare a detailed statement on the effects of proposed federal actions that will significantly affect the human environment.

Clinton's EO 12898 called for improved methodologies for assessing and mitigating health effects from multiple and cumulative exposure. It also provided for collection of data on low-income and minority populations that may be disproportionately at risk. The order further called for environmental health impact studies on people who subsist on fish and wildlife, and it encouraged the affected populations to participate in the various phases of the NEPA assessment and mitigation process, including data gathering, analysis, mitigation, and monitoring, as well as identifying alternatives to the proposed project.

In 1995, a national environmental justice and transportation conference was held in Atlanta to examine some of these conflicts and their resolution.[32] Co-sponsored by the Federal Highway Administration, Federal Transit Administration, Federal Railroad Administration, and Clark Atlanta University, the conference was a follow-up to Clinton's environmental justice Executive Order. Over 250 grassroots environmental justice and transportation equity leaders, civil rights advocates, legal experts, planners, academicians, and government officials attended from thirty states. The four major themes of the conference were: ensuring greater stakeholder participation and public involvement in transportation decision-making; directing resources to identify and address discriminatory outcomes, disproportionate impacts, inequitable distribution of transportation investments, and their civil rights implications; improving research, data collection, and assessment techniques; and promoting interagency cooperation in transportation planning and development.

Then, in April 1997, the Federal Department of Transportation issued its "Order on Environmental Justice," requiring the state DOTs to comply with EO 12898 within the framework of existing laws, regulations, and guidance.[33] In December 1998, the Federal Highway

Administration issued an order requiring the FHA to incorporate environmental justice in all its programs, policies, and activities.

The executive orders, laws, and regulations are only as good as their enforcement. Quite often, people of color have to keep demanding that their rights be protected and services provided even when there are clear-cut mandates. In short, having the laws and regulations is not enough. More important, it helps if communities and nongovernmental organizations understand and have a working knowledge of the transportation planning process. Having information and knowing how to use it is empowering.

What started out as local community-based grassroots struggles against toxics, facility siting, transport of hazardous material, highways and freeways, fare hikes, and disparate transit services have now blossomed into a national environmental justice movement.[34] Environmental justice means different things to different people, but fundamentally, it embraces the principle that all people and communities are entitled to equal protection of our environmental, health, employment, housing, transportation, and civil rights laws. The EPA's Office of Environmental Justice defines environmental justice as follows:

> The fair treatment and meaningful involvement of all people regardless of race, color, national origin, or income with respect to the development, implementation, and enforcement of environmental laws, regulations, and policies. Fair treatment means that no group of people, including racial, ethnic, or socio-economic group should bear a disproportionate share of the negative environmental consequences resulting from industrial, municipal, and commercial operations or the execution of federal, state, local, and tribal programs and policies.[35]

Generally, environmental justice concerns arise where people of color and the poor receive more than their fair share of the negative impacts, while receiving few benefits from transportation projects and investments. Environmental justice provides a framework under which transportation planning can avoid, minimize, and mitigate negative impacts and enhance the livability of communities for residents. The framework rests on an analysis of strategies to eliminate unfair, unjust, and inequitable conditions and decisions. It is also about making sure that groups get their fair share of benefits.

Transportation Equity

Transportation equity analysis incorporates the principles of environmental justice into its overall analysis of transportation policy. Transportation equity analysis examines the negative environmental consequences or costs of transportation and scrutinizes discrepancies in resource allocation and investment. Transportation equity focuses on the distribution of benefits and enhancements among the various population groups—especially among low-income and people of color communities.[36] Unraveling transportation equity issues requires an understanding of how different effects relate to each other, trying to understand direct and indirect impacts as well as the cumulative or counterbalancing impacts of various effects.

Indirect project impacts are the additional side effects caused by direct impacts. Indirect impacts often occur later in time or further in distance than direct impacts. On the other hand, cumulative impacts represent incremental impacts of an action added to other past, present, or reasonably foreseeable future actions. All three types of impacts, especially cumulative impacts, have special significance for people of color and low-income communities—where a disproportionately large share of locally unwanted land uses are found.

How transportation equity is defined and measured can often determine how it is evaluated.[37] One approach delineates three general types of transportation equity. Horizontal Equity focuses on fairness of cost and benefit allocation between individuals and groups who are considered comparable in wealth and ability. Vertical Equity With Regard to Income and Social Class is concerned with allocation of costs between income and social classes. Vertical Equity With Regard to Mobility Need and Ability focuses on how well an individual's transportation needs are met compared with others in their community.[38]

Transportation equity also seeks to address disparate outcomes in planning, operation and maintenance, and infrastructure development. Concerned with factors that may create and/or exacerbate inequities, transportation equity focuses on measures to prevent or correct disparities in benefits and costs.[39] Transportation-induced inequities include infrastructure that physically isolates communities; inequitable distribution of environmental nuisances such as maintenance and refueling facilities (contributing to poor air quality) and airports (noise); lack of sufficient mitigation measures to correct inequitable distribution of negative impacts (for example, noise or displacement of homes, parks, and cultural landmarks); the age and condition of the transit fleet; and the availability and condition of facilities and services at transit stations, such as information kiosks, seating, cleanliness, rest rooms, and condition of the roadways.

Disparate transportation outcomes can be subsumed under three broad categories of inequity: procedural, geographic, and social.[40]

Procedural Inequity analysis directs attention to the process by which transportation decisions may or may not be carried out in a uniform, fair, and consistent manner with involvement of diverse public stakeholders. Procedural Inequity questions ask: Do the rules apply equally to everyone?

Geographic Inequity analysis investigates the negative and positive distributive impacts transportation decisions will have geographically and spatially (for example, rural vs. urban vs. central city). Geographic Inequity questions ask: Do transportation systems address outcomes (diversity and quality of services, resources and investments, facilities and infrastructure, access to primary employment centers, et cetera) that disproportionately favor one geographic area or spatial location over another?

Social Inequity analysis considers the distribution of transportation amenities (benefits) and disamenities (burdens) across population groups. Social Inequity questions ask: Are the benefits and burdens equally distributed across social groups?

Conclusion

Grassroots groups are challenging transportation racism, and demanding that local, metropolitan, state, and federal transportation agencies contribute to the development of just, healthy, and sustainable communities with benefits to all sectors. Adopting a "follow the dollars" approach to organizing, activist groups discover who is important and who is not and which communities count and which do not simply by following the transportation dollars. Local leaders are beginning to track the flow of transportation funds through the various sectors and jurisdictions in their region. Many of these self-trained community analysts are not pleased with what they are discovering. Too often, low-income and people of color voices are muted and the lion's share of transportation dollars flow elsewhere—away from their communities.

Community leaders are demanding an end to racist transportation policies and practices that favor white suburbanites over people of color—policies that use tax dollars to subsidize suburban sprawl and spur the demise of urban inner-city neighborhoods. Even when middle-income people of color make the move to the suburbs, transportation dollars and investments do not follow them as in the case of middle-income whites. Racial and economic redlining—practices closely

akin to those commonly directed at black inner-city neighborhoods—
strangle these black suburbs.

Cities from coast to coast offer fertile ground for grassroots
transportation equity organizing. Some grassroots groups have
organized to block freeway construction, "dirty" diesel bus facilities,
and light rail lines that disrupt and displace residents and businesses,
while other groups are demanding energy-efficient and cleaner
burning public transit vehicles, and a fair and equitable share of
transportation investments, services, and benefits that accrue to
transit-oriented development projects.

Grassroots leaders are working on strategies to eliminate
discriminatory and exclusionary practices that limit low-income
and people of color participation in transportation decision-making.
People must be at the table to speak for themselves. However, it is not
enough to have a place at the table; community leaders' voices must
be heard and their views respected—even when these views may
conflict with the dominant viewpoint.

Transportation is a key ingredient in any organization's plan to
build economically viable, healthy, and sustainable communities.
Many of the economic problems in urban areas involving lack of
mobility could be eliminated if existing transportation laws and
regulations were vigorously enforced in a nondiscriminatory way.
The solution to institutional racism, whether in transportation,
housing, land use, or any other areas, lies in the realm of equal
protection of all individuals, groups, and communities. State DOTs
and MPOs have a major responsibility to ensure that their programs,
policies, and practices do not discriminate against or adversely and
disproportionately impact people of color and the poor. Transportation
equity is not an unfunded mandate. It is the law.

Some groups have taken legal action to accomplish their goals,
while others have chosen different routes. Litigation is just one tool
in an assorted arsenal of weapons available to citizens, groups, and
communities working on social justice and transportation issues. But
legal action is no substitute for having a well-organized, disciplined,
and informed populace. Transportation racism is easy to practice
but difficult to eliminate, and there is no cookie-cutter formula
for dismantling discrimination and unjust policies and practices.
Passionate, committed, broad-based grassroots organizing based on
the principles of environmental justice and civil rights for all is the
foundation of the transportation equity movement.

notes

1.   For an in-depth account of the *Plessy v. Ferguson* court case, see Brook Thomas, ed., *Plessy v. Ferguson: A Brief History with Documents* (New York: Bedford/St. Martin, 1997).

2.   Keith Weldon Medley, "The Sad Story of How 'Separate but Equal' Was Born," *Smithsonian Magazine* (February 1994): 106.

3.   Justice Henry Billings Brown, "Majority Opinion in *Plessy v. Ferguson*," in *Desegregation and the Supreme Court*, ed. Benjamin Munn Ziegler (Boston: D.C. Heath and Company, 1958), 50–51 .

4.   Aldon D. Morris, *The Origins of the Civil Rights Movement: Black Communities Organizing for Change* (New York: The Free Press, 1984), 17–25.

5.   Ibid., 52.

6.   Robin D. G. Kelly, "Freedom Riders (The Sequel)," *The Nation* (February 5, 1996): 18–21.

7.   For a detailed history of the Montgomery Bus Boycott, see Roberta Hughes Wright, *The Birth of the Montgomery Bus Boycott* (Southfield, MI: Charro Press, 1991).

8.   James Melvin Washington, ed., *A Testament of Hope: The Essential Writings and Speeches of Martin Luther King, Jr.*, repr. (San Francisco: Harper Collins, 1991), 325–326. Dr. King's essay was first published posthumously in January, 1969.

9.   Morris, *The Origins of the Civil Rights Movement*, 58.

10.   Ibid., 233.

11.   Ibid.

12.   Cornel West, *Race Matters* (New York: Vintage Books, 1994).

13.   Ralph Ellison, *The Invisible Man*, 2nd ed. (New York: Vintage Books, 1995).

14.   Robert D. Bullard, *Invisible Houston: The Black Experience in Boom and Bust* (College Station, TX: Texas A&M University Press, 1987).

15.   Joe R. Feagin, *White Racism: The Basics* (New York: Routledge, 1995), 7.

16.   See Robert D. Bullard, ed., *Confronting Environmental Racism: Voices from the Grassroots* (Boston: South End Press, 1993); Robert D. Bullard, "The Threat of Environmental Racism," *Natural Resources & Environment* 7, no. 3 (Winter 1993): 23–26; Bunyan Bryant and Paul Mohai, eds., *Race and the Incidence of Environmental Hazards* (Boulder, CO: Westview Press, 1992); Regina Austin and Michael Schill, "Black, Brown, Poor and Poisoned: Minority Grassroots Environmentalism and the Quest for Eco-Justice," *The Kansas Journal of Law and Public Policy* 1 (1991): 69–82; Kelly C. Colquette and Elizabeth A. Henry Robertson, "Environmental Racism: The Causes, Consequences, and Commendations," *Tulane Environmental Law Journal* 5 (1991): 153–207; Rachel D. Godsil, "Remedying Environmental Racism," *Michigan Law Review* 90 (1991): 394–427.

17.   Robert D. Bullard, J. Eugene Grigsby, and Charles Lee, eds., *Residential Apartheid: The American Legacy* (Los Angeles: UCLA Center for African Studies, 1994), 3.

18. Luke Cole and Sheila Foster, *From the Ground Up: Environmental Racism and the Rise of the Environmental Justice Movement* (New York: New York University Press, 2000).

19. St. Claire Drake and Horace R. Cayton, *Black Metropolis* (1945; repr. Chicago: University of Chicago Press, 1993).

20. Kenneth B. Clark, *Dark Ghetto: Dilemmas of Social Power* (New York: Harper & Row, 1965), 11.

21. Kerner Commission, *Report of the National Advisory Commission on Civil Disorder* (New York: Viking Press, 1969).

22. Douglas S. Massey and Nancy A. Denton, *American Apartheid: Segregation and the Making of the Underclass* (Cambridge: Harvard University Press, 1993).

23. Derrick Bell, *Faces at the Bottom of the Well* (New York: Basic Books, 1993), ix.

24. Joe R. Feagin and Melvin P. Sikes, *Living with Racism: The Black Middle Class Experience* (Boston: Beacon Press, 1994), 15.

25. Bullard, Grigsby, and Lee, eds., *Residential Apartheid.*

26. See Joe R. Feagin and Clairece B. Feagin, *Discrimination American Style: Institutional Racism and Sexism* (Malabar, FL: Krieger Publishing Co., 1986); Robert D. Bullard and Joe R. Feagin, "Racism and the City," in M. Gottdiener and Chris G. Pickvance, eds., *Urban Life in Transition* (Newbury Park, CA: Sage, 1991), 55–76.

27. Robert D. Bullard and Glenn S. Johnson, eds., *Just Transportation: Dismantling Race and Class Barriers to Mobility* (Gabriola Island, British Columbia: New Society Publishers, 1997).

28. Robert D. Bullard, *Dumping in Dixie: Race, Class and Environmental Quality* (Boulder, CO: Westview Press, 2000).

29. United Church of Christ Commission for Racial Justice, *Toxic Wastes and Race in the United States* (New York: United Church of Christ, 1987).

30. See Bullard, *Dumping in Dixie*; Bullard, *Confronting Environmental Racism*; Bullard and Johnson, *Just Transportation.*

31. US Congress, *The Civil Rights Act of 1964*, Title IV.

32. Environmental Justice Resource Center, "Environmental Justice and Transportation: Building Model Partnerships" (Conference Proceedings, Clark Atlanta University, Atlanta, GA, May 11–13, 1995).

33. US Department of Transportation, "Order to Address Environmental Justice in Minority and Low-Income Populations," *Federal Register* 62 (1997): 18,377.

34. See Robert D. Bullard, *Unequal Protection: Environmental Justice and Communities of Color* (San Francisco: Sierra Club Books, 1996).

35. US Environmental Protection Agency, *Draft Guidance: EPA Environmental Justice in EPA's NEPA Compliance Analyses* (Washington, DC: US EPA, 1995).

36. Shannon Cairns, Jessica Creig, and Martin Wachs, *Environmental Justice and Transportation: A Citizen's Handbook* (Berkeley: Institute of Transportation Studies at University of California at Berkeley, 2003).

37.   Todd Litman, *Evaluating Transportation Equity* (Victoria, British Columbia: Victoria Transport Policy Institute, 1997), 1.

38.   Ibid.

39.   David J. Forkenbrock and Lisa A. Schweitzer, *Environmental Justice and Transportation Investment Policy* (Iowa City: Public Policy Center, University of Iowa, 1997), 68.

40.   For an in-depth discussion of equity, see Bullard, *Just Transportation*, 1-6.

On October 5, 1996, members of the Los Angeles Bus Riders Union held a mass protest and rally.

TWO
Los Angeles Bus Riders
Derail the MTA
Eric Mann

L os Angeles County is one of the nation's most populous counties, with over 9.5 million inhabitants spread over 4,081 square miles. Covering 470 square miles within LA County is the fabled City of Angels—Los Angeles, California—the second largest city in the United States, with a population of 3.2 million.[1] Los Angeles could easily fit the combined areas of St. Louis, Manhattan, Cleveland, Minneapolis, Boston, San Francisco, Pittsburgh, and Milwaukee within its city boundaries.

Known widely for its automobile culture, Los Angeles also boasts the second largest bus system in the country.[2] The Los Angeles County Metropolitan Transportation Authority (MTA) plans, builds, coordinates, and operates public transit within a 1,433-square-mile service area.[3] As of September 2002, the MTA operated 2,346 buses in its total fleet, with 2,058 in service on an average weekday. The buses covered 185 routes with 18,500 stops. The MTA also operated 60 miles of Metro Rail service at 50 stations. Los Angeles is home to the LA Bus Riders Union, an organizing and movement-building-organization dedicated to carrying on the legacy of civil rights in transportation as established by the Freedom Riders of the 1960s.

This chapter details the legal battle that the Labor/Community Strategy Center (LCSC), the Bus Riders Union (BRU), and their allies waged against the transit racism practiced by the MTA during the 1990s. It details the civil rights and transportation justice victories that the LCSC and BRU achieved in federal court before and after the April 2001 US Supreme Court *Alexander v. Sandoval* decision that limited the use of arguments based on disparate impact as previously provided by Title VI of the Civil Rights Act of 1964. The Los Angeles case is the best example that Title VI, civil rights, and justice, though wounded, are not dead and can still be fought for and won.

Birth of the "Bus Versus Rail" Debate

LA County lacks the areas of density needed to justify the high costs of rail construction as a viable public transit option. Even if an entire rail system were built, it would only serve 11 percent of the population— those who live within a half mile of a rail station. Consequently, most transportation planners are split between the view that rail is an outright misuse of public funds for a city like Los Angeles, and those who argue that rail is, at best, a supplementary component of a multimodal system of which buses must be the mainstay.

Since 1976, the agency that oversees public transit and highway policy in LA County has been the Los Angeles County Transportation Commission (LACTC). At one time, the Southern California Rapid Transit District (RTD) operated a rapid transit bus system separately from the LACTC. The RTD merged with the LACTC based on the argument that two supposedly complementary entities could manage regional transportation development together. However, each kept its organizational title, and both continued to support their different and competitive agendas: the LACTC for rails and the RTD for buses. The catch was that the LACTC was given financial control over the RTD. This establishment of a "bus versus rail" structure led to a growing polarization of the funding for predominantly low-income, inner-city communities versus predominantly higher-income, white suburban communities. Consequently, the discriminatory policies that took the form of a "bus versus rail" debate were institutionalized from the beginning.

The Los Angeles bus system can either ameliorate or exacerbate the poverty among the area's population of color. For decades, the city's "two-tiered" transit system was divided between private transportation (cars) and public transportation (buses). While most Angelenos of all races drove cars, the bus system was understood to be the avenue of last resort for the urban poor, the elderly, the disabled, and students, and as LA's urban poor became increasingly Latino, black, Asian, and Pacific Islander, so did most of the bus riders.

Even within the bus system, however, racial discrimination was reflected in policy. For many years, bus lines to predominantly white suburbs, from Pasadena to the San Gabriel Valley to the San Fernando Valley, had better service, more direct express routes, and newer buses. For many years, the fight of LA's low-income communities of color for equal protection of the law and equal access to public services took place within the RTD, since it was the agency that handled the vast majority of LA's public transit, the bus system. While the issues of transit equity in Los Angeles reach back for decades and have taken a variety of forms, the fight against transit racism has centered on the "bus versus rail" struggle.

A half-cent sales tax created by Proposition A in 1980 provided a temporary boost to the bus system, with $340 million per year being allocated in transit funds. Proposition A allocated 35 percent for rail construction and operations, 40 percent for discretionary transit money for bus or rail, and 25 percent for transit flows to cities (essentially funds to individual cities to help create a mandate for the passage of the Proposition). For the first years after Proposition A passed, 20 percent of its funds were allocated to reduce bus fares from 85 cents to 50 cents. The fare decrease generated dramatically increased bus ridership. The increase reinforced our understanding that in a city of very low-income people—the vast majority of whom are people of color and 57 percent of whom are women—overall bus ridership is highly dependent on fare structure.

Annual ridership rose from a low in 1982 of 354 million unlinked, one-way trips a year, just before the fare subsidy was implemented, to a peak of 497 million in 1985—the last year of the subsidy. After 1985, the funds previously dedicated to bus fare subsidies were used for rail construction, while additional discretionary funds (which were abundantly available) were never sought to maintain the 50-cent fare. Instead, the fare was returned to 85 cents and then further increased to $1.10. Naturally, service cuts followed the fare increases. Bus ridership plummeted more than 20 percent to below 376 million rides per year.

In 1990 Proposition C passed, authorizing a half-cent sales tax to expand public transportation in Los Angeles County. Proposition C mandated 40 percent as discretionary funds for transit, ridesharing, and bicycle programs, 25 percent for streets and highways (primarily for High-Occupancy Vehicle lanes), 20 percent for local governments, 10 percent for commuter rail or high-speed buses on freeways, and 5 percent for transit security.

Proposition A and Proposition C both attempted to create clear guidelines for the dispersal of funds between bus and rail. However, a great deal of the transportation funds were not actually locked in, and there was enormous spending flexibility. Discretionary spending for Los Angeles public transportation has meant spending the vast majority of funds on rail projects while consistently defunding the bus system and claiming business hardship. Public transit in Los Angeles represents a classic case of transportation racism and reflects how government rewards primarily white and affluent constituencies, and punishes primarily low-income constituencies of color.

Public transportation riders in Los Angeles are profoundly poor, with over 60 percent of them residing in households with total incomes under $15,000. The plaintiffs recognized that the dramatic increase in the cost of public transportation would have a disproportionate and irreparable impact on the county's transit-dependent communities. Any increase in transit costs would result in a severe burden evidenced by substantially decreased income and mobility for the vast majority of Los Angeles County's 400,000 daily bus riders.

The Fight for Transportation Equity Begins

In 1991, the Labor/Community Strategy Center began a transportation equity project which would later become the Bus Riders Union. This group focused its membership work on the needs of working people, low-income people, and bus riders, the vast majority of whom were Latino, black, Asian, and Pacific Islander, as well as working-class white. The organizing was motivated by a philosophy of environmental justice, the primacy of the needs of the working class, and a challenge to the corporate domination of society—especially in what should be a public arena. In our view, there is a causal relationship between mobility and a potential escape from poverty.

After a year of intense study, the group sharpened its vision of mass transportation and focused on a "Billions for Buses" campaign. The campaign, led by Bus Riders Union members and organizers, advocated for a first-class, clean-fuel, bus-centered public transportation system in Los Angeles. Almost as soon as the campaign began, the battle over "discretionary funding" and issues of racial discrimination took center stage. In the fall of 1992, the RTD was experiencing a budget shortfall of $59 million. Arguing they had done all they could do to save money, the RTD asked the LACTC to allocate $59 million from Proposition C discretionary funds to cover the shortfall. Since Proposition C funds came from the sales taxes of all Los Angeles residents (and there were nearly half a million riders on the bus system and less than 65,000 riders on rail projects), the LCSC agreed that covering the shortfall was a fair allocation of Proposition C funds. In fact, the LCSC argued that defunding the RTD, thus creating a "budget shortfall," was an illegal use of public funds to benefit a small rail ridership and to punish bus riders.

The LCSC raised the issue of taking public funds specifically paid for by all Angelenos and using them to fund the suburbs and defund the inner city. Through LCSC's intervention, the vast majority of the shortfall was restored without the threatened alternatives of fare increases and service cuts—but the LACTC, rather than use discretionary funds from possible rail projects, instead took some funds from future RTD bus purchases. Even though there was no fare increase at that time, the structure of the argument was framed—the LACTC wanted to use discretionary funds solely for rail projects, thereby creating shortfalls in bus funding that could be solved through fare increases and service cuts.

Partially as a result of this continued conflict between the LACTC and the RTD, in 1992, the California State Assembly established a new mega-agency, the Los Angeles County Metropolitan Transportation Authority (MTA). Unfortunately, the unresolved equity issues between the LACTC and RTD merely changed hands. The battle for transportation equity moved full force to the MTA.

Fare Hikes, Bus Passes, and Service Cuts

In August 1993, as the MTA approved a $3.7 billion budget, it allocated $97 million for a Pasadena Blue Line Rail extension, a project that was still on the drawing board. MTA's decision to allocate funding for the first leg of a rail project with an overall projected budget of $871 million—a decision that did not take into account the purchasing of rail cars or cost overruns, and that did not include a plan for how to complete the project in the following years—followed a familiar pattern. It was predicted that the rail line would siphon funds for bus service.

In December 1993, State Assemblyman Richard Katz, chairman of the Assembly Transportation Committee, whose bill had brought the MTA into existence through state law, criticized the MTA for again sacrificing the needs of inner-city bus riders. Before the fare increases and service cuts, there was repeated criticism of the MTA, this time by the very state legislator who authored the bill that created it. Public criticism was leveled at the MTA for the deterioration of bus service; the diversion of sales tax revenue from bus to rail; fiscal mismanagement; abdicating the attempt to provide equality and equity in the mass transit system; and the acknowledgement by the MTA board's CEO that the politics of the board were responsible for the diversion of funds away from underrepresented inner-city communities.

In April 1994, the MTA held a federally-mandated public hearing on its proposed fare increases and service cuts. What followed was an unprecedented outpouring of public concern from a wide variety of organizations representing many constituencies for whom the proposed fare increases would cause irreparable harm.

Elderly groups testified that they felt imprisoned in their homes because the MTA buses were so slow and the connections and transfers so difficult. Low-income workers explained that the existing bus schedules were so unreliable that they had to leave for work hours before they had to clock-in, for fear of being late and losing their jobs. Representatives of low-income workers testified that for workers making $10,000 to $15,000 annually, even the $42 monthly bus pass was a lot of money and that any increase in the bus pass, or its elimination, would cause significant hardship. Urging the MTA to increase bus service, a number of groups representing the blind talked about the difficulties and dangers of standing on street corners waiting for buses for almost an hour.

Many night-shift workers, such as janitors and service-sector workers, talked about waiting an hour for a bus and then having to travel as much as two hours to locations outside the inner city to find better paying work. Families talked about the expenses of buying bus passes for two children (students) and two adults on one income of less than $15,000, and urged the MTA to find alternatives other than raising fares and decreasing service.

Many MTA board members did not attend the hearing; those that did stayed for only an hour or two and talked to each other during most of the testimonies. When many of the 800 people present asked the MTA board members to respond to their concerns, they were told that since it was a "public hearing" the board was there to listen, not to respond.

On July 14, 1994, the MTA board voted to raise the bus fare from $1.10 to $1.35, a 23 percent hike; eliminate the $42 pass altogether; and reduce bus service on several lines. The board argued that the fare increases and service cuts would save the MTA $32 million per year out of a total budget of $2.9 billion.

Los Angeles Times reporter Bill Boyarsky, who attended the meeting, wrote a scathing critique of the MTA board:

> The MTA's actions hurt the poor in ways that have long-term effects. You could see this at Wednesday's hearing. Some of the speakers said they used adult student passes to attend night school to learn English, and the increase would make the trip to class more expensive. "We want to have a better life," one of them said. "We want to speak with the teachers and help [our children] with their homework."[4]

The following week, the MTA approved a $2.9 billion 1994–1995 budget that included an expenditure of $123 million for the Pasadena Blue Line light rail system. The $123 million expenditure for the light rail nearly matched the MTA's stated $126 million operating bus system deficit. The MTA proceeded to spend money for rail projects while imposing fare increases upon its own ridership. Clearly, the MTA was carrying out discriminatory policies with full awareness of their consequences. The two-tiered, separate but unequal policies of the MTA used its $2.9 billion annual budget to undermine the functioning of the mass transit system, and to subject a low-income ridership to undue hardship.

A public discussion around the MTA's plans eventually led the LCSC to file for a temporary restraining order against the MTA's actions. The discussion centered on riders expressing their daily displeasure with traveling on a deteriorating, inner-city bus system that was considered a stepchild of the MTA. To add insult to injury, the fact that separate, unequal, and second-class service was being provided to an inner-city bus ridership comprised overwhelmingly of people of color was openly acknowledged by the then–MTA CEO, a US congressman, and the local media. Furthermore, the aggressive efforts of the LCSC to place a moratorium on funding, pending a full accounting—warning the MTA that its expenditures on rail would cause future fare increases and service cuts for buses—was ignored. Despite the LCSC's warning and the *Los Angeles Business Journal's* reporting, the MTA pushed ahead with funding for rail projects and refused to even discuss the motion LCSC presented.

In the first legal victory for LA's bus riders, Federal District Judge Terry Hatter issued a six-month temporary restraining order that stopped the MTA from increasing bus fares. Judge Hatter also imposed a "compromise" pretrial fare settlement—he raised the monthly bus pass to $60 a month, and kept the one-way bus fare at $1.10. This was in fact a setback for the most transit-dependent, who utilized the unlimited-use bus pass for as many as one hundred rides a month. In the first of many negotiations between the BRU and MTA, we got the MTA to drop the bus pass back to $49, and in return we agreed to allow them to raise the one-way bus fare to $1.35, which they wanted more. This negotiation was done with the full consultation and support of one hundred of the most active bus riders, who felt the reduction in the monthly bus pass price was essential, whereas the one-way fare was restricted to those who used the bus less frequently. During the negotiations we began to function as a "class representative," a bargaining agent for an entire class of bus riders, and with the assumption of this role, we took on enormous responsibility to be both representative and effective.

The Grassroots Community Challenges the MTA

It was evident that MTA policies substantially discriminated against bus riders who, overwhelmingly, are low-income members of communities of color—black, Latino, Asian, and Pacific Islander. Los Angeles County is a multiracial political jurisdiction of 9.5 million residents, of whom 68.9 percent are people of color. The vast majority of LA County's low-income residents of color live in inner-city communities.

In September 1994, the LCSC and Bus Riders Union initiated a class-action civil rights suit on behalf of LA's 400,000 poor bus riders of color. Represented by the NAACP Legal Defense and Educational Fund, the LCSC and BRU were joined by the Korean Immigrant Workers' Advocates and the Southern Christian Leadership Conference as co-plaintiffs. Together, the groups challenged the proposed imposition of the new MTA policies. The MTA was planning to increase the one-way cash fare for a bus ride from $1.10 to $1.35; eliminate the existing $49 unlimited-use monthly bus pass, requiring passengers to purchase separate tickets for each ride; and set up a zone system on the Blue Line rail system that would raise the fares more than 100 percent for over 50 percent of the passengers.

Elements of the Consent Decree

In October, 1996, the class action lawsuit against the MTA, *Labor/ Community Strategy Center, Bus Riders Union, et al. v. Los Angeles County MTA*, was settled through a consent decree, a pretrial settlement strongly pushed by the federal judge whose provisions fell under the jurisdiction of the federal court for its entire ten-year duration.[5] A consent decree is a mechanism used often in class action lawsuits in which a government agency or corporation agrees to wide-ranging remedies to repair a past injustice. Often, the benefit for the discriminatory party, in this case the MTA, is to avoid having a finding of racial discrimination entered against them.[5] The ten-year, multibillion dollar consent decree settlement improved mass transportation for all bus riders, and set a public policy precedent for grassroots organizers in every city in the US. Specific elements of the settlement include the following.

The monthly, general unlimited-use bus pass was reduced from $49 to $42. This reduction set the precedent that bus pass prices can go down as well as up, and that needs-based rather than market-based pricing of public services paid for with public funds must drive transportation fare policy. In a nation where a minimum wage of $5.25 an hour requires a public policy debate, and many workers in Los Angeles are forced to work in sweatshops for even less, reducing the price and protecting the unlimited-use bus pass is a major achievement of this agreement. It cannot be stressed enough that, before the LCSC and BRU went to court in September 1994, the MTA had just voted to eliminate the general bus pass altogether.

The LCSC and BRU argued that one obstacle to greater mass transit use was the prohibitive price of the bus pass and the burden on families of accumulating $49, or even $42, on the first of the month, the same time the rent was due. Under the past system, a person who could not afford the $49 monthly pass had to pay $53 a month for a pass, in two $26.50 biweekly installments. The biweekly general bus pass was reduced from $26.50 to $21. The settlement clearly established the precedent that to encourage public transportation use, the government, not the consumer, must absorb the costs of "administrative fees" that otherwise would make purchasing two biweekly passes more expensive than a monthly pass.

A new, unlimited-use, $11 weekly pass was instituted. In urban centers throughout the United States, when a growing percentage of working people labor at minimum wage, even a $21 biweekly pass creates obstacles to public transportation use. Painfully, the result is not that people do not use public transportation, but in their desperation to get to work, the poor get poorer, paying for each fare at $1.35 plus a 25-cent transfer because they can't accumulate $42 and $21 at any given time. Finally, when low-income people have completely run out of money, they just do not go places. As such, their lives are reduced to "home to work," and they are denied the right to go to church, to visit family or friends, to attend cultural and educational programs, or even to look for better jobs.

The $11 weekly pass was a major tangible breakthrough in public transportation policy that will cause shock waves in San Francisco, New Orleans, Chicago, and New York if groups there are capable of building on this victory. The $11 weekly pass will get a growing number of low-wage workers who drive gas-guzzling cars with no insurance out of their cars and back on public transportation. Moreover, this establishes the principle that governmental policy, which too often subsidizes the rich and penalizes the poor, must approach the important environmental goal of reducing auto and fossil-fuel use. This could be achieved by providing incentives for voluntary reduction in auto use by prioritizing services to those who most need them.

This is an important victory for the LCSC's work, because the organization has vehemently opposed "pricing" theories advocated by many mainstream environmental groups to discourage auto use. The LCSC has argued that efforts to "stop the externalization of costs" of the auto by charging more for gasoline or "congestion pricing" on highways will not deter those who are wealthy or even comfortable. In the absence of a first-class public transportation system, the affluent will simply pay the tariff to continue to use their cars, while those who are transit-dependent will pay more for inadequate public transportation.

Thus, a principal objective of the LCSC's work is to use coordinated, grassroots organizing by groups like the BRU to require the government to offer low-income people incentives to use public transportation. In a small but significant way, the achievement of this goal increases public support for the public sector.

With regard to reducing overcrowding, the LCSC and BRU wanted the MTA to simply agree to purchase 1,000 or more new buses over five years to reduce overcrowding and accommodate rider demand. In the settlement process the MTA resisted this proposal and as a result, a compromise was reached. The MTA agreed to purchase 102 buses over the next two years to decrease overcrowding and increase service on the most congested lines. It also agreed to reduce standees from a present level of 20 or more on a bus with 43 seats, to an average of 8 standees during peak hours by 2002. In 1997, 2000, and 2002 there were substantial, verifiable goals which when not met, involved "reallocation" (the MTA's dreaded word) of funds from "other sources" (meaning rail) to buses to increase bus service and reduce overcrowding. So far, after years of legal wrangling, the MTA has been forced through grassroots pressure and court orders to expand its fleet by 350 buses.

Expanded bus service to new areas was another major victory. The BRU and LCSC were able to convince the court-appointed mediator that Los Angeles did not want a "ghetto and barrio bus improvement plan," but rather a comprehensive regional transportation plan for all races and classes. Service was needed both within and outside of East LA, Koreatown, Pico Union, South Central, Disneyland, the San Gabriel and San Fernando Valleys, and Orange County. The MTA did not just want suburban riders taking express buses and trains into the central business district (where only 8 percent of the jobs are presently located), but instead a bus-centered, multimodal system that could create new bus transportation to employment, cultural, recreational, medical, and family centers throughout Los Angeles County and beyond.

The consent decree created a framework for the development and implementation of a new five-year service plan. In the first victory for the new service component of the consent decree, the MTA agreed to a pilot project in which it would purchase fifty new buses which would run from inner-city areas to medical, job, and recreational centers. Based on the provisions in the consent decree, the Bus Riders Union developed a plan to put into service 500 new expansion buses to meet transit needs across the county.

MTA Appeal and Delay Tactics

The MTA has resisted the consent decree nearly every step of the way. It has appealed rulings based on the consent decree five times since 1996. MTA's appeal and delay tactics have failed to wear down the Bus Riders Union or to break its resolve. In its resistance to expanding its bus fleet, the agency has spent more than a $1 million in legal fees. The court-appointed mediator Special Master Donald Bliss, Federal Judge Terry Hatter, and the Ninth Circuit en banc have all ruled against the MTA and in favor of the Bus Riders Union. Additionally, the United States Supreme Court rejected MTA's final appeal.

The MTA has been slow to implement the consent decree provision related to overcrowding. In March 1999, Special Master Donald Bliss found that the MTA failed to comply with the consent decree's requirements to reduce the number of passengers forced to stand in buses during peak periods of service. He ordered the MTA to buy 532 new compressed-natural-gas buses and to hire additional drivers and mechanics to relieve the chronic overcrowding plaguing the nation's second largest bus system. Bliss also ordered the MTA to correct a host of problems that afflict its bus service, including inoperable buses, a lack of drivers, breakdowns, missed trips, poor adherence to schedules, and insufficient capacity.[6]

Bliss wanted the dispute between the MTA and the BRU to be resolved. He ordered the MTA to provide additional staff, conduct point checks twice monthly on the twenty most heavily used bus lines, and provide detailed quarterly reports including overcrowding data. Overall, the Bus Riders Union saw this as a major win. The agency's failure to meet the consent decree's first overcrowding reduction by the end of 1997 was a clear signal that the MTA needed to be ordered to comply as soon as possible.

That initial deadline called for having an average of no more than fifteen passengers standing for any twenty-minute period during rush hours. The next deadline was June 2000, by which time there should have been no more than an average of eleven passengers standing. The ultimate goal was that an average of no more than eight passengers would be without a seat by 2002.

In January 2002, the MTA board voted eight-to-four, with one abstention, to pursue a final appeal to the US Supreme Court.[7] The MTA appeals were an attempt to take the heart and soul out of the consent decree and leave an empty shell. Los Angeles Mayor James K. Hahn, who now serves on the MTA board, voted against continuing the appeal and harshly criticized the MTA's actions. Hahn stated, "I am disappointed we are continuing to have this battle in court." Hahn also argued that the MTA should stop its appeals and concentrate on "working to provide better bus and better transit service to the people of Southern California."[8] In March 2002, the US Supreme Court handed the MTA another crushing defeat by refusing to hear their case, resulting in further legal proceedings in the lower courts to determine the number of additional buses needed to reduce overcrowding.

It is important to note that several of the Bus Riders Union's court victories came after the unpopular April 24, 2001, US Supreme Court *Alexander v. Sandoval* decision that limited the use of arguments based on disparate impact in Title VI lawsuits. Essentially, *Sandoval* established that only discriminatory *intent*, and not *impact*, can be challenged under Title VI of the 1964 Civil Right's Act. It is much more difficult to prove that an agency intended to discriminate, than that its actions had the effect of discriminating. The *Sandoval* decision is another of the flagrant examples of the Scalia-majority rewriting of the civil rights laws by fiat, as the stinging dissent by Justice Brennan pointed out.

Under Title VI of the 1964 Civil Rights Act, "No person in the United States shall, on the ground of race, color, or national origin be excluded from participation in, be denied the benefits of, or be otherwise subjected to discrimination under any program" of local or state governments. The act allowed the federal government (through the Justice Department and the then Department of Health, Education, and Welfare) to bring antidiscrimination suits against the government based on complaints from "private parties," that is, individuals or groups who felt they had been discriminated against. But the law also allowed those private parties, represented by civil rights groups such as the NAACP Legal Defense and Educational Fund, or individual attorneys, to file suit on their own—such as that brought in 1994 by the Labor/Community Strategy Center, Bus Riders Union, Korean Immigrant Workers Advocates, and the Southern Christian Leadership Conference.

In the *Sandoval* case, a Latina woman who had been denied her drivers license in Alabama because the drivers test was in "English only" filed a suit arguing that the denial of her language rights constituted a violation of Title VI. Her appeal was upheld by the Eleventh Circuit Court of Appeals, ruling that the State of Alabama had to administer the tests in Spanish. The state appealed, not on the merits of the case, but rather, on a far broader claim that Ms. Sandoval did not have the right to bring her case in the first place. Title VI, the state argued, only empowered the federal government to bring the case, and had never intended to allow individuals such as Sandoval to seek redress against the government.

In a classic five-to-four decision, the Scalia/Thomas/Rehnquist majority overturned thirty-six years of legal precedent, and argued that the 1964 act had never authorized groups to bring suits. Then, in a complex maneuver, the majority argued that individuals, or aggrieved groups, could still bring suits independent of the federal government, if they could prove *intentional* discrimination, not simply "disparate impact" by which the actual effect of a government action is racist and discriminatory. Leaving aside a broader discussion of the outrage of this decision, the failure of the civil rights establishment to fight it, the silence of the Democrats, and the implications for future antiracist work, even in light of the *Sandoval* decision, the LCSC was able to withstand an MTA effort to overturn our entire consent decree for several legal reasons. First, while we were of course a private party, we had brought our case against the MTA based on both intentional and disparate impact discrimination. Secondly, given that the MTA signed a legal contract in order to get out of a finding of liability and to avoid a trial, the consent decree was governed by both civil rights and contract law, that is, the MTA could not get out of a signed agreement by quoting *Sandoval* ex post facto.

The Bus Riders Union was able to withstand the legal onslaught of the MTA, a $3 billion transit agency that has over 8,000 employees. The Los Angeles case provides a clear-cut example of government foot-dragging, delay tactics, and outright resistance to complying with civil rights laws—even when it has been ordered to do so by the courts. It also shows the lengths to which one of the nation's largest transit agencies will go to avoid providing first-class transit services to its own ridership—largely poor and working-class people from communities of color.

Conclusion

The Bus Riders Union, whose membership is primarily black, Latino, Asian, and Pacific Islander with significant participation of antiracist whites, and most of whom are bus riders who live throughout Los Angeles, challenged the racism within the MTA and won. While BRU's members come from all walks of life, they are all supporters of mass transit. The legal fight against the MTA dealt with blatant separate and unequal transit racism. The BRU's legal tactic was driven by its organizing strategy. The legal strategy was the tool the BRU needed to force the MTA to deliver quality transit services to the poor and people of color. It forced the MTA to sit down with the BRU and negotiate. What emerged was a consent decree that ordered the MTA to stop discriminating against its bus riders and to correct the bus–rail service disparities it knowingly created.

Outside of the legal fight, the BRU has continued to organize bus riders and hold actions across the city. Throughout its campaign, the BRU has been clear that its goal is to build an independent base of organized working-class, predominately people of color around racial justice and improved public transportation. BRU members were integral in shaping the Title VI lawsuit against the MTA and have been consistently engaged in the negotiations around the case. Their work has demonstrated how an organization can combine direct action with litigation to apply pressure for change.

The BRU members and organizers are in the struggle for the long haul as long distance runners, not sprinters. As the Labor/Community Strategy Center and Bus Riders Union have evolved from embryonic to substantial forces in Los Angeles County, a new arena of the struggle is now being confronted—a transitional stage characterized by attempts at co-optation and tokenism by the MTA, which too many groups confuse with social change. The Labor/Community Strategy Center and the Bus Riders Union are using this transitional stage, which offers the advantage of far greater access to and dialogue with top MTA staff and key elected officials, as a means of applying more direct organizing pressure and sharpening of the groups' programmatic demands.

notes

1. Los Angeles Almanac (2002), "Historical Residents Population, City and County of Los Angeles, 1850 to 2000," http://www.losangelesalmanac.com/topics/population/po02.htm.

2. Jeffrey L. Rabin, "MTA Told to Buy 532 Buses to Ease Crowding," *Los Angeles Times*, March 9, 1999.

3. Metropolitan Transportation Authority, "MTA Profile," http://www.mta.net.

4. Bill Boyarsky, *Los Angeles Times*, July 17, 1994.

5. Richard Simon, "Settlement of Bus Suit Approved," *Los Angeles Times*, October 29, 1996; David Bloom, "Bus Riders Beat MTA on Fares, Service," *Daily News*, October 29, 1996.

6. Michael Coit, "Bus Riders Win Big: MTA Given Deadline to Expand Fleet," *Daily News*, March 9, 1999.

7. Kurt Streeter, "MTA to Again Appeal Bus Service Agreement," *Los Angeles Times*, January 10, 2002.

8. Ibid.

MATEC protester voices opposition to fare increase in front of MARTA headquarters on June 19, 2000.

THREE

Dismantling Transit Racism in Metro Atlanta

Robert D. Bullard, Glenn S. Johnson, and Angel O. Torres

Transportation has always played an important role in Atlanta's history and development. Landlocked and basically flat, Atlanta has no mountains or major bodies of water to constrain its outward growth. The Atlanta of today doesn't resemble its humble beginnings as the Indian village "Standing Peachtree." Located at the confluence of Peachtree Creek and the Chattahoochee River, the village was considered a strategic location in the area, leading the Georgia legislature in 1836 to authorize a surveyor to locate a site between the Chattahoochee River and the City of Decatur as the terminal point for the Georgia-Tennessee Railroad.[1] With a railroad cutting through the mountains of Tennessee, the legislature expected trade links to be opened to the Midwest through connections with the Tennessee, Ohio, and Mississippi Rivers.

In 1837, the place now called Atlanta was christened Terminus because it was the terminal point for the railroads. In 1845, the name was changed to Atlanta, a name associated with the Western and Atlantic railroad companies.[2] A state law in 1847 precisely established the corporate boundaries of Atlanta to be exactly one mile from the state depot in every direction, making Atlanta a perfect circle. The city later expanded through annexations. By 1980, Atlanta covered 131 square miles.

Most of the city's boundaries are found entirely within Fulton County, except for a small portion that extends into DeKalb County. Atlanta has not been involved in any significant annexation of surrounding developments since 1967. The city of Atlanta is an incorporated entity within fixed boundaries. Atlanta's inability to annex has contributed to uneven growth and development of the area. The growth pattern has had important social and economic implications for the mostly black central-city core and the rapidly expanding mostly white suburban ring.

Though burned to the ground by Union forces in 1864, city officials were successfully promoting Atlanta as the "Gateway to the South" in the 1880s. By 1895, Atlanta was celebrating its rebirth as the "Capital of the New South."[3] A century later, Atlanta and its suburban neighbors are still capitalizing on the region's "growth machine" imagery. Over the past half century, Atlanta emerged as the commercial and financial center of the southeastern United States. Atlanta is the center for federal government operations in the region, as well as the center of communications and transportation. CNN beams around the world from its Atlanta home base, and it is hard to fly South without passing through Atlanta's Hartsfield International Airport, the busiest airport in the nation. Unfortunately, all of Atlanta's growth has its downside. Though it is considered the "capital" of the New South,[4] it is also the "poster child" for sprawl.[5]

Atlanta has also been touted as the black Mecca.[6] Over 500,000 blacks moved into the region in the 1990s. Atlanta has the sixth largest African American population in the country. The 1990s also saw Atlanta become more ethnically diverse. In 2002, the region was home to over 500,000 Latinos and 175,000 Asians. This chapter analyzes the impact of race on the Atlanta metropolitan growth pattern and on transportation planning.

Regional Growth

Black Atlanta has a well-established middle class, business elite, mainstream civil rights establishment, and a sophisticated political machine. The city is home to twenty-nine degree-granting colleges and universities, including the Atlanta University Center—a consortium of six historically black colleges and universities enrolling some 15,000 black students.

Metropolitan Atlanta has experienced constant growth since the 1900s. The region has grown in population at an annual rate of 2.9 percent since 1950. The 1960s were considered the boom years in which Atlanta established its regional dominance. The 1970s and 1980s were characterized as a time when the city became increasingly black. During this same period, Atlanta experienced a steady decrease in its share of the metropolitan population, housing, and jobs as compared to 1960.

In 1980, Atlanta captured about 40 percent of the region's jobs. The 1990s saw the region's city-suburban jobs gap widen. In

1990, Atlanta's share had slipped to 28.3 percent and in 1997 to 19.08 percent.[7] Over 348,000 jobs were added to the region between 1990–1997, with most of the new jobs and newcomers settled outside Atlanta, leaving the city lagging far behind its job-rich suburbs.

Metropolitan Atlanta continued to experience record growth in the 1990s. The region grew from about 3 million residents in 1990 to almost 4 million in 2003. An average of 69,100 people moved into the metropolitan area each year during the 1990s, compared to 61,788 in the 1980s.[8] In just one twelve-month period (from April 1998 to April 1999), metro Atlanta grew by 94,300 people—the second-largest increase in the region's history. On the other hand, the city of Atlanta grew by only 900 people during this same period.[9] Population growth was one hundred times greater in Atlanta's suburbs than in Atlanta's urban core.

The boundaries of the Atlanta metropolitan region doubled in the 1990s. The region measured 65 miles from north to south in 1990. Today, Atlanta's economic dominance reaches well beyond 110 miles from north to south.[10] Much of the region's growth in the 1990s was characterized by suburban sprawl and economic divestment in Atlanta's central city.[11] Leading the nation in residential construction during the 1990–1996 period, the record number of building permits contributed to the region being dubbed "Hotlanta."

Atlanta's northern suburbs reaped the lion's share of jobs and economic development. The 272,915 jobs that were added to the mostly white Republican-voting northern suburbs accounted for 78.4 percent of all jobs added in the region from 1990–1997. Another 70,582 jobs, or 20.3 percent, were added in the southern suburbs of the region. On the other hand, only 4,503 jobs were added in the region's mostly black, Democrat-voting central core of Atlanta, representing only 1.3 percent of all jobs created during the height of the region's booming economy.[12]

Thousands of entry-level jobs go unfilled in the mostly white suburban counties while black Atlanta has a 35 percent poverty rate, one of the highest in the country. Georgia Tech economics professor David Sjoquist described the "Atlanta paradox" as "a paradox of extreme racial and economic inequality—of abject poverty in a region of tremendous wealth, of a poor and economically declining city population in the face of dramatic economic growth, and of a black Mecca in a 'city too busy to hate' (a slogan adopted in 1955 by Mayor William Hartsfield), confronting a highly racially segregated population and the substantial problems associated with racism and poverty that pervade the city."[13]

Flight of jobs and middle-income families to the suburbs has contributed to and exacerbated both economic and racial segregation in housing and schools. Central city Atlanta has become increasingly black and poor white inner-city neighborhoods have been passed over by the region's expanding economy. Blacks comprise 66.8 percent of Atlanta's 400,000 residents.[14]

Some black Atlantans have made the move to the suburbs. In 1970, only 8 percent of Atlanta's suburban population was black. By 2000, blacks made up 25 percent of Atlanta's suburban population—surpassing Washington, DC, as the largest concentration of blacks in its suburban ring. However, black suburbanization has not automatically translated into residential integration. Most blacks have become re-segregated in Atlanta's suburbs. Many middle-class blacks are choosing to live in black suburban neighborhoods to avoid having their children and themselves subjected to white racism, which ranges from subtle to overt.

Suburbanization of home and work has widened social and economic inequities between metropolitan Atlanta's blacks and whites. These problems are exacerbated by persistent racial discrimination in housing and employment, residential segregation, and inadequate public transportation.[15]

MARTA – Moving Africans Rapidly Through Atlanta

Race-shaped land-use planning and public transportation in metro Atlanta has created a divided region. Racism has maintained those economic and geographic divisions. These divisions are physically evidenced by the area's transit system—the ten-county Atlanta metropolitan area has a regional transit system in name only. The Metropolitan Atlanta Rapid Transit Authority (MARTA) serves just two counties, Fulton and DeKalb. MARTA was built on deceit, broken promises, and racism. Because Atlanta's white business elites wanted MARTA, it was built—whether or not it met the needs of the region or was accepted by the community.

The original plan called for a five-county regional transit system. In the 1960s, MARTA was hailed as the solution to the region's growing traffic and pollution problems. Atlanta's white economic and political elites pushed for a rapid-rail system that they felt would market Atlanta as a "cosmopolitan" New South city. In 1967, rapid-rail lines were under construction in San Francisco, Seattle, Los Angeles, and Washington, DC. Atlanta's leaders did not want the city to be left behind as they marketed the city's progressive image.

From the earliest stage, disparities in service between white and black neighborhoods were built into MARTA's design. MARTA was a business-led initiative, more about money and politics than transportation and mobility. A 1968 rapid-rail referendum that proposed more rail service to white areas of Atlanta to black areas was soundly defeated. Not surprisingly, blacks did not support a plan that shortchanged their communities. Black areas voted 2-1 against the measure. The vote in the suburban counties hinged on white residents' fear of being "overrun" with blacks from Atlanta.[16] Many whites jokingly referred to MARTA as "Moving Africans Rapidly Through Atlanta."

Not accepting defeat lying down, the white business elite went back to the MARTA drawing board. They sought black support by promising the black community more rail service, minority contracts, and low fares for a fixed period.[17] A second four-county rapid-rail referendum was presented to voters in 1971. Largely because of black support, the referendum was passed in the city of Atlanta, and in Fulton and DeKalb counties. The plan called for a 52.1-mile rapid-rail system with forty stations, 17.6 miles of dedicated bus-only lanes (busways) connecting with eight rail stations, an 86 percent expansion of the already existing bus system, and a 15-cent fare.

One of the key provisions of the MARTA proposal that secured black support for the 1971 referendum was a specific promise white elites made to Atlanta black leaders. In proposing the expensive northern rail line, the white elite promised a rail line to connect the downtown area to the Perry Homes public housing development—an Atlanta Housing Authority development located five miles on the far west side of the city and housing 3,000 low-income black residents.[18]

The Perry Homes line was a promise that was never kept. Apparently, the plan was proposed only to manipulate the black vote—and it worked. The real MARTA implementation plan gave priority to MARTA rail lines in the mostly white northern suburbs, while providing only buses for the mostly black areas, including Perry Homes and the other 12,000 residents living in isolated public housing developments. Essentially, the referendum translated into an expensive rail system for whites and a network of cheap buses for blacks. Perry Homes Resident Association President Mary Sanford waged a gallant campaign to have MARTA keep its promise. Her cries fell on deaf ears. The MARTA planners had no intention of running a rail line to the mostly black public housing project.

Over the past two decades, MARTA officials have amended the rapid-rail plan to make it next to impossible for the Perry Homes branch line to receive priority ranking to be built. The Perry Homes proposal was not even in contention when MARTA's latest round of expansions were being considered in the 1990s. Perry Homes tenants were denied a MARTA rail branch, and now have had their homes sold from under them by the Atlanta Housing Authority (AHA). The Perry Homes housing development no longer exists.

In 1999, the Atlanta Housing Authority won a federal grant to move the 2,500 low-income black residents out of Perry Homes, demolish the existing housing, and build a new 1,000-unit complex. A $340 million, upscale mixed-income development, West Highlands, was built on the 343-acre site where Perry Homes once stood. Plans for the West Highlands development include 1,000 houses, 700 apartments, shops, a charter school, library, YMCA, and a Jack Nicklaus golf course.

Approximately 228 homes will be set aside for public housing. Perry Homes residents were relocated in 2000 and West Highlands will be ready for occupancy in 2003. Taking issue with the small number of public housing units planned for West Highlands and fearing wholesale displacement, Mary Sanford stated "I don't really know what is going to happen to those who cannot help themselves."[19]

There is no guarantee that any former Perry Homes residents can move back to the West Highlands development. Past experience in Atlanta reveals that only about one in ten former tenants are successful in securing units in redeveloped public housing. There is no question that the Atlanta Housing Authority has transformed several of its dilapidated public housing developments into model housing. However, this transformation has come at the price of displacement of low-income tenants in favor of those tenants who can pay full market rent. Before all of the redevelopment, Atlanta had 14,500 units of public housing. Today, there are 9,500 public housing units in the city.[20]

It is no secret that white suburbanites did not want public transit or blacks in their communities. A 2000 Brookings Institution report on metro Atlanta found "public transit, overwhelmingly relied upon by minorities and low-income people who tend to live in the southern parts of the city and region, is relatively underfunded and constrained by suburban resistance."[21] Transportation planners responded to suburban attitudes and transit dollars flowed along a path determined by white racism.

Although the mostly white Gwinnett and Clayton counties opted out of MARTA and the one-cent MARTA sales tax on their residents, the two counties were given representation on MARTA's board of directors. Even state officials were given representation on the MARTA board, even though the state provides no funds to MARTA. Many black leaders and community activists in Atlanta and Fulton and DeKalb counties condemned this practice as "representation without taxation." [22]

Today, MARTA is the ninth largest transit system in the United States. During the 17 days of the 1996 Centennial Olympic Games in Atlanta, MARTA carried more than 25 million passengers—1.5 million passengers a day. With a $300 million annual budget, MARTA operates 702 buses and 248 rail cars. The rail system operates 38 rail stations spanning 48 miles of rail and the bus system operates 154 bus routes that cover 1,500 miles. Of the 702 buses in its fleet, 222 are clean-fuel Compressed Natural Gas (CNG) buses.[23]

Just how far and where MARTA rapid-rail lines will extend has proved to be a thorny issue that is hotly debated among diverse neighborhood constituents in Atlanta, Fulton and DeKalb counties. Competition between MARTA's service-area "haves" and "have-nots" will likely intensify in the future.[24] At present, 28.2 percent of Atlanta's black males and 35 percent of black females take public transit to work. On the other hand, 4.4 percent of white male and 6.7 percent of white female Atlantans take MARTA to work.[25] Additionally, MARTA planners are considering a light rail transit (LRT) initiative. Like the initial MARTA plan, racial inequities appear to be built into the various LRT proposals. With several proposals to extend MARTA rail lines under consideration, there is no agreement on where MARTA should go next.[26]

Talk of expanding the MARTA system into the suburbs still raises a red flag among many white suburbanites.[27] MARTA is equated with blacks and elicits negative attitudes among many white metro Atlantans. Consequently, discussion of building a rail system without using MARTA can generate some agreement among suburban homeowners.[28] As it stands, only residents of Fulton and DeKalb counties pay for the upkeep and expansion of the system with a one-cent MARTA sales tax. The regular one-way fare that cost 15 cents in 1972 is now $1.75. MARTA provides nearly 26,000 parking spaces at 38 rail stations. Parking at MARTA lots is free except for the overnight lots that cost $3 per day. It is becoming increasingly difficult to find a parking space in some MARTA lots. A recent license tag survey, "Who Parks-and-Rides," covering the period 1988–1997, revealed that 44 percent of the cars parked at MARTA lots were from outside the Fulton/DeKalb County service area.[29]

The parking issue became a sore point with many taxpayers from Fulton and DeKalb counties who appeared to be subsidizing people who live in outlying counties. Many white suburbanites struggle against MARTA and have been successful in keeping it out. Some of these same suburbanites drive to and park their cars at the MARTA satellite park-and-ride lots, and ride on MARTA trains into the city and to the airport. MARTA is a bargain to them since they do not pay the one-cent sales tax to support MARTA, and parking at the MARTA lots is free. The only cost to them is the $1.75 one-way fare for a 45-minute ride that usually takes up to two hours in a car.

Fulton and DeKalb County MARTA riders, rich and poor, pay the same $1.75 one-way fare if they travel one stop or ten stops, plus a one-cent MARTA sales tax. The fare structure, suburban subsidies, and board representation all raise transportation equity concerns. These concerns resurface from time to time at MARTA board meetings and hearings—especially when fare hikes and service cuts are involved.

The way MARTA funds are invested has also taken on equity overtones. It is widely known that transportation investments can spur economic development and neighborhood revitalization. Many black Atlanta neighborhoods have waited decades for the economic benefits associated with MARTA stations. They are still waiting. A 1997 study found MARTA had no significant impact in shaping the region's development pattern. On the other hand, sprawl development and highways were cited as the dominant players. These factors have also hindered transit-oriented development (TOD) around many MARTA stations. Of particular concern is the significant decline in employment in central city neighborhoods.[30]

In recent years, MARTA has begun to take a more active role in encouraging development around its rail stations. MARTA and the Atlanta Development Authority (ADA) have identified nine sites for mixed-use developments.[31] TOD got a shot in the arm in 1999 when BellSouth (one of the area's largest employers) announced that it would move 13,000 of its employees to new offices to be built near the MARTA Lindberg station.[32] BellSouth's plan would also consolidate much of its suburban operations in offices near MARTA's North Springs, Doraville, and College Park stations.[33] Still, all of the MARTA's TOD projects are located north of I-20—the historical demarcation between north and south in the region, with whites concentrated largely to the north and blacks concentrated largely to the south.[34]

Separate Buses for Suburban Atlanta

Cobb County created it own transit system in 1991. It opted not to join MARTA. Cobb Community Transit (CCT) operates forty-one buses that cover 345 miles. The suburban system carries an average of 9,300 passengers on weekdays. The one-way fare inside Cobb County is $1.25. The fare to a MARTA connection is $3 one way and $4 round-trip (both include MARTA transfers). CCT has limited links to MARTA. However, CCT buses take riders directly into several MARTA stations and stop at the curb in front of major employers. CCT also operates express routes that run from park-and-ride lots. The two systems do not share funds when riders transfer.

Gwinnett and Clayton counties voted in 1998 and 1999, respectively, to start bus systems. Both systems became functional during the latter part of 2001. Clayton County's C-TRAN is operated by MARTA and it began operations in October 2001. With a daily ridership of more than 1,700 riders on twelve buses, C-TRAN numbers surpassed any prior expectations.[35] Buying and running the buses for three years is expected to cost $30.7 million—80 percent is covered by the federal government, 10 percent by the state, and 10 percent by the county.[36]

Gwinnett County Transit became operational in November 2001. The system operates sixteen express buses. The new 35-seat buses feature reclining seats, directional air and lighting, and overhead compartments for laptops or briefcases. They feature racks for luggage and bikes, and access for people with disabilities.[37] Gwinnett is spending $79.5 million to buy and operate a fleet of seventy-four buses and vans through 2007. Local routes started in 2002 and are scheduled to be expanded in 2005. About $41.5 million will come from federal sources, $8.5 million from the state, $20.5 million from Gwinnett County funds, and about $9 million from fares, which will be $2 one way, with various discounts.[38]

In January 2002, the Georgia Regional Transportation Agency (GRTA) board announced that it was negotiating with thirteen metro area counties to start a regional express bus system by the year 2003, although it has yet to be implemented.[39] In preparation for the new service, board members voted unanimously to purchase forty-eight buses and apply for a $20 million federal grant to launch the service. At peak operation, forty-three buses will be rolling between downtown Atlanta and major centers in eleven metro counties during morning and evening commute hours.

Out of the thirteen counties governed by GRTA, eleven opted into the new regional bus system. Fayette and Cherokee counties decided against this new bus system. In exchange for contributing operational costs for the buses, the counties that opted in will collectively receive a half billion dollars for road improvements and other transportation costs. According to GRTA, by the year 2010 there will be 113 regional buses, 88 of which will be in operation at peak hours. The bus fleet will be phased in during the next eight years.[40]

Fulton and DeKalb residents are waiting to see how this new regional approach to transit will work. Because of MARTA budget shortfalls and the region's need for a seamless and coordinated transit system, a few elected officials have floated the idea of a state takeover of MARTA. However, the lack of state financial contribution to MARTA, and the failure of metro Atlanta suburban counties to participate in taxation, places an unfair burden on the residents of Atlanta, Fulton, and DeKalb counties who have carried MARTA's taxing burden for four decades.[41]

Black Coalition Fights Back

Although Atlanta has a long and rich civil rights history, it has lagged behind in dismantling the vestiges of transportation apartheid. When the Environmental Justice Resource Center (EJRC) first brought environmental justice and transportation racism issues to the larger Atlanta community in 1995, few local civil rights groups had specific strategies to address the racism that permeated MARTA's decision-making.

Metro Atlanta, unlike Los Angeles with its Labor/Community Strategy Center, did not have a single organization that was willing to serve as a convener, facilitator, initiator, or coordinator of transportation equity activities. In 1999, the EJRC, by default, served this role through the development of the Atlanta Transportation Equity Project (ATEP) with funding from several private foundations.[42] Through the ATEP, research, workshops, and training sessions were conducted with a dozen local black organizations to bring them up to speed on transportation planning in general and MARTA in particular. These black groups later formed the core of the Metropolitan Atlanta Transportation Equity Coalition (MATEC).

In an effort to expand the knowledge base and horizons of MATEC members, ATEP organized a field trip of ten MATEC members (four citizen-leaders, four MARTA union leaders, and two EJRC staff members) to Los Angeles to visit with representatives from the Labor/

Community Strategy Center and Bus Riders Union. On two separate occasions, ATEP brought Labor/Community Strategy Center director Eric Mann and several members of his staff to Atlanta to work with MATEC members. There was no reason to reinvent the wheel since Atlanta and Los Angeles had a lot in common when it came to transit racism. MATEC activist Sherrill Marcus summed up the Atlanta transit dilemma:

> When MATEC began its work, metropolitan Atlanta led the country in sprawl development. All of the adverse impacts from it increased congestion, worsened air quality, and made it more difficult accessing jobs. Improvements were made only after we came together to address these problems. Now, MARTA has as its top priority an extension of the west rail line that serves a minority area. The diesel-only bus garage that serves a mostly black area is also scheduled for retrofits to provide natural-gas-fueled buses.[43]

ATEP also hosted a premiere of Academy Award winner Haskell Wexler's *Bus Riders Union* documentary for MATEC and the public. The film and Los Angeles organizers were used as a "hook" to get more Atlantans aware of modern-day transportation racism and the link to transportation as an historical civil rights issue. The events, held at Clark Atlanta University, also generated heightened interest among students and faculty within the Atlanta University Center. The film showed that it is possible to win a modern civil rights victory against transportation racism.

In nearly four decades, MARTA had five general managers—all of whom were white males. In December 2000, after intense pressure from MATEC members and some key black elected officials, MARTA selected its first African American general manager, Nathaniel Ford.[44] However, it was made clear that having a black face at the helm of MARTA was not enough. The MATEC group wanted real change in dismantling transportation racism at MARTA.

It is ironic that several days before the MARTA board selected its first African American general manager, MATEC filed a discrimination complaint against the agency with the US Department of Transportation on behalf of their minority and disabled members.[45] One of the first items Nathaniel Ford had to deal with was MATEC's discrimination complaint. The MATEC groups charged MARTA with racial discrimination under Title VI of the Civil Rights Act of 1964.

They also cited MARTA for failing to comply with the federally mandated Americans with Disabilities Act (ADA). The complainants included a broad array of groups, including some well-known black civil rights organizations (SCLC, NAACP, and Rainbow/PUSH Coalition), neighborhood organizations, a disabled persons advocacy group, an environmental organization, a youth group, and a labor union that represents MARTA drivers.[46]

The coalition claimed that MARTA's services to minority communities were not on a par with the services provided to white communities. They pointed out that a disproportionate number of MARTA's overcrowded bus lines were located in minority communities, and minority communities did not receive a proportionate share of clean Compressed Natural Gas (CNG) buses and bus shelters. They contended that the rail stations located in minority neighborhoods were poorly maintained and fewer amenities were provided in comparison to those located in white communities. Additionally, the group charged the agency with providing inadequate security at the rail stations serving minority riders.

Unfair Fare Hike

On June 19, 2000, the MARTA board approved a $307 million operating budget that raised its one-way cash fare from $1.50 to $1.75—a 16.7 percent increase. The weekly transit pass jumped from $12 to $13 (an 8.3 percent increase); monthly passes increased from $45 to $52.50 (a 16.7 percent increase); and half-price senior citizens fares went from 75 cents to 85 cents (a 13.3 percent increase). Local groups argued that the fare increase would have a negative, disproportionate, discriminatory effect on MARTA's largely poor, people of color, and transit-dependent riders.

The MATEC group and its allies pleaded with the MARTA board not to raise its fares at a time when its ridership was showing an upward trend.[47] The groups cited studies that show ridership increased more than 5 percent between 1999 and 2000.[48] They also cited MARTA's failure to arrive at real budget alternatives to the fare hike, such as considering charging for parking, raising the parking fee at its overnight lots, increasing advertising, and seeking funds from the state. MARTA is the only major regional transit agency in the country that does not receive state funds.

The fare increase would raise approximately $12 million per year for MARTA to support the opening of two new suburban train stations (Sandy Springs and North Springs) on the North line. The two new suburban stations would add just two miles of track at the cost of $464 million in construction and $4 million annually to operate. The expensive, northern suburban rail expansion was being funded on the backs of Atlanta's poor, transit-dependent, and largely black transit riders. Once again, decisions to "go northward" that had been made decades earlier were playing out in the fare hike, while basic services to MARTA's core ridership in Atlanta and the South were declining. Atlantans were subsidizing the expansion of rapid-rail to the northern suburbs.

Whites comprised over 89 percent and blacks 9 percent of the populations living within a one-mile radius of MARTA's five north rail stations. This compares to 35 percent of whites and 62 percent of blacks who live within a one-mile radius of MARTA's stations system-wide.[49] A 1995 report prepared by Georgia Tech professors concluded that the residents who travel on MARTA's northern-tier rail lines are "more working ages, typically male, of higher income and typically white (by more than two to one)" as opposed to passengers who travel on the southern-tier rail lines. They also are more likely than all other MARTA riders to own a car, drive alone and travel long distances to MARTA stations, and pay cash or tokens.[50]

MARTA's northern-tier customers are "more sensitive to MARTA service than to fares." Georgia Tech Professor Nelson and his colleague concluded that as MARTA expands, northern-tier ridership will likely increase regardless of fare hikes.[51] MARTA's own rider surveys show that African Americans made up 77 percent of its customers in 1995 and 73 percent in 1999.[52] On the other hand, white MARTA riders increased from 22 percent in 1995 to 24 percent in 1999. On average, African Americans in the Atlanta region who ride MARTA have lower incomes, spend more per capita on transportation, and are more likely to be car-less than their white counterparts. Only 6.3 percent of whites compared to 26.5 percent of blacks who live in the MARTA service area are car-less.

MATEC entered into alliances with transportation experts at Clark Atlanta University and technical consultants who worked on the *Labor/Community Strategy Center, Bus Riders Union, et al. v. Los Angeles County MTA* case in California.[53] An independent transportation consultant, Thomas A. Rubin (who worked on the Los Angeles MTA case), was retained to review MARTA's budget figures and the impact of the fare increase. Rubin's findings confirmed what most Atlantans already knew: a fare hike would hit low-income African Americans and other people of color the hardest.[54]

For nearly a year, the MATEC groups insisted that MARTA's decision to raise its fares would have a negative, disproportionate, and discriminatory effect on the system's largely black, transit-dependent riders, and would cause them irreparable harm.[55] A May 2000

MARTA fare hike vote failed by one vote.[56] The fare vote passed a month later.[57] The fare hike went into effect on January 1, 2001.

Disabled People of Color Riders

Disabled people of color face the same challenges as other individuals with disabilities. They also face the "double jeopardy" of racial and disability discrimination. The coalition charged MARTA with denying disabled riders equal access to public buses, entitling them to relief under Title II of the ADA and Section 504 of the Rehabilitation Act. Disabled riders had not been accommodated in a timely manner and were disadvantaged due to malfunctioning equipment and the failure to provide alternate transportation promptly to those who require lift equipment. As a result, a disabled rider might have to wait several hours for lift-equipped buses.

In 2000, MARTA served 12,939 disabled patrons and roughly 30,000 customers who pay the senior/disabled fare on its regular route service. It served 2,800 paratransit-eligible customers. MARTA served 600 paratransit riders per day, 78.8 percent of whom are African American. Noncompliance with the ADA hits the African American MARTA riders especially hard, since many are transit-dependent and have low incomes. The disabled utilizing MARTA's paratransit services were subjected to long delays and excessively long trips before reaching their destinations. Additionally, MARTA failed to assure their riders that its personnel is trained to properly assist disabled patrons and to offer services in a respectful and courteous way, as required by the ADA.

In November 2001, attorneys for the Disability Law and Policy Center of Georgia, Inc., filed a civil action suit against MARTA. This lawsuit was the first formal action against MARTA for ADA violations. Represented by attorneys for the nonprofit Disability Law and Policy Center and cooperating counsel from the Decatur law firm Hill, Lord and Beasley, the six plaintiffs in the class action suit allege consistent, blatant discrimination against MARTA riders with disabilities. More specifically, the suit alleges noncompliance with the ADA and the Rehabilitation Act of 1973, which provide a specific set of guidelines for public transportation systems serving people with disabilities.

In October 2002, the plaintiffs won a preliminary injunction against MARTA. The court ordered MARTA to hire an independent consultant to do "testing" on the system (similar to fair housing testing) and report back, documenting ADA noncompliance issues that needed to be addressed by MARTA. MARTA was also ordered to redesign its website to make it user-friendly for the visually impaired and new customer service procedures were implemented to comply with the ADA.

Dumping "Dirty" Diesel Buses in Black Communities

In 2000, MARTA's bus fleet was comprised of approximately 698 buses, 118 of which were clean-fuel CNG buses. The bus fleet was housed at three garages: Laredo (249 buses), Perry (239 buses), and Hamilton (210 buses). MARTA's bus fleet distribution raises equity concerns considering that the Hamilton garage, which serves predominately black South Atlanta, is allocated the smallest bus fleet and minority routes suffer disproportionately from overcrowding. Additionally, the current and planned allocation of types of buses raises some special equity and Title VI concerns.

Of the three MARTA garages, the Hamilton facility serves by far the largest concentration of minority bus routes. All of MARTA's bus routes in the Hamilton garage service area are minority routes. All of the buses housed at the Hamilton garage are "dirty" diesel buses, which are the oldest, most dilapidated, and most pollution-generating buses. In 2000, MARTA had no plans in the next several years to bring clean-burning CNG buses to its mostly black areas served by the Hamilton garage. This meant that MARTA customers on bus routes with the largest concentration of blacks would have to wait the longest for the CNG buses, which are the newest, cleanest buses, equipped with the latest technology. On the other hand, the two MARTA garages with the largest concentration of nonminority bus routes are either currently served by a full fleet of CNG buses (the Perry garage), or plans are underway to accommodate CNG buses (the Laredo garage).

Clearly, the benefits and the burdens of MARTA's bus fleet are not equally distributed across MARTA's service area. The benefits of CNG buses disproportionately accrue to MARTA service areas with the greatest concentration of nonminority bus routes. Bus routes serving a large share of white passengers, such as the Emory University route, are serviced by newer buses only.

Residents in predominately black South Atlanta are disproportionately burdened by the environmental hazards and potential health effects created by MARTA's older diesel-only bus fleet, which are both housed in and travel through their communities. MARTA's allocation of CNG buses and its plan to retrofit the depots to accommodate CNG buses (with the all-minority bus routes in South Atlanta served last) points to a pattern and practice of discriminating against blacks.

Disparate Shelter Distribution and Station Conditions

MARTA has failed to provide adequate bus shelters in people of color communities. According to MARTA's latest Title VI Compliance Program report, submitted in August 1997 to the US Department of Transportation's Office of Equal Opportunity, there were 576 bus shelters located inside of the MARTA service zone. The bus routes were classified as minority or nonminority according to FTA guidelines. MARTA reported 267 (46.4 percent) nonminority and 309 (53.6 percent) minority shelters.

Minority routes averaged 8.45 miles in length while nonminority routes averaged 3.99 miles. Minority routes averaged 3.68 shelters per route with a ratio of .46 shelters per mile, while nonminority routes averaged 6.14 shelters per route with a ratio of .70 shelters per mile. Among the individual routes, there is one 4.26-mile nonminority route that does not have shelters. Six minority routes are without any shelters at an average length of 5.66 miles and ranging from 2.87 to 6.98 miles.

The longest nonminority route extends for 20.89 miles and has 15 shelters while the longest minority route extends for 17.32 miles and has only one shelter. Additionally, MARTA's practice of placing used bus shelters in minority communities while placing new bus shelters in nonminority communities raises additional Title VI concerns surrounding allocation of bus shelters.

Are MARTA stations created equally? MATEC members asked this question. It was also asked by *Atlanta Journal-Constitution* staff writer Stacy Shelton. She found that MARTA riders grade the train stations from "arty to dingy."[58] Generally, MARTA's newest Sandy Springs and North Springs stations get the most positive responses, while many of the older stations located in inner-city and people of color neighborhoods get the worst ratings in terms of cleanliness, safety, ambiance, and signs.

Another *Atlanta Journal-Constitution* staff writer, Martha Ezzard, also observed disparities in MARTA rail stations. In her 2001 article, "Moving Art," she writes:

> I closed my umbrella with a shiver on a recent gloomy workday. Time to enter the cavern. That's the way I think of the Five Points MARTA station, which can make a gray day grayer. No color. Little light. Lots of litter. Twenty-eight

minutes later, I arrive on a different planet. Glistening white tile and shiny chrome make the Sandy Springs MARTA station, bathed in artificial light, feel like the top of the world, though it's as underground as any of MARTA's thirty-seven stations. Once I stepped off the train onto the platform, my eyes automatically followed the geometric modules of Katherine Mitchell's 12-foot-high "ziggurats" upward—the colorful pyramids-like art that adorns the station's mammoth architectural space. The Sandy Springs station invites lingering.[59]

People of color transit riders do not need newspaper reporters to know that they are being shortchanged by MARTA when it comes to maintenance, amenities, and security at MARTA rail stations in their communities. The northern-tier MARTA rail stations located in predominately white communities are well maintained and have an abundance of visible security personnel (station managers) at all times. In contrast, the southern-tier and west-end MARTA rail stations located in predominately black communities are poorly maintained and security personnel has either low visibility or is entirely absent.

The disparities at rail stations go well beyond art and decoration. According to MARTA's Title VI Compliance Program report, schedule information telephones (SITs) are located at twenty-three MARTA rail stations. Of the thirteen rail stations without SITs, nine are located in mostly minority areas. SITs have direct access to MARTA's customer information center.[60]

There are also disparities in the provision of TraveLink kiosks at the rail stations. TraveLink kiosks are informational computers accessed by touching a screen. The kiosks provide travelers with information about bus and rail carriers, airlines, state highways, weather, and hotels. MARTA provides bus schedules, fare information, itinerary planning, and the next bus available to the customer.

MARTA has twenty-three rail stations equipped with TraveLink kiosks and thirteen without. Of those thirteen rail stations without kiosks, eleven are located in mostly minority areas. Additionally, there are racial disparities in the provision of covered parking, weather protection on rail platforms and walkways, informational displays, and atmospheric comforts such as art and music. MARTA's failure to equalize the amenities provided at its rail stations constitutes disparate treatment of minorities in violation of Title VI.

Faulty Public Participation Process

MARTA failed to follow the public participation process that the DOT has adopted for assessing transportation equity issues in the

Atlanta area, as expressed in the DOT's Assessment of Environmental Justice Issues and Public Involvement in the Atlanta Metropolitan Area (Phase I Equity Analysis).[61] The standards adopted by the DOT require a public participation process that reaches, empowers, and takes into account low-income and communities of color in transportation decision-making.

The standards set by the DOT require MARTA to assure full and fair participation by all communities in the fare restructuring process, which encompasses timely and effective notification of public meetings and measures to assure equal opportunity to participate at public meetings. MARTA failed in this very basic public participation standard by not providing timely and effective notification of the public hearings on the fare increase to all impacted communities, and failed to assure equal opportunity for participation at the hearings.

The proposed-fare-increase ads ran in the *Atlanta Journal-Constitution* in English only, and were posted on MARTA's web page, also in English only. MARTA failed to provide notification of the public hearings on the proposed fare increase to Atlanta's non-English speaking Latino community residents. MARTA did not take the time to alert Latinos in Atlanta of proposed changes. Public notices and announcements were not included in local Spanish language media, including newspapers and radio. The result was an alarming lack of participation by Latinos in the public hearing process.

During the three public hearings held on the proposed fare increase, not a single member of the Latino community testified, even though one of the largest Latino communities in Atlanta is located near MARTA's headquarters at the Lindberg rail station. Additionally, MARTA failed to make English-Spanish translation services available at the public hearings even though MARTA received considerable advance notice that a segment of the Latino community would need translation services for meaningful participation.

Due to MATEC's efforts, MARTA has taken steps to remedy the disparity in service toward Latino riders. Currently, MARTA provides Spanish-English literature and flyers at train stations and public meetings. A Spanish-English interpreter is now available at all board meetings and public hearings. Also, MARTA's customer service hotline is now able to provide assistance to Spanish-speaking customers.

Conclusion

MARTA has a long history of shortchanging its black customers. The system was created and built on empty promises and the deceiving of blacks in order to get their vote. Having an active community-based organization such as MATEC has made a difference in the way MARTA delivers transit services and responds to its low-income and people of color riders. Many of the changes, improvements, and enhancements that MARTA has instituted since November 2000, the date MATEC filed its Title VI and ADA complaint, can be directly attributed to concessions won through federally supervised mediations between MATEC and MARTA, and grassroots mobilization of black Atlantans.

Originally, the complaint was forwarded to the FTA's office in Washington, DC. The complaint was transferred to the Chicago and Boston offices, respectively, of the FTA, before finally reaching the Atlanta FTA office in April of 2002. This major delay (fifteen months) in investigation and action on the part of the FTA allowed the solidification of the fare increase on the part of MARTA. In September 2002, the FTA advised the complainants to enter mediation talks with MARTA representatives. After extensive internal discussions, the MATEC members agreed to mediation.

Mediation proved more difficult and frustrating than the MATEC groups had anticipated. Mediation was completed in mid October 2002. The parties agreed on mediating only the Title VI issues—the ADA issues against MARTA were already being debated in court because of the class action lawsuit filed by under the ADA and the Rehabilitation Act in November 2001. Over twenty months passed from the time of the filing of the complaint to the mediation. The extended time between the two events proved devastating for MATEC efforts, since many of the issues raised in the complaint were less relevant than at the time of filing. Also, during that period the new administration at MARTA began steps toward addressing many of the issues in the complaint, leaving MATEC with very little room for negotiation. It was also clear that MARTA had no budget for the mediation. The items that MATEC demanded that would increase costs for the agency were quickly eliminated from the discussion both by the FTA and MARTA.

Some changes at MARTA were cosmetic and mere window dressing. Others are more substantive. Getting black Atlantans to challenge the powerful white business elite and black political elite was not easy. Black politicians recognized that ordinary citizens far outnumber the elites and carry the majority vote at the end of the day. Grassroots community pressure persuaded the Atlanta City Council and the Fulton County Commission to pass resolutions in 2000 opposing MARTA's unpopular fare hike.

As mentioned earlier in this chapter, in 2000, the MARTA board shattered a four-decade "glass ceiling" for blacks and selected its first African American general manager. Nathaniel Ford, former executive vice president of operations at MARTA, was selected after a national search. In the same year, the MARTA Police Department initiated a new program designed to reduce crime in the system. The new program, called MPPACT (MARTA Police Proactively Attacking Crime Trends), utilizes crime statistics to show trends in customer complaints, crimes, calls for service, and disorder in the system. Using this analysis, MARTA plans to utilize the existing police force more efficiently. Also, MARTA customers can report a crime by dialing #MPD on their cell phone and connect directly to the MARTA Police Department Communications Center.

A year later, MARTA received fifty new "clean diesel" buses to replace old buses (some more than twelve years old and with more than 600,000 miles) at the Hamilton garage, which serves the mostly black South Fulton County. While this concession does not provide clean CNG buses in the mostly black service area, this is the first time in over ten years that this facility received new buses. The previous practice was to move the old buses to the Hamilton garage and place the new buses at the other two garages. MARTA is currently trying to secure funding for the conversion of the Hamilton garage from housing diesel buses to CNG buses.

Several train stations in minority areas have received upgrades and maintenance such as Hamilton Holmes (new roof), West End (power scrubbings), and Ashby Street (elevator and escalator repairs). MARTA has begun a program to install 600 shelters and 300 benches, giving minority, low-income, and transit-dependent areas priority placements. It established the SMART Team program. This program uses a number of the agency's employees to identify, assess, and recommend solutions to maintenance problems in and around MARTA's train stations.

MATEC has received assurances and a commitment from MARTA for resolving overcrowding on specific bus lines. Currently, customers can call MARTA's hotline and report overcrowding on specific bus routes. MARTA's personnel agreed to conduct assessments on such routes and initiate corrective actions when appropriate.

Finally, no regional transit system can work in metropolitan Atlanta without having MARTA at the core. MARTA is the most comprehensive transit system in the region—operating both buses and rail. This mature transit system has taken four decades to develop—with only two of the counties in the thirteen-county region paying for the system. Race still matters in planning transit in metropolitan Atlanta. Until racism is reined in, the Atlanta region will continue to have a patchwork of unlinked, uncoordinated, and "separate but unequal" transit systems feeding into and feeding off MARTA.

notes

1. Metropolitan Planning Commission, *Up Ahead: A Metropolitan Land Use Plan for Metropolitan Atlanta* (Atlanta: Metropolitan Planning Commission, 1952), 12.

2. Bradley R. Rice, "Atlanta: If Dixie Were Atlanta," in *Sunbelt Cities: Growth since World War II*, eds. Richard M. Bernard and Bradley R. Rice (Austin: University of Texas Press, 1983), 31–57.

3. Ibid., 31.

4. See Robert D. Bullard, *In Search of the New South: The Black Urban Experience in the 1970s and 1980s* (Tuscaloosa, AL: University of Alabama Press, 1991).

5. Robert D. Bullard, Glenn S. Johnson, and Angel O. Torres, eds., *Sprawl City: Race, Politics and Planning in Atlanta* (Washington, DC: Island Press, 2000).

6. Marshall Ingwerson, "Atlanta Has Become a Mecca of the Black Middle Class in America," *Christian Science Monitor*, May 29, 1987, 1; Bullard, *In Search of the New South*.

7. Ibid.

8. The 1998 Atlanta Regional Commission estimates are based on the 1990 US census, building permits, and other growth formulas.

9. David Firestone, "Suburban Comforts Thwart Atlanta's Plans to Limit Sprawl," *The New York Times*, November 21, 1999, 30.

10. Christopher Leinberger, "The Metropolis Observed," *Urban Land* 57 (October 1998): 28–33.

11. David Goldberg, "Regional Growing Pains," *Atlanta Journal-Constitution*, March 10, 1997, E5.

12. Ibid.

13. David L. Sjoquist, ed., *The Atlanta Paradox* (New York: Russell Sage Foundation, 2000), 2.

14. Atlanta Region Minority Population by County, 2000, 1990 and 1980

	2000	1990	1980
City of Atlanta	66.8%	69.6%	68.1%
Atlanta Region	41.2%	30.7%	27.1%
Cherokee County	7.6%	2.8%	2.7%
Clayton County	62.1%	27.9%	9.1%
Cobb County	27.6%	12.7%	6.2%
DeKalb County	64.2%	47.0%	29.8%
Douglas County	22.7%	9.2%	6.3%
Fayette County	16.1%	7.6%	5.6%
Fulton County	51.9%	53.2%	53.1%
Gwinnett County	27.3%	9.2%	4.1%
Henry County	18.6%	11.4%	18.7%
Rockdale County	24.3%	9.7%	10.1%

US Census Bureau, "Table 7 from Census 2000 Summary File 1" in *Atlanta Region Outlook* (Atlanta Regional Commission, 1998).

15. Bullard, Johnson, and Torres, eds., *Sprawl City*, Chapter 2.

16. Margaret Edds, *Free at Last: What Really Happened When Civil Rights Came to Southern Politics* (Bethesda, MD: Adler and Adler, 1987), 75.

17. Larry Keating, *Atlanta: Race, Class, and Urban Expansion* (Philadelphia: Temple University Press, 2002).

18. Ibid., 114.

19. Quoted in Milo Ippolito, "Planned Community May Bring New Life to Stagnant Corner of City," *Atlanta Journal-Constitution*, November 11, 2002, B1.

20. Mara Shalhoup, "Atlanta Housing Authority Shell Game," *Creative Loafing Atlanta*, November 6, 2002.

21. The Brookings Institution, *Moving Beyond Sprawl: The Challenge for Metropolitan Atlanta* (Washington, DC: The Brookings Institution Center on Urban and Metropolitan Policy, 2000), 22.

22. Metropolitan Atlanta Transportation Equity Project, "Title VI Administrative Complaint Against MARTA," November 30, 2001.

23. Metropolitan Atlanta Transportation Equity Project, "Media KIT: Fact Sheet," http://www.itsmarta.com/newsroom/martafacts.htm (accessed May 1, 2003).

24. Bill Torpy, "Haves, Have-Nots Battle over MARTA Access," *Atlanta Journal-Constitution*, May 25, 1998, E1.

25. Sidney Davis, "Transportation and Black Atlanta," in *Status of Black Atlanta*, ed. Bob Holmes, 79 (Atlanta: The Southern Center for Studies in Public Policy, 1994).

26. Ibid., Susan Laccetti Meyer, "Where Should MARTA Go Next," *Atlanta Journal-Constitution*, December 5, 1998, A18.

27. Bill Torpy, "MARTA Proposal Spurs Anger," *Atlanta Journal-Constitution*, October 30, 1998, F2.

28. David Goldberg, "Atlanta Suburbanites Thinking Regionally," *The Neighborhood Works*, November/December 1997, 14.

29. Metropolitan Atlanta Rapid Transit Authority, *Tag Survey 1988-1997* (Atlanta: MARTA Division of Planning and Policy Development, Department of Research Analysis, 1999); Goro O. Mitchell, "Transportation, Air Pollution, and Social Equity in Atlanta," in *Status of Black Atlanta*, ed. Bob Holmes (Atlanta: The Southern Center for Studies in Public Policy, 1994), 120.

30. Research Atlanta, Inc., *The Impact of MARTA on Station Area Development* (Atlanta: School of Policy Studies Georgia State University, 1997), 17.

31. David Pendered, "MARTA Aims to Help Shape Development," *Atlanta Journal-Constitution*, October 19, 1998; David Pendered, "MARTA Makes Its Move," *Atlanta Journal-Constitution*, March 29, 1999.

32. Joey Ledford, "Beating Traffic Woes by Moving to Town," *Atlanta Journal-Constitution*, February 5, 1999, C2.

32. David Pedered, "A Bold New Frontier for MARTA," *Atlanta Journal-Constitution*, February 1, 1999, F3.

34. See Bullard, Johnson, Torres, eds., *Sprawl City*, 39–68; Robert D. Bullard, Glenn S. Johnson, and Angel O. Torres, "Atlanta Megasprawl," *Forum for Applied Research and Public Policy* 14, no. 3 (Fall 1999): 17–23; Robert D. Bullard, Glenn S. Johnson, and Angel O. Torres, "The Routes of American Apartheid," *Forum for Applied Research and Public Policy* 15, no. 3 (Fall 2000): 66–74.

35. Henry Farber, "C-TRAN Marks Six Months of Success on the Road," *Atlanta Journal-Constitution*, April 11, 2002, J11.

36. Henry Farber, "GRTA Gears up to Put Buses on the Road in Clayton County," *Atlanta Journal-Constitution*, September 26, 2001, B1.

37. Doug Nurse, "Gwinnett Transit Gears up for Riders," *Atlanta Journal-Constitution*, August 30, 2001, A1.

38. Ibid.

39. Christopher Quinn, "Burbs Steered to Bus System," *Atlanta Journal-Constitution*, January 17, 1999, A1.

40. Julie Hairston, "GRTA OKs Purchase of 48 Buses for New Service," *Atlanta Journal-Constitution*, March 11, 2002, C3.

41. Jim Galloway, "2002 Georgia Legislature: Atlanta Debate, State Takeover of Airport Assailed, but MARTA's Reins Up for Grabs," *Atlanta Journal-Constitution*, January 23, 2002.

42. The Environmental Justice Resource Center at Clark Atlanta University built the Atlanta Transportation Equity Project with grants from the Public Welfare Foundation, Turner Foundation, Surdna Foundation, and Ford Foundation.

43. Sherrill Marcus, lead organizer with the Metropolitan Atlanta Transportation Equity Coalition, interview, May 30, 2003.

44. Stacy Shelton, "MARTA Appoints New Chief," *Atlanta Journal-Constitution*, December 1, 2000, D16.

45. Metropolitan Atlanta Transportation Equity Coalition to Ron Stroman, US Department of Transportation, Office of Civil Rights and Nuria Fernandez, Administrator of the Federal Transit Administration, complaint letter, November 28, 2000.

46. Ernie Suggs, "Complaint: MARTA Hike Based on Bias," *Atlanta Journal-Constitution*, December 7, 2000, D5.

47. John McCosh, "Smog, Fare Fights Swirl Around MARTA," *Atlanta Journal-Constitution*, May 25, 2000, C1.

48. Robert D. Bullard to William Mosley, MARTA Board Chairman, memorandum, April 17, 2000, commenting on the impact of the proposed fare hike on low-income, transit-dependent, and minority riders.

49. Goro O. Mitchell, "Transportation, Air Pollution, and Social Equity in Atlanta," in *Status of Black Atlanta*, ed. Bob Holmes, 105–139 (Atlanta: Clark Atlanta University, 1999).

50. Chris Nelson, et al., *MARTA Impact Study, North and Northeast Lines Travel Market Analysis* (Atlanta: Georgia Institute of Technology, 1995), 11.

51. Ibid.

52. Metropolitan Atlanta Rapid Transit Authority, *5th Annual Quality of Service Survey*, (Atlanta: MARTA Division of Customer Development, Department of Planning and Analysis, 1999).

53. Eric Mann, "Confronting Transit Racism in Los Angeles," in *Just Transportation: Dismantling Race and Class Barriers to Mobility*, ed. Robert D. Bullard and Glenn S. Johnson, (Gabriola Island, British Columbia: New Society Publishers, 1997), 68-83.

54. Thomas A. Rubin, *Report on the Impact of the MARTA Fare Increase* (January 2000), submitted to the Environmental Justice Resource Center at Clark Atlanta University as part of the Atlanta Transportation Equity Project.

55. John McCosh, "As MARTA Grows, So May One-way Fare to $1.75," *Atlanta Journal-Constitution*, February 18, 2000, A1.

56. John McCosh, "MARTA Fare Increase Stalled by One Vote," *Atlanta Journal-Constitution*, May 26, 2000, C1.

57. David Pendered, "MARTA to Start 2001 with Fare Hike," *Atlanta Journal-Constitution*, June 20, 2000, A1.

58. Stacy Shelton, "Riders Grade MARTA Stops from Arty to Dingy," *Atlanta Journal-Constitution*, May 31, 2001.

59. Martha Ezzard, "Moving Art," *Atlanta Journal-Constitution*, February 25, 2001.

60. Metropolitan Atlanta Rapid Transit Authority, *Title VI Compliance Program* (August 1997) report submitted to the Office of Equal Opportunity. Stations have been added to the MARTA system since this report was filed.

61. US Department of Transportation, *Assessment of Environmental Justice and Public Involvement in the Atlanta Metropolitan Area* (Washington, DC: US Department of Transportation, Office of Civil Rights, 2000).

FOUR

Burying Robert Moses's Legacy in New York City
Omar Freilla

Over the course of forty-four years, Robert Moses turned the powers of mundane government agencies into his own personal empire of construction. Elected by no one, Moses held everyone from mayors and governors to presidents in check. His power came from the skillful manipulation of the spoils from the many titles that he often held simultaneously: New York City (NYC) Construction Coordinator; NYC Parks Commissioner; New York State (NYS) Council of Parks Chair; NYS Public Works Department Chair; Long Island State Parks Commissioner; NYC Slum Clearance Committee Chair; and commissioner for a host of public authorities such as the Triborough Bridge and Tunnel Authority. The public authorities were the economic engine that powered his empire since they provided him with an independent source of revenue. Tolls collected at Triborough's bridge crossings were funneled directly into the agency's coffers to be spent as Moses saw fit. The lack of accountability to the public allowed by these various organizations provided him with plenty of room to move about in secret. Those he trained were spread like frosting over a host of other bureaucracies such as the NYC Housing Authority, extending his reach even further. From 1920 to 1964, Moses was the ultimate power broker, involved, from beginning to end, in creating over $27 billion worth of public works projects, earning him the title "master builder."[1]

He oversaw the construction of highways, parkways, parks and playgrounds, bridges, and housing developments all over New York State, and is credited with having shaped the face of the modern American city more than any other person. But for communities that wound up in his path, Robert Moses was the very symbol of everything wrong with government planning. For these communities, Moses's legacy is one of racism and classism, forced removals, the splitting of neighborhoods, economic depression, and increased pollution. Conservative estimates place the number of people forced from their homes for his highways at 250,000—a number that jumps to almost half a million when factoring in the homes bulldozed to make way for "urban renewal" and other projects.[2] Not surprisingly, poor Latinos and African Americans made up a disproportionate share of those kicked into the street to make way for Moses's vision. His application of federal "urban renewal" and "slum clearance" programs reshuffled the neighborhoods of New York City, creating new housing opportunities for wealthy whites. But the net effect of his projects was even greater than could have been imagined and was to have far-reaching consequences.

Moses's celebrated highways unleashed forces that gutted stable neighborhoods and sent marginal ones careening over the edge. They provided the city's white middle class with an escape route made of long, clean stretches of road to the mythic garden paradise of suburbia, just as the city's manufacturing base was beginning to erode. The gap between rich and poor ballooned, and the entire city suffered as statewide political power shifted north and east, following the white exodus into suburban single-family homes. New York City would be left isolated for decades with a crumbling infrastructure, a traffic-jammed nightmare of roads, and a deserted population not found on anyone's agenda at the state .

New York City's turnaround over the years has been portrayed in the wider press as a recent phenomenon, a product of the Giuliani Administration. But in reality, the city's rebound from the aftermath of the Moses era has been a slow process of recovery involving a wide spectrum of players. If anyone is to receive credit for NYC's recovery, it ought to be, first and foremost, the grassroots community groups that sprang from the ashes of burned-out apartment buildings and vacant lots to meet the needs that the city and state ignored. Over the years, many other organizations working to rebuild their communities within the physical limits imposed by Moses's highways have developed and joined with those early grassroots groups.

Those of us involved with the NYC environmental justice movement have found that working around the limits imposed by highways has necessitated a radically different approach. Through open collaborations between communities, we are attempting to confront the Moses legacy head-on with the shared goal of physically removing the very highways that have caused so much grief. This chapter tells the story of two NYC neighborhoods—one in Southwest Brooklyn and the other in the South Bronx—their decimation by Moses, and their determination to reclaim and transform their worlds.

Moses the Butcher in Brooklyn

Before the opening of the Gowanus Parkway in 1941, Third Avenue was the heart of Brooklyn's Sunset Park—a tree-lined street with movie theaters, restaurants, small shops, few cars, and an elevated subway line. When residents of the time found out the subway line was to become the right-of-way for a highway, they pleaded with Moses to move his plans just one block west to Second Avenue, away from businesses and homes. Everyone in the neighborhood knew that Second Avenue was the dividing line that kept the blight of the waterfront's warehouses, factories, and seedy piers at bay. But Moses dismissed the community's calls to move the road, responding that Sunset Park was "a slum" not particularly worth saving.[3] It didn't matter that Sunset Park's residents, who were predominantly poor European immigrants with a sprinkling of Puerto Ricans, didn't agree with Moses's characterization of their neighborhood.

Unlike the elevated subway tracks, the Gowanus's solid, wider roadbed draped Third Avenue in a curtain of darkness. The parkway displaced over one hundred stores and 1,300 families. As a wave of divestment crashed over the neighborhood, longtime residents packed their bags and moved out. Abandoned buildings and vacant lots spread like a virus as alcohol and drug use increased.[4]

Moses's authority at the time did not permit him to build highways, only parkways, which by definition excluded trucks. But something had to be done about the trucks that would soon be bellowing out of the mouth of the Brooklyn Battery Tunnel that Moses was building into Manhattan. His solution was to steer trucks onto Third Avenue underneath the Gowanus Parkway. With the opening of the tunnel in 1950, Sunset Park became more accessible than ever to trucks and the industries that depended on them. Residential side streets became inundated with trucks slicing their way to the waterfront. The Gowanus transformed the sounds of Third Avenue from friendly chatter to a cacophony of rumbling tractor-trailers, blasting truck horns, and screeching brakes. And people wondered, what was it all for?

The Gowanus became jam-packed as soon as the Brooklyn Battery Tunnel (at one end) and the Belt Parkway (at the other) were opened. All over the city Moses began to widen many of the roadways he had only recently built and build new ones wherever he could fit them, all in a desperate but vain attempt to reduce congestion. It wasn't until the 1960s that Moses would make his way down the list to the Gowanus. Reclassifying it as an expressway (Interstate Highway I-278, as it is known today), Moses widened the Gowanus (as well as Third Avenue) right up to the windows of adjacent buildings. [5] But the widening did nothing to alleviate congestion. To the contrary, adding new lanes merely added new lanes of congested traffic.

The decline that came about as a result of the Gowanus's construction was compounded by changes in the shipping industry during the 1960s that reduced the number of port-related jobs in the community.[6] The prevailing policies of financial institutions further isolated Sunset Park. Federal housing policies of the time encouraged the infamous practice of redlining, denying loans to neighborhoods with even a trace of people of color. Those who had to live in the "new" and declining Sunset Park were those that couldn't afford to leave or who were routed to the neighborhood by a combination of cheap rents and racist housing policies.

Federal low-interest home loans were restricted to new single-family housing. The combination of cheap loans and construction of new homes created jobs for construction workers, the vast majority of whom were white, and made racially segregated suburbs affordable.[7] The policy was, in effect, a massive welfare program for the white working class. Neighborhoods like Sunset Park, where older multifamily homes were the rule and the concentration of people of color was steadily rising, were completely abandoned. According to these federal restrictions and bank rating systems, if you were a homeowner in Sunset Park and wanted to renovate your home or building in the decades after the Gowanus was built, you wouldn't have been able to get a loan to do it.

While Sunset Park may not have been a slum to its residents before the Gowanus, it certainly became one to many after. Moses's classification of Sunset Park as a slum would be put to use in other neighborhoods again and again. According to Moses, a slum had no right to exist and its residents had no rights that the government was bound to respect. Not that he particularly respected any community's rights, particularly those that voiced an objection to his plans, but he certainly knew which communities the press and his colleagues respected. Whenever a neighborhood contained people whose income, language, or skin color placed them outside the gates of power in New York City, conjuring up the image of a "slum" became a surefire tactic to avoid having to preserve anything or be accountable to anybody.

In effect, the label was a license to demolish. The label's most destructive effects would soon be seen in another part of the city, the South Bronx. The combined construction of the Cross-Bronx, Major Deegan, Bruckner, and Sheridan Expressways instigated a chain of events that turned the South Bronx into the premier poster ghetto of America for at least three decades.

Moses the Butcher in the Bronx

What overwhelmed the South Bronx about Moses's highways was the sheer magnitude of construction. Four major interstate highway projects occurred practically simultaneously between the 1950s and early 1960s.[8] The concentration of highways in the Bronx was by and large a result of geography. The Bronx is the only one of the five NYC boroughs that is actually a part of the US mainland. The remaining four (Manhattan, Brooklyn, Queens, and Staten Island) are either part of an island or an island unto themselves. But the decision to rip through dense residential areas and evict thousands of people in order to create a network of highways for suburbanites speaks volumes about the low regard Moses had for the residents of the Bronx.

Most of the areas affected were racially and ethnically mixed communities. In his book *The Power Broker*, Robert Caro paints an in-depth and disturbing portrait of what happened along a one-mile section of the Cross-Bronx Expressway known as East Tremont and to the 1,530 evicted families in this mixed neighborhood of Jews, African Americans, and Puerto Ricans. The tragedy of East Tremont was repeated along each mile of Moses's highways in the Bronx. One particular segment of the Bronx's spaghetti bowl of highways, a short stub of a highway known as the Sheridan Expressway, has special relevance today.

At one and one-quarter miles long, the Sheridan Expressway (I-895) is the shortest stretch of highway in the New York metropolitan region. Moses originally planned to extend it another six miles and connect it with I-95 somewhere near the northern border of the Bronx. On the way it would have carved up even more neighborhoods than it already had in the short distance it traveled. But before reaching I-95, the Sheridan would have had to pass through the Bronx Zoo, something the zoo's wealthy benefactors were not about to allow without a fight. [9] Fortunately for them, the early 1960s were the final years of power for Moses. He was slowly being stripped of his many positions in a game of political chess being played with then governor Nelson Rockefeller over who would control the future of New York.

The groups opposed to Moses's plan were successful in stopping the highway in 1962. Two years later Moses was completely stripped of all power. By 1972 Governor Rockefeller would officially declare that there would be no extension of the Sheridan.[10]

Those north of the zoo were spared the onslaught of bulldozers. But those who lived to its south were victims of a highway construction binge that devoured homes and businesses—consuming entire communities and livelihoods. In the aftermath of so much destruction, what remained was a useless fragment of a highway that has seen little use since it first opened. In addition to displacing people, that fragment of highway (along with the Cross-Bronx and Bruckner Expressways) managed to cut off access to the meandering urban oasis known as the Bronx River. North of the Bronx Zoo, the river is fully accessible to everyone. For those living in the South Bronx, only a small island of park, sandwiched between the Sheridan and a few weeping willows on the river's banks, offers a glimpse of the distant past. The portion of the river that extends into the South Bronx has been solidly encased in a box of concrete and abandonment. The only way for those of us in the South Bronx to view the Bronx River is by standing on a bridge or highway overpass. And while the river itself can at times seem somewhat serene, the concrete plants and garbage-covered lots along its banks and the floating bits of trash make for a sorry sight.

There are still people in the South Bronx who remember a time before the highways drove wedges between communities. They are the ones who stayed while the South Bronx burned during the 60s and 70s. The burning—much of it directly caused by landlords who found it more profitable to burn their apartment buildings and collect the insurance benefits rather than maintain their properties—was a by-product of the widespread abandonment which Moses's highways played no small part in creating. In spite of all the pain and suffering that residents of the South Bronx were forced to bear, the highways (with the exception of the Sheridan) would end up sharing the same status as Brooklyn's Gowanus Expressway—that of a moving parking lot—proving that you can't "build your way out of congestion."

Growing out of a community vision and using unconventional methods, a grassroots environmental justice movement, intent on demolishing the Sheridan and Gowanus Expressways and burying Robert Moses's legacy, has formed.

Brooklyn Resurgence

Occupying a small storefront one block from the Gowanus Expressway is the office of the United Puerto Rican Organization of Sunset Park (UPROSE). Its walls and windows are covered with signs demanding an end to environmental racism in Sunset Park: "Paz Para Vieques" slogans that recall the successful campaign to end US military bombing exercises on the Puerto Rican island of Vieques; posters documenting Palestinian uprisings; and a photo of Malcolm X. Founded as a social service agency in the 1960s for the area's Puerto Rican community, the organization has expanded to serve a broader mix of the neighborhood's growing numbers of Palestinian, Mexican, Dominican, and Chinese residents. Consequently, the group's executive director, Elizabeth Yeampierre, prefers to go strictly by their acronym, UPROSE. Since she came to the organization in 1996, Elizabeth has been vigorous about community and youth organizing, especially when it comes to environmental justice. As a member of the New York City Environmental Justice Alliance, a network of community groups fighting for environmental justice, UPROSE has become an important voice for environmental justice in the city. UPROSE's very active youth group, Youth Justice, always makes their presence known in the neighborhood—from marching into public hearings with banners, matching T-shirts and hats to on occasion wearing Puerto Rican and Palestinian flags as masks. Due to its immense size and impact on the community, what to do about the Gowanus Expressway is a question UPROSE and Youth Justice have had to spend a lot of time thinking about.

For decades, the Gowanus has maintained absolute domination over the southwest Brooklyn waterfront, the local skyline, and local ears and lungs. Daily traffic counts average 175,000 vehicles at the highway's most congested point.[11] Its bumper-to-bumper traffic pushes cars and trucks onto local streets. The incredible volume of vehicles creates an invisible mist of fine particles that most residents associate with high asthma rates. According to the local hospital, Lutheran Medical Center, the greatest concentration of people hospitalized for asthma attacks in Sunset Park live within the shadow of the Gowanus.[12]

At sixty-one years old, the Gowanus Expressway is in bad shape and desperately crying out for help. How to replace its corroded and badly weakened roadbed has been the subject of New York State Department of Transportation (NYS DOT) and Federal Highway Administration (FHWA) meetings since 1985.[13] But no plan was provided to the communities that line the Gowanus until the environmental assessment was released in 1994, nine years later. When the plans were finally made available, residents were stunned at the "solution." The NYS DOT was proposing a major reconstruction effort that would dump almost a quarter of the highway's traffic onto local streets for ten years. Residents moved from stunned to outraged when they read the conclusion of the project's seven-volume environmental assessment which declared that, since the project would create no increase in capacity, there would be "no significant impact" on the community. The project was referred to as a mere "replacement-in-kind."[14]

The strategy seemed to be lifted directly out of Robert Moses's playbook: create an illusion that a project either costs less than it actually does or that it will not disrupt local life. When he first built the Gowanus Expressway, Moses used deception to convince elected officials that the project would involve no property takings and would incur minimal costs since it would rely on the support beams of Third Avenue's elevated train. But he failed to mention having to demolish vast stretches of housing and businesses to accommodate the road's width, and the need for on- and off-ramps. In a similar vein, NYS DOT played down the fact that lane closures would divert an estimated 50,000 vehicles per day from the Gowanus to Third and Fourth Avenues.[15] As if crossing Third Avenue's ten lanes of traffic wasn't already hard enough, the NYS DOT's traffic mitigation plan called for eliminating curbside parking on Third Avenue and speeding up traffic lights. The Gowanus repair plan was devised purely from a "behind the steering wheel" perspective, with no real thought given to the needs of the people in the neighborhoods which the traffic would pass through. What little efforts were made to address the impacts on residents relied on other agencies to provide the remedy. Meanwhile, the NYS DOT failed to engage any of those agencies, and did not have any plans to do so.

It is estimated that the reconstruction effort would have forced local communities to bear up to $2 billion worth of hidden costs in the form of congestion, traffic accidents, air and noise pollution, vibration, and pavement damage, as well as 1,100 additional accidents per year from the vehicles diverted onto local streets.[16] By the end of 1996, emergency repair work was already inundating local streets with new traffic, giving residents a taste of the proposed reconstruction effort.[17] The NYS DOT's failure to respond to communities' concerns only served to galvanize more residents as fear spread of the consequences getting worse.

With the release of the NYS DOT's deceptive environmental assessment, neighborhood organizations became desperate for a way to keep their streets from becoming mini-highways. Coming together as the Gowanus Expressway Community Coalition (GECC), UPROSE, and other community organizations and residents rallied support against the NYS DOT's plan. Fortunately, reforms since Moses's time have provided communities with more opportunities to influence the planning process. The groups used the reforms to their advantage and filed a complaint with the FHWA that challenged the basis of NYS DOT's environmental assessment. The GECC convinced the federal agency of the righteousness of their cause. As a result the NYS DOT announced in 1996 that it would begin a full Environmental Impact Study (EIS) on the project the following year.[18] With the help of the Regional Plan Association (RPA), the GECC was able to develop an alternative to the NYS DOT reconstruction proposal that garnered widespread support—the removal of the elevated Gowanus Expressway and its replacement with an underground tunnel. The tunnel would enable the treatment of vehicle exhaust and finally open up Third Avenue to the sunlight it had been denied for over sixty years.

The RPA brought modern boring techniques (imagine a giant mechanical earthworm) to the attention of the GECC. Using new technology, it would be possible to build a tunnel directly underneath the existing Gowanus without affecting the highway's ability to operate at full capacity.[19] Outside of the United States, the technique has become a popular tool for tunnel construction. It has been used to build underground tunnels with great success in cities such as Paris, Cairo, Hamburg, Berlin, London, Tokyo, Sydney, Singapore, and Oslo.[20] The RPA has estimated the cost of a Gowanus tunnel to range between $1.5 and $2.5 billion, an amount greater than the $1 billion cost of the conventional reconstruction plan offered by the NYS DOT. However, over the course of its longer lifespan (roughly double that of an elevated highway), the tunnel's one-time cost is equivalent to the multiple reconstructions that would be needed for an elevated Gowanus.[21] The tunnel's longer life, lower maintenance costs, and community benefits clearly make it the better choice.

The NYS DOT has been cool to the tunnel concept since it was first proposed. Their initial response was to argue that the tunnel was prohibitively expensive. They based their estimates on a labor-intensive, disruptive, expensive, and archaic technique, known as "cut and cover," which literally means cutting a trench and covering it. In an effort to break the state engineers' vice grip on technical knowledge and dispel the NYS DOT's mythology of construction, the RPA hosted a briefing in 1998 by a team of tunneling experts from around the world for the Brooklyn borough president's Gowanus Expressway task force.[22] The briefing successfully challenged the NYS DOT's technical authority and helped legitimize the tunnel in the eyes of skeptics.

In contrast to the NYS DOT's reconstruction plan, the tunnel proposal acted like a crack in a dam, unleashing an outpouring of support from every possible sector. The support was evident at public hearings held in 1997 in which comments were supposed to be recorded and incorporated into NYS DOT's Draft EIS. Yet despite the tidal wave of requests for a study of the tunnel and an assessment of the economic and social impacts of all options, the NYS DOT's Draft EIS went no further than what was originally proposed—a few different variations of the same reconstruction plan.

The failure to incorporate the communities' comments did not come as a surprise to most. At one of the public hearings, the NYS DOT did not even bother to record public statements, sending a clear message to all in attendance that they were merely talking to a brick wall. The agency's treatment of public comments would soon come back to haunt it. Later that year, members of the GECC sued the NYS DOT, the FHWA, and the New York Metropolitan Transportation Council (NYMTC)—the official metropolitan planning organization for the region—for failing to include the tunnel alternative in the Draft EIS despite the fact that it was repeatedly requested during the scoping phase of the EIS. After a four-year legal battle, the two sides reached a groundbreaking settlement agreement in 2001.[23]

The NYS DOT agreed to an enhanced EIS that would include an economic impact assessment of each of the proposed alternatives and an analysis of the tunnel option; payment of $375,000 to the community coalition to hire a technical advisor to follow the EIS process; a consensus-building process that included community groups, NYS DOT and local elected officials; and coordination of the project's public participation efforts by the GECC. Getting the state to pay for a technical advisor was seen by the coalition as a major win. It provided the GECC with the skilled resources they needed to analyze the mountains of data that agencies typically throw at their opposition in order to overwhelm and intimidate them. The settlement agreement is the closest the coalition's members have come to getting the NYS DOT to place the tunnel proposal on equal footing with reconstruction. The agreement challenges the antidemocratic practices that have been handed down from the Moses era and that are used widely by most city and state planning agencies and public authorities.

The agreement also goes beyond typical air quality requirements. Pollution levels for each of the proposed alternatives are to be compared to each other and to federal emissions standards. Pollution from tunnels will be modeled on ventilation systems that have emissions controls installed. Air pollution impacts will be assessed at both the local and regional levels. This is an important victory because agencies usually focus solely on the regional level, an approach that serves to ignore local impacts.

Looking into the future, a new Third Avenue without the elevated expressway offers a variety of different land uses: park space, bike lanes, new housing, as well as commercial and transit opportunities. However, a vibrant Third Avenue also offers the potential for gentrification that would immediately replace working-class residents with higher-income ones. Some would argue that gentrification is natural and bound to happen. However, those of us on the receiving end of gentrification know that it acts as a gatekeeper for environmental racism and classism. Gentrification forces low-income people and people of color to move from one polluted neighborhood to another. In a twisted game of real-estate musical chairs, developers stop the music and pull recovering neighborhoods out of the mix for a wealthy and mostly white elite, leaving those behind to search once again for a place among the scraps.

Confronting the potential for gentrification is an issue that remains to be addressed in the communities fighting to bury the Gowanus Expressway. Environmental justice groups are in a position to ensure that affordable housing is a part of any redevelopment plan we propose. Environmental justice groups realize that we not only have to fight to transform our communities, but also have to fight to keep them ours. Such a perspective is also beginning to come together in the South Bronx, where communities are engaged in a similar fight against the Sheridan Expressway.

South Bronx Rising

Through my work with the New York City Environmental Justice Alliance (NYCEJA—pronounced knee-jah), I was involved with two alliance member organizations in the South Bronx—The Point CDC and We Stay/Nos Quedamos—in challenging the NYS DOT's effort to expand the Bronx's Sheridan Expressway. The two community groups were also joined in this fight by the Tri-State Transportation

Campaign and the Pratt Institute Center for Community and Environmental Development. At a NYS DOT public meeting in the Bronx, in the spring of 1999, the agency announced its plan to create a short stretch of a bike path, or, as it's known in transportation lingo, a greenway, along a bank of the Bronx River. It had been less than a year since we first heard word through the grapevine about the Sheridan expansion plans. As a result we looked at the NYS DOT's greenway plan with suspicion and seized the opportunity to turn the crowd gathered at the meeting against any possible efforts by the NYS DOT to connect the greenway to acceptance of a Sheridan expansion.

At the meeting I met Alexie Torres-Flemming, who worked with young people in her organization, Youth Ministries for Peace and Justice. They were an energetic group involved in an effort to revive the Bronx River. Their work was similar to that of the NYCEJA alliance member organization The Point CDC—an arts-centered community group that was involved in reclaiming the waterfront and battling waste transfer stations in the Hunts Point section of the South Bronx, an area just south of where Youth Ministries was based. At the time the group was working out of the basement of a church across the street from the Bronx River housing projects—projects famous in hip hop lore as the home of DJ Afrika Bamabatta's early Zulu Nation parties, back in the days when hip hop was in its infancy, a partial product of the South Bronx's desolation created by Moses's highways. Alexie and a group of young people started the organization in 1994 as a response to the torching of a church by drug dealers. Since then they have expanded beyond their initial anti-drug campaign to embrace a spectrum of issues facing the community, everything from environmental justice and affordable housing to police brutality. This was after all the same neighborhood where Amadou Diallo was brutally gunned down in front of his home in a hail of forty-one police bullets.

Since 1996, Youth Ministries' RIVER team (Reaching and Including youth Voices for Environmental Rights) and The Point CDC have been at the forefront of getting residents onto the Bronx River in canoes to make the lack of parks and other green places in communities of color a frontline issue. Their combined work has resulted in the removal of over twenty-two cars and ten thousand tires from the muck of the river's bottom. But their shared vision for breathing new life back into the river has mushroomed ever since they shifted their glance from the river to the Sheridan, and everything in between.

Compared to every other highway in the city and even some of the Bronx's local streets, the Sheridan doesn't get much use—about 37,000 vehicles a day.[24] By contrast, the Cross-Bronx expressway handles five times that number. Moses's original plans for the Sheridan have long since been abandoned as politically unworkable. By the time Youth Ministries joined NYCEJA and the fight against the Sheridan, the state's plans for the roadway could best be described as a desperate scramble to justify the road's continued existence. Instead of expansion, the focus had shifted to the Sheridan's northern and southern interchanges, where the NYS DOT argues that the highway must be brought up to current safety standards in an effort to reduce accident rates. It is a worthwhile goal considering that the Bruckner-Sheridan Interchange has an accident rate that is twice the national average.[25] However, the NYS DOT was adding to the upgrade a batch of new connections to other roads, sending up a red flag that the agency was attempting to entice more drivers onto a road that wasn't getting much use.

At the southern interchange, the NYS DOT's plan called for a road leading directly into the Hunts Point food market—the world's largest food distribution center and a local magnet for diesel truck traffic.[26] Considering the volume of truck traffic at the market that uses local streets, the proposal was not an inherently bad one. However, at its northern interchange with the Cross-Bronx Expressway, the NYS DOT proposed to build a ramp that would connect the Sheridan Expressway to the Bronx River Parkway, a parkway parallel to the Sheridan.[27] At two to three stories high, the proposed ramp would have passed before the bedroom windows of a row of houses and apartment buildings just a few blocks away from the East Tremont neighborhood detailed in Caro's *Power Broker.*[28]

The NYS DOT's package for the safety upgrades and new ramps totaled upwards of half a billion dollars, approximately $5,523 for each inch of road.[29] It's no wonder that this project has had trouble getting off the ground since it was first promoted in 1978 by the Carter Administration. Faced with the opportunity to influence the Sheridan's fate, the environmental justice and technical support groups that came together to challenge the NYS DOT's plans for the Gowanus proposed a radically different alternative, one that disputes the Sheridan's very right to exist. Naming ourselves the Southern Bronx River Watershed Alliance (SBRWA), our proposal was to completely demolish the Sheridan, effectively solving the interchange safety problems. It made sense; after all, 80 percent of households in the South Bronx do not even own or lease an automobile,[30] and it is well documented that the Sheridan does not get much traffic.

The NYS DOT's best argument for keeping the highway has been the need to provide direct access for trucks into the Hunts Point Market. The neighborhood around the Hunts Point Market is inundated with upwards of 11,000 truck trips a day.[31] Most of them are destined for the market or one of the nearly thirty waste facilities in the neighborhood. The trucks constantly barrel down residential streets with engines rumbling at street lights and exhaust pipes spewing clouds of soot that one can only connect to a child's or friend's asthma. Hunts Point has the second-highest rate of hospitalizations for asthma in the entire city, one that is six times greater than the national average.[32] But none of that has much to do with the Sheridan Expressway, since most truckers heading to Hunts Point Market don't use it.

According to a NYS DOT survey of truck drivers at the Hunts Point Market, 80 percent of respondents said they rely on the Bruckner Expressway, not the Sheridan, to get into and out of the market.[33] In spite of their reliance on the Bruckner, there is no exit off of the Bruckner Expressway within a mile of the market. As a result many truckers spend a good deal of time weaving their way through residential streets. The SBRWA has proposed an alternative transportation plan that, while meeting the needs of the drivers, places its focus more squarely on the communities being driven through. It calls for the creation of on- and off-ramps from the Bruckner Expressway instead of the Sheridan. With improvements to the Bruckner, it would be possible to remove the Sheridan and dedicate the land underneath its surface to a more productive community use. For one-tenth the cost of the proposed state plan, the SBRWA's plan would provide direct access to the Hunts Point Market from the Bruckner, making it easier for trucks to get to their destination without getting lost and winding up under someone's kitchen window. It would also include traffic calming to prevent local streets from being used as shortcuts. Additionally, the SBRWA has called for an increase in rail freight usage in order to minimize the need for trucks in the first place.

What should take the place of the Sheridan Expressway is a question best left to a real community planning process—something the NYS DOT has yet to engage in. To present a community with a blank page and no lines and say, "What would you like to see?" is a radical approach for an agency that is still deeply mired in the Robert Moses school of planning, where plans are drawn up years beforehand and word is allowed to leak out just before construction begins, or at best, nowadays, just before an environmental impact study is underway.

With the help of the Tri-State Transportation Campaign, Youth Ministries' RIVER team developed and administered a survey to people living near the Sheridan asking them what they would prefer to see in its place. Approximately 40 percent said they would prefer a park, 20 percent wanted housing, and another 20 percent wanted a mixture of the two. The remaining 20 percent had their own ideas for what should utilize the Sheridan's 1.25 mile right-of-way. Through rallies, guerilla theater, door knocking, and media coverage, the SBRWA has been able to spread the message that taking down the Sheridan Expressway is not only possible but necessary.

Neighborhoods next to the Sheridan have one-twelfth to one-fourth the nationally recommended 6.5 acres of park space. New York City averages about 2.25 acres of green open space for every 1,000 people, an abysmal amount. But that number pales in comparison to the .4 acres for every 1,000 people within a half-mile of the Sheridan, or the .87 acres per 1,000 people within a mile and a half.[34] There are five public schools that border the Sheridan, all drowning in an ocean of concrete and asphalt.

Momentum against the Sheridan picked up once the NYS DOT announced its fast-track proposal to build a "temporary" truck road connecting the Sheridan Expressway to the Hunts Point Market, through an adjacent, abandoned concrete plant along the Bronx River. The SBRWA received word about the temporary road in the spring of 2001, just a few months after Youth Ministries had succeeded in getting the abandoned plant turned over to the Parks Department.[35] Youth Ministries—which had long since joined the SBRWA in the campaign against the Sheridan—and members of the alliance immediately rose to challenge the NYS DOT's temporary road. Youth Ministries' RIVER team paraded through the neighborhood in makeshift cardboard cutouts of a dying river and a "truck monster." Theatric commandos took over church sidewalks and bus stops spreading word of impending doom. In the face of intense community pressure, the backers of the temporary road retracted their support and asked the NYS DOT to develop an alternate means to provide access for trucks into Hunts Point. By the end of the following year the temporary road was officially dead. In a major victory, the $9 million federal allocation for the road was shifted to the Parks Department to aid in the redevelopment of the former concrete plant as a park.

But the NYS DOT's larger plans for the Sheridan still remained. Fortunately, the SBRWA was able to convince the New York

Metropolitan Transportation Council—the agency through which federal transportation dollars are distributed—to coordinate a series of meetings between the environmental justice groups and the NYS DOT in an effort to better address transportation problems in the Bronx. These meetings have turned into forums that have brought in a number of additional players, from rail freight operators, law enforcement agencies, and environmental regulatory agencies to businesses and business development groups. Since these discussions began the state has increased attention to, and funding for, rail freight infrastructure as an alternative to heavy truck traffic.

In spite of all the organizing and meetings that had taken place, the NYS DOT's Sheridan expansion plan was still not yet officially underway. In February 2003, almost five years after the NYS DOT first announced its plan, the agency sent out the official notice for a public scoping meeting for the Sheridan's highly anticipated EIS. A public scoping meeting is intended to be the first opportunity for community groups to influence what that particular study will include. In this case, the community was given fewer than 45 days to prepare its response.

Had it not been for the early warning received years before, environmental justice groups and the communities they belong to would not have been able to come up with a serious counterproposal to the NYS DOT's plan. But since so much time had elapsed, much of the groundwork necessary to develop both a serious argument for taking down the Sheridan Expressway and a better plan for addressing local traffic problems had already been done. We also learned that the NYS DOT had dropped the portion of its original proposal that involved extending the Sheridan's northern interchange, and had included removal of the Sheridan as an element to be considered. But plans for connecting the Sheridan's southern interchange with Hunt's Point remained the central focus, and the DOT's proposal for removal of the Sheridan was not associated with any of the additional alternatives that would have made it feasible.

We were fighting for the whole package—complete removal of the Sheridan—and recognized that we needed to have a strong show of support at the public scoping hearing in order to be taken seriously. We decided to hit the streets again, going from door to door with petitions, hosting community meetings and individual meetings with community groups, business leaders, and local elected officials. By this point, the leadership of the campaign to remove the Sheridan had expanded to include two key community groups that also worked on environmental justice issues and became central to the organizing effort, Mothers on the Move and Sustainable South Bronx. At the public scoping meeting, which took place on an evening in March 2003, everyone's efforts paid off. The recently renovated and spacious local Hunts Point library was jam-packed with supporters, from both the residential and business communities, of what had become known simply as "the community plan."

While the turnout at the Sheridan hearing was certainly a major milestone, the experience of communities along Brooklyn's Gowanus Expressway demonstrates that the SBRWA is still facing an uphill battle with the Sheridan. We are still confronting bureaucratic inertia, misplaced priorities, and skepticism of anything that radically differs from the status quo.

Confronting Gentrification

Replacing old highways with new land uses is a concept that is being put into practice in several US and Canadian cities.[36] In Portland, Oregon, a highway on the city's waterfront was dismantled in 1974 after it was made redundant by a parallel highway. A thirty-seven-acre waterfront park with basketball courts, hiking and cycling trails, a dock, public art, and restrooms replaced it. The City of San Francisco took advantage of a 1989 earthquake that knocked down part of the Embarcadero Freeway to replace the freeway with a waterfront promenade, complete with bike path. Inspired by San Francisco's success, the City of Toronto moved in May 2000 to tear down a 0.9-mile segment of the elevated Gardiner Expressway East in order to redevelop a vast stretch of waterfront. In 1999 the mayor of Akron, Ohio, announced his desire to demolish a half-mile section of the Innerbelt Freeway in order to get to twenty-five acres of waterfront land. The mayor of Milwaukee has also made known his plans to demolish the Park East Freeway—which carries 54,000 vehicles a day, 69 percent more than the Sheridan—and replace it with housing, shops, and offices. The removal of the highway, which borders downtown, is seen by Milwaukee officials as a way to entice development in the downtown region.

Unfortunately, all of this highway demolition for creative land use development also means gentrification. As soon as California's DOT announced it would knock down the Embarcadero Freeway, nearby property values skyrocketed 300 percent. Since then hundreds of development projects have been attributed to the freeway coming down. Milwaukee was inspired to demolish its highway because of the success of a real estate developer in taking abandoned land, cleared for portions of the highway that were never built, and turning it into luxury rental apartments—$500,000 condominiums and a supermarket, all on the waterfront.[37]

Freeing up large tracts of contiguous land is a real estate developer's dream. The success of environmental justice efforts will undoubtedly whet the appetites of developers eager to reap tremendous profits off of the grassroots efforts spent to revitalize communities. Across the country, the very people responsible for building the community gardens and neighborhood centers that have allowed their communities to bounce back are being priced out by the value changes they created. It will take a carefully coordinated community-development process to ensure that gentrification is not the final outcome.

To that end, environmental justice activists have begun promoting several means by which residents of today will not be forced out tomorrow. The work of the Bronx based organization We Stay/Nos Quedamos provides an example of how ensuring affordable housing enables existing low-income residents to own their own homes, thus stabilizing a neighborhood's most economically vulnerable. Nos Quedamos formed as a community response to an urban renewal plan that, in typical Robert Moses fashion, would have razed the entire South Bronx neighborhood of Melrose and thrown thousands out onto the streets. Melrose residents reacted by conducting their own community planning process, which led to the Melrose Commons Plan. Unlike the city's plan for mostly market-rate housing, the Melrose Commons Plan has kept housing affordable, and prioritized the needs of existing residents. The plan makes room for both renters and homeowners, and provides for the elderly, the homeless, and even asthmatics. After a ten-year tug of war with the city, Nos Quedamos is now overseeing construction and turning the community's dream of housing itself into a reality. Another means available to grassroots organizations to exert independent control over the future of freed land is the creation of community land trusts, whereby land is placed under the control of a trust that can designate appropriate uses of the land. Taken together, these two ideas provide a holistic means of retaining community control of land and protecting nearby residents from the unintended consequences of their own efforts to improve their neighborhoods, all within the context of environmental justice.

The Demolished Road Ahead

Making transportation infrastructure compatible with a community's needs was never a part of Robert Moses's agenda. Enabling communities to direct a process that shapes the future of their neighborhoods was perhaps the last thing he would ever have wanted to see happen. Such a process would not only ensure that local needs are met, but would also empower marginalized communities—a frightening concept to the predominantly white and middle-class world of transportation engineers. What environmental justice activists are doing in both Sunset Park and the South Bronx is challenging future investments in highways that have caused suffering. Instead, they are advocating for their demolition and reuse of freed-up land to meet real community needs. As urban highways across the country are nearing the end of their useful life, opportunities abound for community groups to undo the legacy of the Robert Moses era, a legacy that shaped not only New York City but cities across the United States.

In New York City, we have been able to build momentum for the demolition of old highways for a number of reasons. One key component has been our ability to convey to others in our community the history of how things got to be the way they are—of identifying Robert Moses's influence and showing in very clear terms the ways in which the needs of local communities were deliberately sacrificed. Another factor has been the collaborations between grassroots community groups and organizations that provide technical assistance. These collaborations have enabled our groups to transform ideas into very real, well-developed proposals that have been carefully crafted and analyzed, and presented in a way that is friendly to the eye and clear to the mind.

However, it is important to recognize that it isn't enough to present a well-articulated argument and hope that policymakers will be impressed by our data and swayed by our sheer brilliance. From the onset of all of our efforts, we have realized that highways will not come down in our communities unless we have first built an aggressive mass movement featuring a large coalition of supporters from a broad spectrum of the community. This means not only organizations and other institutions, but also direct organizing of local residents that aren't members of any group. We are waging an uphill battle. Building a base of support is the most critical part of our effort, one that all of the groups mentioned in this chapter continually work to create.

One other critical component in our efforts is the importance of seizing opportunities to present an alternate vision. The community proposals for both the Sheridan Expressway and the Gowanus Parkway have gained visibility and legitimacy because we have used the public participation process mandated as part of the environmental impact studies currently underway for both highways. Our task is to get the NYS DOT to make the removal of the Sheridan and the burying of the Gowanus the two alternatives the state opts to pursue at the conclusion of its studies. Once the decisions have been made, the resources can be marshalled. Ironically, the same federal government that made possible the highway construction frenzy of the 1940s, 50s and 60s may now provide funds for the deconstruction of these very same highways.

The fact that the potential for gentrification is a subject of discussion within both campaigns goes to show that people believe that the highways will eventually come down, and in their place will be something communities can finally enjoy. But gentrification is a very real possibility; developing measures to protect against it is a vital step we must take to ensure that we can afford to raise our children in the same neighborhoods we seek to create.

Most of us involved in the struggles of the Sheridan and Gowanus live, work, or have grown up within earshot of the highways we now hope to demolish. What drives us is the potential within our communities that has been locked away, buried underneath a mountain of neglect, poverty, and concrete.

Recently Majora Carter, executive director of Sustainable South Bronx, was sitting on the couch of her new storefront office in Hunts Point. Taking advantage of the light from the morning sun, rising over a row of apartment buildings, she read through a stack of newly arrived letters. The letters were from third and fourth graders at P.S. 48, the local elementary school. The children all wrote about how much they wanted a park and a place to play by the river, and about how great it was that she wanted to help green the neighborhood and rip up streets. Still holding onto the letters, she called me with a teary-eyed laugh, saying, "I just needed to share them with somebody, they're so beautiful." In one of the letters, a nine-year-old boy named Daniel Loftin had scribbled on the side margin a message that summed up both the tragedy of the lack of resources in our neighborhoods and the sense of freedom that comes from ignoring imposed limits in order to meet your real need. The note read: "Run and play, the streets are free."

notes

1. Robert Caro, *The Power Broker: Robert Moses and the Fall of New York* (New York: Vintage, 1974).

2. Ibid., 19–20.

3. Ibid., 520–525.

4. Ibid.

5. Ibid., 749, 895–896; and Auto-Free Zone, *Deconstructing Highways* (Ottawa: Auto-Free Ottawa, January/February 1993).

6. Southwest Brooklyn Industrial Development Corporation, *Sunset Park: Beyond the Gowanus Expressway Competition* (Brooklyn: SBIDC, 1999).

7. Douglas S. Massey and Nancy A. Denton, *American Apartheid: Segregation and the Making of the Underclass* (Cambridge: Harvard University Press, 1993), 51–54.

8. Caro, *The Power Broker.*

9. Tom Topousis, "Boondoggle Highway," *New York Post*, October 2, 2000, 5.

10. Ibid.

11. New York State Department of Transportation, *Traffic Volume Report for Kings County* (2000), http://www.dot.state.ny.us/tech_serv/high/countfiles/kings.pdf.

12. Lutheran Medical Center Asthma Clinic, *Distribution of Asthma Hospitalizations* (1994).

13. Stipulation of Settlement, *Transportation Alternatives, Inc., et al. v. New York Metropolitan Transportation Council, et al.*, 97 Civ. 7021 (E. D. N. Y.) (Gershon, J. 2001), http://www.transalt.org/press/testimony/010119gowanus.html.

14. New York State Department of Transportation, *Gowanus Expressway (I-278) Rehabilitation Project, 92nd Street-BBT-Hamilton Avenue Interchange, Borough of Brooklyn, Draft Design Report Environmental Assessment Draft, Section 4 (F Evaluation), PIN X729-94*, vol. 1–7 (1994).

15. Auto-Free Zone, *Deconstructing Highways.*

16. Tri-State Transportation Campaign, *The Environmental Costs of Rebuilding the Gowanus Expressway* (September 22, 1994).

17. Tri-State Transportation Campaign, "Gowanus Chaos Premieres at Prospect Interchange," *Mobilizing The Region*, no. 108 (December 13, 1996).

18. Testimony of Joanne Simon on behalf of Gowanus Expressway Community Coalition before the New York State Assembly Committee on Transportation and the Legislative Commission on Sustainable Transportation Issues in the Metropolitan Area (August 19, 1999); Tri-State Transportation Campaign, "Brooklyn Activists Win Environmental Review of Gowanus Project," *Mobilizing The Region*, no. 103 (November 1, 1996).

19. Regional Plan Association, *A Gowanus Tunnel: An Initial Feasibility Study*, http://www.rpa.org/publications/gowanus-project.html.

20. Ibid.; Tri-State Transportation Campaign, "Brooklyn Activists Win Environmental Review of Gowanus Project," *Mobilizing The Region*, no. 103 (November 1, 1996).

21. Regional Plan Association, *A Gowanus Tunnel: An Initial Feasibility Study.*

22. Tri-State Transportation Campaign, "Tunnel Experts Say Underground Gowanus Obstacles Exaggerated," *Mobilizing The Region*, no. 195 (November 6, 1998).

23. Memorandum of Understanding between *Transportation Alternatives, Inc., et al. and the New York Metropolitan Transportation Council and Federal Highway Administration* (January 19, 2001).

24. Southern Bronx River Watershed Alliance, *Redundant Roadway: Deconstructing the Bronx's Sheridan Expressway* (May 1999).

25. Ibid.

26. New York State Department of Transportation, *Bruckner/Sheridan Expressway Interchange Improvement–Expanded Project Proposal, D007389, PIN X730.39* (October 1997).

27. New York State Department of Transportation, *Interchange Improvements at East 177th Street/Bronx River Parkway*, presentation by Tams Consultants, Inc., October 15, 1998.

28. Javier Gomez, "Se oponen a construcción de Puente elevado," *El Diario La Prensa* (November 19, 1998).

29. Tom Topousis, "Boondoggle Highway," *New York Post*, October 2, 2000, 5.

30. US Bureau of the Census, *1990 Census of Population and Housing*, http://www.census.gov/main/www/cen1990.html

31. Mothers On the Move, *Protecting Our Hunts Point Neighborhood from Dangerous Truck Traffic: A Community Led Initiative to Create Safe Streets* (February 2001).

32. NYC Childhood Asthma Initiative–NYC Department of Health, *Asthma Facts*, (1999), http://www.ci.nyc.ny.us/html/doh/pdf/asthma/facts.pdf.

33. New York State Department of Transportation, "Summaries of Truck Origin-Destination Survey," Technical Memorandum, no. 2, *Bruckner/Sheridan Expressway Interchange Improvement–Expanded Project Proposal Preparation*, D007389, PIN X730.39, Appendix B, part 2 (June 1996).

34. New York City Environmental Justice Alliance, *Green Space Ratios for Parks: Sheridan Expressway Area and New York City*, based on 1990 Census population data and 1998 NYC Tax Block and Lot File.

35. Jose Martinez, "Riverfront Plan Still Parked," *Daily News*, Bronx edition, May 29, 2001, Metro, 1.

36. Lisa Schreibman, "On a Tear," *Planning* (January 2001).

37. Ibid.

BOSS organizer, Malik Abdul, leads coalition activists in a protest on July 19, 1999 during the Measure B campaign.

FIVE

Transportation Choices in the San Francisco Bay Area

Stuart Cohen and Jeff Hobson

L ike other regions across the country, the San Francisco Bay Area is plagued by low-density sprawl development that draws investment and life away from its urban core. Taxpayer-subsidized highways attract jobs and houses to the suburbs and agricultural areas, gobbling up open space and forcing residents to use cars for nearly every trip. As a result, the share of all Bay Area trips made on public transit has steadily declined—more than 60 percent over the past three decades—while the number of miles the average resident drives has skyrocketed.[1] This chapter describes the development of the Transportation and Land Use Coalition (TALC) and the ways it has merged environmental and equity agendas to combat these trends.[2] We will describe some of TALC's successes as well as the obstacles we encountered, and use these case studies to draw some conclusions about how organizations can work together to build a coalition that focuses on a socially just and environmentally sustainable transportation system.

Obstacles to Coalition Building

Changing regional transportation priorities is a formidable task. Transportation planning can seem inaccessible to grassroots organizations: the decision-making bodies are regional, the meetings are usually held in the middle of the day, and the agendas are often extremely technical and filled with jargon. There are few opportunities to express the everyday concerns of people who need the bus to get to work or bring their children to school. At the same time, environmentalists who have been involved in these decisions are often perceived by transportation planners as being overly idealistic, hoping to pass a purely environmental agenda despite the popularity of new highways and expensive rail extensions in the more suburban portions of the country.

Another fundamental problem is that the immediate goals of social justice and environmental groups are often different.[3] Social justice groups focus on more frequent bus service, increasing late-night and weekend transit service, making transportation more affordable, or keeping speeders from turning neighborhood streets into dangerous highways. Environmentalists have long focused on stopping suburban freeways from paving over open space, getting commuters out of their cars to improve air quality, and making the streets safe for bicycles and pedestrians. Merging these various areas of concern requires both constituencies to broaden their thinking about transportation.

Some issues of primary concern to environmental and social justice groups have naturally overlapped in the past. Diverse interests have teamed up to stop proposed urban highways and support public transit in urban centers, or to support cleaner, less-polluting trucks and buses after research showed disproportionately high rates of asthma in urban communities. Until the 1990s, collaboration between environmental and social justice groups tended to be short-term and single-issue oriented.

To affect long-term change, environmental and social justice organizations must reach beyond single issues and find common ground to merge their agendas. The rise of sprawl and the counter movement for smart growth are now creating a context where diverse groups from across the country are beginning to collaborate.

Forging a Coalition

TALC first formed in 1997 as the result of a grant from the Hewlett Foundation to the Surface Transportation Policy Project (STPP), a Washington, DC-based research and advocacy group. The intention of the grant was to plant the seeds of collaborations in a few major metropolitan areas. After four meetings, TALC decided to focus its first campaign on the 1998 regional transportation plan (RTP). Updated every three years, the RTP is a document that defines transportation spending priorities for the nine-county Bay Area for a twenty-year period. The Bay Area's RTP is developed by the Metropolitan Transportation Commission (MTC), the Bay Area's metropolitan planning organization.

The 1998 RTP draft would have forced four transit operators to expect a collective deficit of $375 million, resulting in some combination of fare increases and service cuts. At the same time, the plan included $10 billion for road and highway projects. TALC members analyzed the RTP and came up with an alternative proposal that would fully support the transit operators by cutting funding for six particularly damaging highway projects. But when TALC introduced their "100% funding for transit" proposal at a June meeting of MTC and the county transportation agencies, they were met with surprised silence and the occasional snicker. Coalition leaders had succeeded in piercing the MTC's technical shield, crunching the numbers and wading through the stacks of policy documents, but they didn't have the political firepower needed to get decision makers to listen to their suggestions.

At that time, TALC's forty member groups were mostly environmental and planning groups. The major exceptions were Urban Habitat, a regional leader on social justice issues and founding member of TALC, and the Latino Issues Forum. Then in June 1998, community organizers from Building Opportunities for Self-Sufficiency (BOSS) approached TALC's leaders. BOSS is a Berkeley-based group that primarily provides services and shelter to homeless and very-low-income people, but its organizing team also works on related policy issues such as welfare reform. BOSS leaders had been surprised when a client survey indicated that inadequate transportation was one of their top concerns. When organizers began looking into the issue, they were struck by the sums of money contained in transportation budgets. "What caught my eye was that huge number—88 billion dollars—there just isn't money like that in our typical issues," said Dawn Phillips, then-director of BOSS's Community Organizing Team. "We knew our communities had to get our fair share."

Phillips's interest in transportation issues led her to TALC. But BOSS's members had some reservations about joining forces with TALC: "The coalition looked like they were mostly white environmentalists, so it brought up fears about whether our issues would get lost in the shuffle," Phillips said. "We went ahead because we knew we needed TALC's technical and policy expertise and we thought it was an interesting and possibly great model in the making. We wanted to see how far we could push this coalition to hear our issues and bring equity issues into their agenda." [4]

The leadership at BOSS, for their part, had something powerful to offer the environmentalists: years of experience in community organizing and mobilization. The environmental groups in TALC could argue persuasively about the policy implications of spending money on transit rather than highways and turn out members to meetings. But BOSS and other grassroots groups could deliver firsthand accounts of what bus service meant to their communities. In their hands, "100% funding for transit" ceased being an abstract policy debate and became a discussion about people who would be literally trapped in their homes if they didn't have buses to get them to work, to school, or to the supermarket. When TALC leaders explained that fighting for additional transit funding now, as part of the 20-year RTP, would help them avoid future fights over service cuts or fare increases, BOSS's organizing team responded by making the RTP the year's top priority.

Members of the newly energized coalition began to educate, train, and mobilize local leaders to participate in hearings. As the campaign gained steam and drew media coverage, TALC was able to attract even more groups. Social justice groups led the organizing drive. Their style was louder and more confrontational than the environmental policy analysts were used to, and it completely changed the tenor of the discussion. Hundreds of transit users showed up at hearings that had formerly been dominated by developers and highway interests.

They told the commissioners in personal terms about the impact of underfunded transit on their lives. At one hearing, Hale Zukas, a paraplegic who is unable to speak, painstakingly used a pointer attached to a helmet on his head to tell the nineteen MTC commissioners, "I can't drive. I ride transit, and there are many people in my position."[5] When one of the public hearings was held in Dublin, a distant suburb with poor transit access, a caravan of thirteen vehicles brought over seventy-five of BOSS's clients. Their exuberant, horn-tooting arrival was captured for the nightly news by a clutch of television cameras. They accused government agencies of transportation racism and of deliberately disenfranchising low-income and minority communities.

In an arena in which nearly all the players—agency staff, decision makers, lobbyists, and environmental advocates—are white, the vocal presence of people of color had a powerful impact. Their voices altered the way the RTP process was covered by the press. "Of an overflow Dublin Civic Center crowd of more than 150 people, at least two-thirds were there to implore the Metropolitan Transportation Commission to put pressure on AC Transit to restore East Bay bus routes discontinued in recent years," the *West County Times* reported. "The collection of grassroots citizen groups also called on the MTC to scale back planned freeway expansions."[6]

Initially, some of the more traditional environmental members of TALC were uncomfortable with the intensified rhetoric, which sparked an internal debate about whether the more aggressive tactics would harm the campaign by alienating MTC commissioners. But it was hard to argue with the visibility BOSS's tactics had brought. Leaders and then members of the environmental groups began to support and participate in the demonstrations, and BOSS's leaders began to trust that TALC members were open to viewing transportation from a racial justice perspective.

On the day the MTC was scheduled to approve the RTP, coalition groups packed the overflow room and coordinated testimony. The MTC staff staunchly defended their plan and urged the commissioners not to accept TALC's recommendation. Fifty-six speakers—ranging from homeless moms with their children in their arms to Sierra Club leaders—called for "100% funding for transit." This broad support provided political cover for the US Environmental Protection Agency and the Bay Area Air Quality Management District to speak out in favor of TALC's recommendation. With every major media outlet in the region covering the vote, MTC commissioners rejected the staff recommendation, voting unanimously in favor of TALC's proposal. The crowd erupted into applause. "It was like a lovefest," MTC spokesman Joe Curley told a reporter after the hearing. "I don't think we've ever had a meeting quite like this before."[7]

Merging the Issues

With this initial success drawing headlines such as "Transit Backers Gaining Strength," TALC's members began working to define a merged environmental–social justice agenda.[8] "After the RTP victory we really saw that this needed to be a long-term coalition" said Rachel Peterson, then-executive director of Urban Ecology and co-chair of TALC in 1998 and 1999. "We spent over four months developing a joint platform and identified some key opportunities to continue collaborative campaigns."

What follows are a few examples of how issues that are considered environmental or social justice issues were redefined to become coalition issues, and the challenges that the group faced during the resulting campaigns.

Measure B: Round One

Alameda County, which stretches from the urban centers of Oakland and Berkeley into suburbs and farmlands to the east and south, has felt acute tensions between suburban investment and urban disinvestment. Lower-income urbanites complain that funding for their transit systems and city streets has suffered while highways and commuter rail systems have grabbed the lion's share of regional funding. In 1998, while TALC worked to shape the RTP, tensions in Alameda County came to a head when voters were asked to renew Measure B, the county's transportation sales tax. First passed in 1986, the sales tax had devoted fully two-thirds of its funds to highway expansions that served white-collar commuters. The tax was due to expire in 2002 unless a new round of funding was approved by the county electorate.

The 1998 ballot measure contained more support for transit than the 1986 version, and the transit funding it contained was vital to the region's bus line, AC Transit, which was already suffering from declining federal operating subsidies. If Measure B was not renewed, by 2002, AC Transit would lose $11 million per year in operating funds, forcing the agency to make sweeping service cuts.[9] For these reasons, transit supporters felt the need to give Measure B their reluctant support. Their reluctance had to do with the measure's inclusion of highway funding pushed by business and developer interests. On the other hand, environmental groups, such as the Sierra Club, vigorously opposed the new measure. Their opposition was enough to keep the measure from getting the two-thirds majority it needed to pass.

The "victory" for the environmental groups was bittersweet. They managed to block the passage of a demonstrably flawed measure. But there was no transit-friendly replacement on the table and vital bus services were likely to be cut. Environmentalists had expended their political capital fighting a measure that had the support of many transit users and environmentally-friendly politicians. Neither side really won, and a new approach was clearly needed.

The supporters of Measure B were undoubtedly going to try again in the election of 2000. If the priorities of Bay Area transportation planning were going to change, social justice and environmental groups were going to have work together to form a common agenda.

Measure B: Divided We Lose, United We Win

Given that the transportation sales tax proposal had split the public interest community the previous year, the new coalition faced its toughest test in a potentially divisive struggle over Measure B during the 1999–2000 election season. As Measure B's proponents started gearing up for another election bid, both social justice and environmental leaders recognized that if either group hoped to reshape the Measure B plan into one that both they and the voters could support, they would have to work together. Unanimous support, the groups judged, would be necessary to achieve the two-thirds supermajority needed for a special sales tax.

TALC put together a campaign steering committee composed of the three groups who brought the most bargaining power to the campaign: Sierra Club, Environmental Defense, and BOSS. The environmentalists brought broad name recognition and demonstrated electoral strength from leading the successful 1998 "No on B" campaign. BOSS brought a powerful community organizing team with strong ties to other community groups who would lend support in mass rallies and demonstrations. With the help of TALC staff and input from coalition members, steering committee members wrote a seven-point platform of proposed revisions to the 1998 expenditure plan and secured endorsements from nineteen public-interest groups in the county.[10]

When the Alameda County Transportation Agency (ACTA) held its first meeting in March 1999 to consider another attempt at the ballot, TALC presented its platform. The release immediately shaped the debate. Newspaper headlines reported "Dueling Transit Plans."[11] ACTA officials began negotiating with TALC members about what it would take to get coalition support. Over the next year, organizing for a "Better Measure B" included a survey of over 1,800 low-income residents about their transportation needs and over two thousand letters of support for TALC's platform. Meetings were so packed with TALC supporters that the building management tried to lock protesters out of one meeting, and ACTA had to change venues several times to find a meeting space large enough to hold the crowd.

But TALC's cohesion was tested several times. During the summer of 1999, TALC faced the difficult decision of when, or whether, to accept a compromise package. BOSS leaders were ready to declare victory—they had secured some increases in funding for night and weekend transit service, and the importance of Measure B to AC Transit ensured that the group's membership would ultimately support it. Environmentalists, on the other hand, were still threatening to oppose Measure B if they didn't win more concessions.

The coalition had some tense internal meetings. BOSS's leaders said that opposing the measure would be tantamount to white environmentalists denying transit services to black and brown inner-city residents; the Sierra Club leader shot back that if the package contained significant highway expansion, more children would suffer from asthma and more acres of hillside would be lost to the developers' bulldozers. "That internal debate was really difficult," said Mike Daley, conservation director of the local Sierra Club chapter. "BOSS brought an important grassroots presence and breadth to the coalition. We didn't want to lose that when most of our bottom-line issues weren't resolved yet."[12]

In the end, the groups reached an internal compromise. The environmental groups agreed to develop a clear bottom line and a deadline by which they would make a decision about supporting or opposing the measure, and BOSS's leaders agreed that they wouldn't declare victory yet. "To us, that internal compromise meant the environmentalists weren't just giving us lip service, it was a concrete demonstration of commitment to our issues," said Dawn Phillips. [13]

The agreement showed that TALC had some staying power. "Before that compromise, I don't know if we trusted the environmentalists," said Phillips. "But what saved the day at every point was that we knew the coalition leaders would support us, even if it wasn't the decision they would have otherwise made."

The cohesion paid off. In February 2000, when ACTA adopted a final plan for Measure B spending, the measure included $186 million more for alternative transportation than the 1998 version. The plan included: $95 million more to help expand night and weekend transit service; $44 million more to paratransit for seniors and the disabled; $44 million more for bicycle and pedestrian safety and access; and $3 million for a new program to support transit-oriented development. ACTA had funded TALC's recommendations by going from the fifteen-year plan proposed in 1998 to a twenty-year plan in 2000. Most of the increases went towards elements of TALC's platform, but the plan still devoted 18 percent of its funds to highway projects.

Despite the highway funding, the Sierra Club offered more than nominal support in 2000, making Measure B an electoral priority that earned significant staff and volunteer time. "The Measure B campaign helped push us to change our priorities," said the Sierra Club's Daley. "We recognized that a lot of social justice issues can also be seen as environmental justice issues, and that we need to do a better job of reflecting the needs of those communities."[14]

ACTA officials credited TALC with improving the plan and asked the coalition to help coordinate the grassroots "Yes on B" campaign.[15] Building on unanimous support from member groups, TALC helped secure the endorsements of over three hundred elected officials, community groups, and businesses, and coordinated the efforts of hundreds of volunteers in getting the word out. The new coalition process resulted in Measure B receiving a record-breaking 81.5 percent support at the ballot, 23 percent higher than in 1998.

There was another significant result of the "Better Measure B" effort: the tricky internal negotiations fortified the foundation for a long-term coalition. "Before this campaign, our members thought environmentalists cared more about plants and animals than about people. Some thought we didn't like them because they aren't like us and they sometimes take positions against our issues," said BOSS's Phillips. "But in this campaign, environmentalists stood with us on a crucial issue; that made us trust them more and think that we might be able to ask them for support on other issues of concern to poor urban folks."[16]

Merging Safety Issues

In 1999, Luis Arteaga, associate director of Latino Issues Forum (LIF), received a call from a *Washington Post* reporter asking, "Why are Latino and African American men killed as pedestrians more often than white men?" Although the group is a long-time advocate of public transit and a leading member of TALC, LIF had not previously been engaged in pedestrian safety issues. Arteaga was only able to offer logical rationales and anecdotal information, suggesting that "People of color tend to work more swing shifts, so they rely on their feet or bicycles to get to and from transit, often in areas with no sidewalks and poor lighting."

Arteaga contacted James Corless, STPP's California director and a founding leader in TALC, who was already researching these issues. The analysts were conducting an intensive review of hospital records because the California Highway Patrol did not record the ethnicity of pedestrian victims. STPP's research uncovered that Latinos and African Americans are at the highest risk from pedestrian-vehicle collisions, and that children are particularly vulnerable. The resulting report, *Caught in the Crosswalk*, garnered front page coverage across California.[17]

Pedestrian and bicycle safety had previously been an issue that appealed to a narrow demographic. The membership of bicycle advocacy groups is mostly young and white, and pedestrian issues seemed mostly to concern environmentalists and city planners. STPP worked with TALC to bring the issue to the attention of leaders and parents in urban areas, where local roads are often used as mini-freeways and safety infrastructure is an afterthought. One finding of the research—repeated like a mantra in the ensuing campaign—was that pedestrians accounted for 20 percent of road deaths, yet just 1 percent of the state highway department's safety funding was dedicated to pedestrian safety.[18]

California Assembly member Nell Soto, a member of the Latino legislative caucus, authored a "Safe Routes to School" bill that would dedicate $20 million per year out of the state highway safety budget to planning and implementing safe streets and paths to community schools. STPP and LIF engaged the increasingly organized TALC members as well as other interest groups throughout the state: school principals, health professionals and pastors in low-income communities, bicycle coalitions, and relatives of past victims.

The bill passed both houses of the legislature, but Governor Davis's highway department urged a veto. So groups turned up the grassroots pressure. A statewide "Walk Your Child to School Day" publicized the issue, with newspapers highlighting the impacts on children of color found in the report.[19] In finally signing the bill into law, the Governor noted its tremendous and diverse support—it got more calls and letters than all but one other issue that year.

Taking on BART in Santa Clara County

Environmentalists across the country have long supported suburban rail extensions as a way to attract auto drivers to transit and, more recently, as a way to create the infrastructure for transit-oriented smart growth. Increasingly, some of these systems, as well as the policies that favor expensive suburban rail extensions to the detriment of urban mass transit, have come under fire from social justice groups.[20] While the "highways vs. transit" debate is a natural for environmental and social justice coalition-building, the "transit vs. transit" debate has the potential to destroy a coalition's solidarity.

The Bay Area Rapid Transit (BART) is a regional rail system that connects the suburbs to San Francisco and Oakland and is extremely popular among Bay Area voters. But BART is also expensive to build, costing as much as $300 million per mile for its subway portions. BART has often competed for funding against more cost-effective proposals for bus service or commuter rail that uses existing tracks. BART usually wins these battles.

With calls for transit funding—and BART extensions—intensifying, TALC undertook a process to clarify the coalition's positions on various transit investments and proposals. TALC members spent thirteen months researching, analyzing, and writing *World Class Transit for the Bay Area*, a 120-page document that laid out a more sustainable vision for the region and detailed over

$12 billion in transit investments that TALC would support.[21] In January 2000, every major media outlet covered the report's conclusion: the region should convert 600 miles of commuter and freight tracks to dedicated rapid transit bus lanes before spending billions on more BART extensions.[22]

Just four months later, a half-cent transportation sales tax was proposed by the Santa Clara Valley Transportation Authority (VTA) in the epicenter of the then-booming Silicon Valley. The centerpiece of the proposal was a $4.3 billion BART extension to downtown San Jose, with additional funds for highway projects. In response, TALC authored a new report, *No Justice, No Tax*, that highlighted the importance of bus service to low-income communities of color—as communities of color comprise 70 percent of VTA bus riders—and how that service would be endangered by likely BART cost overruns.[23] Released with the support of a host of community groups, the report was covered by seven television stations. BayRail Alliance, a transit advocacy group, helped TALC develop a positive transit vision—placing European-style rail on existing freight lines that would cost just one-eighth the expense of BART. This organizing paid off when two Santa Clara county supervisors, who had been asked to put the sales tax onto the county ballot, cited social justice concerns and blocked the BART-and-roads measure from getting on the ballot.

The next week, the VTA board surprised everyone by circumventing the county supervisors and placing a "BART tax" on the ballot themselves. As a transit agency, the VTA could only put proposals for public transit on the ballot, not for road funding. So, the $6 billion "Measure A" proposal became a transit-only tax. In addition to $2 billion for BART the measure promised twelve transit improvements, including a 50 percent increase in their bus fleet and light rail to East San Jose, a low-income and largely Latino community. TALC had a dilemma: some groups could not imagine opposing a tax that was entirely for public transit, especially now that the coalition's organizing had helped win a plan that included buses. On the other hand, TALC's executive director cautioned that VTA's figures didn't add up. His analysis showed that the promised bus improvements might never materialize and that the VTA might even cut bus service to cover BART's hidden costs.[24]

Other TALC leaders argued that since BART was hugely popular with voters, elected leaders, and powerful business groups, opposing the measure would weaken future TALC efforts. With election day fast approaching, TALC voted to oppose the tax and led the "No on A" effort. At the ballot, Measure A won because of BART's popularity, skyrocketing congestion, and an effective $2 million advertising campaign, financed by the Silicon Valley's booming high-tech companies, all of which overwhelmed TALC's grassroots opposition.

TALC's transit proposals helped merge the environmental and social justice agenda, but failed to effectively articulate that vision in enough time to influence the broader public. The results of voters passing Measure A may plague the South Bay for years to come. The VTA has already cut bus service three years in a row, and may make total cuts of up to 60 percent by 2006. At the same time the VTA has already siphoned off an extra $800 million from the sales-tax measure to cover the escalating costs of the BART extension, as outlined in the TALC's March 2003 report, *Transportation Injustice*.[25] The situation is grim, but there are signs of hope: a TALC-sponsored protest in May 2003 brought out over 250 angry residents representing low-income transit riders, seniors, the disabled, environmentalists, and transit workers.[26] One month later, with grassroots and media pressure building quickly, the VTA board members adopted a primary recommendation of TALC's Transportation Injustice report and borrowed $80 million from Measure A to avoid a 21 percent bus cut.

Free Transit for Low-Income Families

Transportation is a huge cost for most American households, second only to shelter. And these costs hit low-income residents the hardest: Nationwide, the lowest-income households spend 36 percent of their take-home pay on transportation.[27] In California, the free, yellow-school-bus programs have been decimated—only 11 percent of Bay Area children now ride a school bus to school—leaving many urban students to pay for their ride to school on public transit.[28]

This can mean trade-offs for low-income families, especially toward the end of the month as cash runs low. In public testimony before the MTC, one thirteen-year-old explained that his mother supports five children on one paycheck, saying, "If I choose to eat lunch, I have to walk home."[29] Others testified that they missed school at times because they didn't have bus fare. And school districts' budgets suffer as high absentee rates lead to further cuts in state education funding.

To combat this critical gap in access to education, TALC joined with local legislators to propose a free bus pass for low-income students in the East Bay, including Oakland and Richmond, which have some of the most concentrated pockets of poverty. Youth groups, neighborhood advocates, and school officials turned out in force to support the proposal, and through TALC were able to enlist the support of environmental groups as well. The local Sierra Club chapter featured the proposal several times in its monthly newsletter, highlighting the plight of low-income students cut off from education and urging its members to lobby for the proposal. They also pointed out that car trips to and from school are a major contributor to traffic congestion and air pollution.[30] After a five-month campaign that included three press conferences on the MTC's steps, the commission agreed to help fund a two-year pilot project that will provide free bus passes for 31,000 low-income middle and high school students.[31]

Affordable Housing as an Environmental Issue

Housing has sometimes been a fierce battleground between environmentalists and low-income people's advocates. Successful efforts to block new housing developments are at least part of the reason for the skyrocketing housing costs in the Bay Area. As housing in the urban core and suburban ring has become more expensive, and new developments more politically contentious, growth has leapfrogged into outlying suburbs and farmlands. The dearth of affordable housing has become so severe that the number of people commuting to the Bay Area from outside the region has skyrocketed to 170,000 per day.

In the past few years, Bay Area environmental groups, led by the Greenbelt Alliance, have been recognizing that they can save open space by supporting "infill housing,"—essentially building new homes in existing urban or suburban areas. Environmental and business groups, together with low-income people's advocates, are building housing-action coalitions that are popping up in front of city councils within the larger Bay Area counties to support affordable transit-oriented infill housing.[32]

In 1999, the Association of Bay Area Governments (ABAG), a regional planning agency, announced plans to update its "fair share housing allocations," which tell each city how many housing units should be built within its borders. Urban Ecology, a TALC member group which focuses on sustainable urban development, coordinated a TALC working group to develop a "Fair Share Housing" platform calling for more than 100,000 new units of infill affordable housing to be built.[33] This effort is especially important because it has pushed environmental groups to look beyond their traditional concerns of location and site design. Environmental groups in TALC now regularly support increased mandatory set-asides for affordable housing and zoning rules that require affordable housing to be built along with market-rate developments.

Media coverage of the platform, combined with pressure from TALC member groups, helped convince ABAG to shift some of the expected housing growth away from the distant suburbs and back into urban and suburban centers. To make sure these regional recommendations get implemented at the local level, the Non-Profit Housing Association of Northern California has coordinated a coalition organizing drive to win support for fair-share-housing goals in fifteen high-growth cities.

Coalitions that Last

Finding overlapping interests on individual issues and working on joint campaigns is a crucial step to building a long-term coalition. But cooperation on a series of single campaigns does not make a movement. Without a lasting commitment, these ad-hoc coalitions can fall apart as changes in leadership sever the connections between groups, as new issues challenge the political alignment, and as groups embark on new campaigns that don't require coalition support.

But with a conscious effort to build on initial victories, a succession of collaborative campaigns can become a long-term coalition. The following describes four useful lessons we have learned from TALC.

Clarify a Broad and Specific Platform

Community groups often must work in reactive mode, responding to potentially damaging projects. Ultimately though, a proactive agenda that leads to significant and sustained positive change is needed. For a long-term coalition, the agenda needs to include goals and campaign targets that bind the constituent groups.

Just a few months after its initial victory at the MTC, TALC developed a platform that contained broad goals, specific objectives, and—following each objective—one or two policies the coalition would support.[34] For example, it is easy to say that TALC supports an increase in funding for transit. To make this vague support specific, the platform points to gas taxes and user fees, such as higher bridge tolls, as the most equitable and efficient way to fund transit.

This level of detail, while time-consuming to agree upon, minimizes conflict down the line by reducing misunderstandings and giving members confidence that their priority issues will be worked on in time. It also makes TALC more nimble, allowing TALC representatives to support new proposals that are clearly aligned with the platform.

Develop an Activist Base

While research and dialogue can help frame joint campaigns, it is clearly not enough. For a movement to take hold and win victories, groups need to organize. Organizing takes the movement beyond staff and community leaders to membership and a broader base of citizen activists. Though joint organizing efforts can be frustrating, engaging a variety of groups brings different resources and tactics to the struggle.

To resolve tensions created by different group approaches, TALC leaders respect each group's judgments about what tactics would best energize their own base, yet choose actions that all can support. For example, in the Measure B campaign, BOSS members performed creative street-theater actions, but stopped short of shutting down the MTC's offices when it was clear the environmental groups would not support such an action. On the other hand, environmental groups recognized that their middle-class membership is most willing to write letters and testify during public comment periods. Nonetheless, environmental leaders agreed to participate in and put their names behind the more vocal protests, and eventually were able to engage some of their members in the protests as well.

This acceptance and eventual embrace of a more vocal organizing style by environmental groups strengthened relationships between TALC leaders and member organizations. It also signaled a new understanding of the meaning of "campaign." Sprawl-inducing highways are certainly worth protesting, but cutting the transit safety net for already disadvantaged communities is cause for screaming.

Construct an Inclusive Coalition Infrastructure

TALC's success at merging the social justice and environmental agendas was possible only because it had recognized the structural barriers groups face in considering such a coalition. For example, when coalition leaders first approached foundations for support, TALC explicitly requested funds that would assist social justice groups in contributing to TALC, thereby recognizing the social justice groups' unequal access to resources. TALC has also developed a decision-making structure that strives for inclusion. The elected board of directors tries to maintain a balance of issue interests, reflected in the composition of four social justice groups, three environmental groups (one of which has an urban-design focus), four transportation research and advocacy groups (two of which have a combined social justice and environmental focus), and one progressive central labor council.[35]

Use the Membership's Time Wisely

A well-known rule of coalition building is to select a mix of short-term campaigns to ensure people stay engaged and celebrate victories, while also working on long-term efforts that can create truly fundamental change. Just as important is choosing campaigns that play to the strengths of coalition members. This can be particularly important because transportation planning is characterized by technical discussions and long planning horizons, so even major victories may not produce tangible benefits for many years.

For example, one of TALC's missteps was agreeing to devote significant time to the Environmental Justice Advisory Group (EJAG) convened by the MTC to help the agency develop an equity analysis of the 2001 RTP.[36] The MTC had conducted a similar analysis for the 1998 RTP, but without any public process, and with an analysis that TALC strongly disagreed with. This EJAG, it seemed, was an opportunity to develop an analysis in which inequities of funding and access would become clear.

As it turned out, participating effectively in the advisory group required highly detailed statistical and mapping knowledge. Many community activists found the process confusing and frustrating. Despite months of frequent meetings, the final design the MTC used was not much different than it would have been without community participation. It was often difficult to tell whether the agency was rejecting community suggestions for technical reasons ("The model cannot do this.") or for policy reasons ("We do not want to analyze this.").

Not surprisingly, the agency's final report presented data in a way that put the 2001 RTP in a positive light, claiming that low-income and people of color communities have better access to jobs than the region as a whole, a claim which failed to recognize differing auto-ownership levels in the region. An alternative analysis, using the report's own data, shows that the lowest-income residents have access to 75,000 fewer jobs than the highest-income residents.[37]

In retrospect, many TALC members felt that it would have been better to focus on more direct methods of influencing funding decisions rather than trying to involve large numbers of activists in a mostly technical discussion. "The time I spent in EJAG was worse than a waste of time," reflects Reverend Andre Shumake of the faith-based Richmond Improvement Initiative, a TALC member organization. "Not only did they not accept many suggestions and recommendations from our diverse group, but now MTC can say they consulted the community about environmental justice."[38]

Conclusion

The experience of TALC shows that social justice and environmental groups can go on from single-issue tactical cooperation to promote a comprehensive vision that merges the agendas of both constituencies. This task has not been easy. Although a common platform reduces conflicts and inclusive decision-making helps resolve disagreements as they arise, many forces can still strain a coalition's cohesion. For example, differing interests in Alameda's Measure B made it hard to determine when to accept a compromise solution; in Santa Clara's Measure A, TALC stuck to a principled stance that some members correctly felt would alienate potential allies.

Building and sustaining a coalition that merges the environmental and equity agendas requires that members go in knowing that both sides may change their minds, may have to compromise on issues, may have to change their tactics and style, and probably won't get exactly what they want. By accepting these risks, we can forge powerful coalitions that recognize the interdependence of equity and the environment. With such a collaboration, the Sierra Club can strongly support free bus passes for low-income students and homeless activists can demonstrate against suburban highway expansion for the money it draws away from transit.

By rallying leaders around a common policy platform and coordinated organizing efforts, a broad-based coalition can help local activists extend their influence to the regional level. The joined forces of environmental and social justice groups can help single-issue activists influence decision makers and constituencies who might otherwise dismiss them as an unrepresentative fraction of the public.

If we do the research and talk to each other, we can find the wide areas of overlapping concern to both social justice and environmental advocates on transportation issues. If we build on those common interests with joint campaigns, we can win concrete gains for both constituencies. Through those campaigns, we make personal connections and increase our knowledge of the shared values behind the goals. We can build a lasting coalition that can weather divisive issues. Armed with policy research, grassroots muscle, and a truly merged agenda, social justice and environmental groups can create a movement for transportation justice that can finally take on the powerful and entrenched highway and developer lobbies.

notes

1. Metropolitan Transportation Commission, *San Francisco Bay Area Regional Demographic and Travel Characteristics* (October 1999), http://www.mtc.ca.gov/datamart/stats/baydemo.htm. Compiled from US Census figures.

2. Originally called the Bay Area Transportation Land Use Coalition (BATLUC), the group shortened its name to Transportation and Land Use Coalition (TALC) and incorporated as an independent 501c(3) in September 2002.

3. The term "social justice group" is used here broadly to include community and neighborhood groups from low-income and people of color communities, as well as advocacy organizations that represent those communities.

4. Interview with Dawn Phillips, February 7, 2002.

5. Laura Hamburg, "Extra Funds Recommended for Transit," *San Francisco Chronicle,* October 10, 1998.

6. Sam Richards, "Buses, Not More Freeways, Urged at MTC Forum: Overflow Crowd in Dublin Honks Horns, Advocates Pressure on AC Transit to Restore Discontinued Routes," *West County Times*, September 25, 1998.

7. Laura Hamburg, "Rare Praise for Regional Road Map," *San Francisco Chronicle*, October 29, 1998.

8. Robert Oakes, "Transit Backers Gaining Strength," *Contra Costa Times*, November 15, 1998.

9. Alameda Contra Costa Transit District, "Measure B Transportation Sales Tax Renewal," brochure (undated).

10. Transportation and Land Use Coalition, "Proposed Revisions to Alameda County Sales Tax Expenditure Plan" (March 1999).

11. Tyche Hendricks, "Alameda County Debates Dueling Transit Plans," *San Francisco Examiner*, April 20, 1999.

12. Interview with Mike Daley, February 1, 2002.

13. Interview with Dawn Phillips, February 7, 2002.

14. Interview with Mike Daley, February 1, 2002.

15. Benjamin Pimentel, "Support Builds for Transit Tax in Alameda County: Coalition to Back Revised Measure B," *San Francisco Chronicle*, February 25, 2000; Lisa Vorderbrueggen, "Sierra Club, Coalition Back Transit Tax Plan," *San Jose Mercury News*, February 18, 2000; Sean Holstege, "Diverse Groups Rally Behind Measure B: Many Foes of 1998 Tax Back Latest Proposal," *Oakland Tribune*, February 19, 2000.

16. Interview with Dawn Phillips, February 7, 2002.

17. Surface Transportation Policy Project, *Caught in the Crosswalk: Pedestrian Safety in California* (Washington, DC: Surface Transportation Policy Project, September 1999); Michael Cabanatuan, "Pedestrians Face High Risk in Three of the Bay Area Counties," *San Francisco Chronicle*, September 29, 1999; Douglas P. Shuit, "County Leads State in Pedestrians' Deaths, Study Finds: Report on California Accidents Also Shows That Danger is Higher for Young Blacks and Latinos," *Los Angeles Times*, September 29, 1999.

18. STPP, *Caught in the Crosswalk*. Statistics on safety funding were previously reported in Surface Transportation Policy Project, *Mean Streets*, (Washington, DC: Surface Transportation Policy Project, August 1998).

19. Shawn Hubler, "A Walk for Children's Safety," *Los Angeles Times*, October 4, 1999.

20. Two cases that have led to transportation lawsuits include the Urban League and Straphangers Campaign in New York and the Bus Riders Union in Los Angeles. For details on the New York case, see *New York Urban League et al. v. State of New York and Metropolitan Transportation Authority* or http://www.straphangers.org.

21. Transportation and Land Use Coalition, *World Class Transit for the Bay Area* (January 2000).

22. Michael Cabanatuan, "New Approach to Traffic Problems: We Can Do More with What We've Got, Bay Area Coalition Suggests," *San Francisco Chronicle*, January 14, 2000; Gary Richards, "Halt BART to S.J. and Freeway Widening, Coalition Says," *San Jose Mercury News*, January 14, 2000.

23. Transportation and Land Use Coalition, *No Justice, No Tax* (July 2000).

24. The agency's cost estimates failed to account for nearly $2 billion in bond financing, ongoing maintenance, and other costs. These concerns were originally documented in Transportation and Land Use Coalition, *What's the Rush? Why Santa Clara County Will Benefit by Waiting to Renew Its Transportation Sales Tax* (July 2000). Additional detail was presented in Transportation and Land Use Coalition, *Overextended: An Analysis of the Economic Uncertainties and Environmental Justice Risks of Extending BART to San Jose* (March 2001).

25. Transportation and Land Use Coalition, *Transportation Injustice* (March 2003).

26. San Jose Mercury News Staff, "Protesters Say Poor, Elderly Would Suffer if Transportation Cuts Are Adopted," *San Jose Mercury News*, May 2, 2003.

27. US Bureau of Labor Statistics, "1998 Consumer Expenditure Survey," in Surface Transportation Policy Project, *Driven to Spend* (November 2000).

28. California Department of Education (1997), cited in Transportation and Land Use Coalition, *World Class Transit for the Bay Area*, 62. Of the 955,843 children enrolled in grades K–12 in the Bay Area, only 105,664 use school buses to get to school.

29. Lisa Vorderbrueggen, "Transportation Group Aims to Help Students," *Contra Costa Times*, July 26, 2001; Michael Cabanatuan, "Poor Kids' Pleas for Bus Passes Taken to Heart," *San Francisco Chronicle*, July 26, 2001.

30. Ezra Danciu, "Many School Transit Options Available: Gridlock Multiplies with School Traffic," *Tri-Valley Herald*, August 25, 2001. Contra Costa Transportation Authority, "School Bus Program: In the Communities of Lafayette, Moraga, and Orinda, California," (1994).

31. "East Bay Youths to Test Free Bus Pass," *MTC Transactions* (January 2002).

32. The first and most active Housing Action Coalition was formed in January 1993 under the aegis of the Silicon Valley Manufacturing Group. The goal of the coalition is to support the creation of housing that is well-built, relatively affordable, and appropriately located to meet the needs of Santa Clara County

residents. More information is available at http://www.svmg.org/Committees/Housing/Housing_Action_Coalition.

33. Lisa Vorderbrueggen, "ABAG and Coalition Want Houses in Cities," *Contra Costa Times*, November 16, 2000; Jason B. Johnson, "Urgent Call for Housing in Bay Area," *San Francisco Chronicle*, November 17, 2000.

34. Transportation and Land Use Coalition, *Platform*, first adopted June 1999, last updated December 2002. Available at http://www.transcoalition.org.

35. As of August 2001, the Coalition Steering Committee consists of BayRail Alliance, Contra Costa County Central Labor Council (AFL-CIO), Greenbelt Alliance, Latino Issues Forum, Non-Profit Housing Association of Northern California, Regional Bicycle Advisory Coalition, Richmond Improvement Association, Sierra Club, Surface Transportation Policy Project, Transportation for a Livable City (San Francisco), Urban Ecology, and Urban Habitat. Board members serve three-year terms.

36. Metropolitan Transportation Commission, *Environmental Justice Report for the 2001 Regional Transportation Plan for the San Francisco Bay Area*, September 2001.

37. TALC analysis based on data in MTC's *Environmental Justice Report.* MTC's analysis only presented data comparing auto access between low-income and high-income communities, and between minority and non-minority communities, along with similar comparative data for transit access. This approach ignores the difference in auto ownership between different communities. The report's own data shows that low-income residents are six times more likely to live in a household without a car and that the transit dependent have access to nine times fewer jobs than people with cars. The report also presents job access and auto-ownership data for residents in four income ranges ($0–25,000, $25,000–$50,000, $50,000–$75,000, and over $75,000). Combining job-access data with auto ownership data reveals that the lowest-income residents had access to 75,000 fewer jobs than the highest-income residents.

38. Comments made during "Environmental Justice in Transportation Planning," a workshop held by the California Department of Transportation to solicit advice from community-based organizations, February 8, 2002. Quote confirmed by e-mail correspondence with Reverend Shumake.

SIX

Transit Activism in Steel Town, USA
Brian Nogrady and Ayanna King

D ecades of inequity in the planning, funding, and administration of public transportation facilities in Pittsburgh, Pennsylvania have resulted in a segregated and unequal regional transit system, particularly in the construction of fixed transit guideways. Pittsburgh has two major transit corridors, east and south. The Port Authority of Allegheny County (PAT), the region's public transit agency, has invested a significantly large proportion of the area's limited transit capital funds to build a high-cost, modern, clean, and quiet light rail transit (LRT) system that serves predominantly white and higher-income communities in the southern part of the county. At the same time, in the region's highest transit corridor—the predominantly black and lower-income eastern communities—PAT has built a low-cost highway for the exclusive use of buses, the Martin Luther King, Jr. East Busway (MLK-EB), on which it operates diesel buses. In developing these unequal and separate systems, PAT has invested or allocated seven times more capital dollars per rider in the southern corridor than the eastern one.

In choosing LRT for the south, PAT rejected every cheaper busway option as a "lesser alternative." PAT's planning documents for the LRT expressed concerns over the adverse environmental impact of buses, specifically citing the odor and noise problems that would be created in immediately adjacent residential neighborhoods by the high frequency service along a busway and its station areas. However, in planning for a short extension of the MLK-EB, despite repeated requests from affected eastern residents concerned about environmental impacts, PAT refused to consider upgrading the busway to LRT. PAT also failed to provide the public with information that would allow an informed comparison of the true environmental and monetary cost of any alternatives, besides PAT's pre-ordained buses-only plans for the east. The extended busway will be used by more than 1,500 diesel-bus trips each weekday and will adversely affect adjacent residential neighborhoods, particularly the terminal communities where hundreds of buses will use residential streets to access the busway, projecting noise and pollution into the adjacent schools, homes, and playgrounds. The communities most directly impacted by the MLK-EB include those with the highest black populations in the region.

Prior to the 1980s, regional transit plans called for an integrated, high capacity, rail transit system serving the East End corridor and eastern suburbs, connected to the southern Pittsburgh area. The MLK-EB was planned and built, beginning in the late 1970s by PAT, as a low-cost interim facility with the express representation that it would soon be upgraded. Two decades later, PAT has refused to consider upgrading the MLK-EB, claiming it would be too expensive. Yet PAT continues to accord funding priority to more expensive expansions of the LRT to the south and north that serve fewer riders than the east, including a northern extension that pointedly avoids other black neighborhoods. PAT is also pursuing other high-cost-per-rider projects like the Pennsylvania High Speed Maglev Project, a transportation project that will bypass black neighborhoods altogether, providing an exclusive magnetically levitated train system for white suburban commuters.

In addition to the environmental and health burdens already endured as a result of PAT's discriminatory policies, blacks experience decreased service levels, inferior station facilities and vehicles, and poor downtown access. Moreover, their communities are denied access to the growing regional LRT system, with its future expansions to the Pittsburgh International Airport and elsewhere. They are cut off from the much-needed opportunities for economic development, investment, and employment that an integrated regional LRT system could facilitate.

The large, artistic letter "G" found on all of PAT's vehicles is meant to advertise its "Gold Standard of Service" motto. The glaring disparities in its allocation of transit funds, environmental impacts, and service, particularly between its two major transit corridors, one black and one white, can only be recognized as discrimination, and a "Gold Standard of Service for Some."

Background

Like most of America, Allegheny County is highly segregated by race. According to the 2000 Census, about 75 percent of blacks live in urban neighborhoods east of downtown Pittsburgh and 10 percent live in those neighborhoods just north. Over the past half-century, these East End and North Side communities have borne a disproportionate share of the burdens of many of the region's transportation and urban renewal projects. Highways built to serve suburban commuters severed vibrant black communities of the North Side and the east's Hill District from downtown. These projects displaced tens of thousands from their homes, businesses, and communities. Redlining and the Allegheny County Public Housing Authority, which for decades specifically located black public housing residents into particular communities, further contributed to the region's segregation.

PAT, the nation's fourteenth-largest transit agency, provides public transit service for Pittsburgh and surrounding Allegheny County, carrying a system-wide average of 256,150 passengers each weekday. It maintains a fleet of 1,000 buses for 230 bus routes operating on streets and on 26.7 miles of exclusive bus lanes, High-Occupancy Vehicle lanes, and busways; and 55 LRT vehicles operating on 15.8 miles of track. The rich history of transit service in Pittsburgh includes inclines, commuter railroads, and an extensive electric trolley system that at its peak, encompassed 606 miles and 99 routes. This streetcar system remained largely intact until 1964, when PAT took over operations after acquiring thirty-three independent transit companies. After consolidating the lines, PAT proceeded to convert many trolley lines to diesel buses.[1]

Numerous studies, beginning as early as 1906, have been conducted for the purpose of integrating rail transit with the subway system, building upon the extensive streetcar system. Comprehensive long-range plans developed in the 60s and 70s were meant to guide the development of an integrated rail transit system that would extend east, south, and north. Over three decades, however, PAT's inequitable allocation of capital funding has left behind the plans for rail lines that would serve predominantly black communities in the East End and North Side, even though these areas have the highest transit demand and were assigned priority. Instead PAT has advanced high-cost and lower ridership lines serving predominately white and higher-income communities.

East and South Corridor Disparities

The LRT system that PAT operates from the southern suburban municipalities and city neighborhoods into downtown is comprised of a 10.5 mile South Hills Main Line (running mostly at-grade and in its own right-of-way from the county's southern edge to downtown) with a 5.3 mile Library Line branch. The LRT network was completed in 1987. To create the network, PAT converted parts of the existing South Hills Main Line trolley corridor and Library (trolley) Line into LRT. PAT also constructed a new mile-long downtown subway. The subway system has ten major stations with many customer-friendly features, and six additional subway stations providing convenient access to over 90 percent of downtown. A total of 434 vehicle trips from three different routes operate in the corridor weekdays, carrying an average of 25,527 passengers.[2] The communities adjoining the South Corridor are only 3.7 percent black, compared with 13 percent for Allegheny County. Suburban communities benefiting most from the LRT have an even more uniformly white population, ranging from 0.8 percent to 1.5 percent black residents.

The LRT system cost $520 million to build—approximately an $818 million investment today. PAT is building a $500 million LRT extension in the South Hills and is also designing the North Extension—a $389 million LRT extension to downtown Pittsburgh's North Shore area. With the additional two LRT extensions, PAT's total investment for the South Corridor will be $1.7 billion.

In Pittsburgh's predominantly black and lower-income East End, by contrast, PAT operates the MLK-EB. While reserved lanes for buses in the middle, or at the sides, of an existing expressway or multilane street are sometimes referred to as busways. The MLK-EB is unique. It is an exclusive, grade-separated, concrete, two-lane, buses-only highway with stations, built on a railroad corridor that previously carried interurban commuter rail service. Essentially, this private highway for buses runs for 6.8 miles from Wilkinsburg Borough through various Pittsburgh neighborhoods to the edge of downtown.

PAT operates 434 daily LRT trips and 1,146 bus trips on the existing MLK-EB each weekday on forty-six bus routes. However, this large volume of trips does not provide greater service frequency for East End residents. Only 341 daily bus trips—three of the forty-six bus routes—provide service between MLK-EB stations and downtown. The remaining 805 bus trips made along the MLK-EB are local express and suburban express routes that use the busway as a shortcut. Buses, not serving East End residents, enter the busway and travel nonstop between downtown and the suburbs. Adjacent residential neighborhoods, although not served by the buses funneled onto the MLK-EB, are nonetheless exposed to the harmful diesel exhaust and noise generated by them. Once they reach downtown, the buses leaving the MLK-EB don't have their own right-of-way, like the LRT and subway. Instead, buses exit the terminus of the MLK-EB on the edge of downtown and complete a short loop on congested downtown streets—no different from regular city street bus routes.

Completed by PAT in 1983, the 6.8 mile busway cost $113 million to build, approximately a $175 million investment today. At the six stations along its length, riders wait on simple concrete sidewalks. Despite its inferior service and its shorter length, the high density of the East End Corridor and the high transit dependency of low-income residents combine to give a weekday average of 27,546 passenger trips, 2,000 more than the South Corridor. PAT is finishing a 2.3-mile, $62 million extension of MLK-EB. Including the busway extension, PAT's investment in the East End Corridor, the region's highest-transit corridor, will be a mere $237 million—compared with $1.7 billion for the South Corridor.

The communities adjoining the MLK-EB are 43.9 percent black. The adjacent residential areas most directly impacted by the busway are 54.5 percent black. Additionally, each weekday the 805 bus trips from suburban-express and local-express routes use residential streets to enter and exit the MLK-EB in two particular communities: Wilkinsburg and East Liberty. Wilkinsburg and East Liberty, which clearly bear the greatest burden of the noise, pollution, and traffic impacts, are 68.5 percent and 74.6 percent black, respectively. The specific streets on which hundreds of diesel buses travel—passing homes, schools, playgrounds, churches, and day-care facilities—are over 90 percent black.

Each day hundreds of buses get on and off the MLK-EB in East Liberty and Wilkinsburg. These terminal communities have the county's highest rates of asthma among children. Express bus routes, serving suburban communities and suburban park and ride lots, use residential streets in these communities to access the busway. In stopping and starting at traffic signals, and climbing the East End's steep hills, these buses leave behind maximum levels of pollution and noise in the playgrounds, parks, schools, and day-care facilities they pass. Over 400 such bus trips get off in Wilkinsburg each day, the majority of which do not service the community in any way, but use its streets as a short cut.

LRT systems are generally planned for higher-density corridors where the transit demand is greater, since LRTs provide higher levels of service. On the other hand, low-cost busways are planned for lower-density corridors where the transit demand is less, such as along a suburban highway.[3] That the East End consists of higher-density development than the South Hills is one of the many underlying incongruities of PAT's disparate transit investments. Furthermore, a large percentage of South Corridor riders access the LRT by car at one of its eight free park and ride facilities, whereas most East End Corridor riders walk to transit stations. The East End is the ideal corridor for a high-capacity LRT system, and where such an investment would yield the highest ridership per capital dollar spent.

PAT has often implied that the LRT was built in the South Hills —and not the East End—because the South had trolleys, and thus PAT was simply modernizing the system. But historically, the East End Corridor had the most streetcar tracks in Allegheny County. Within three years of PAT taking over, the streetcar lines had been replaced with diesel buses, marking the start of the segregation in Pittsburgh's transit system.[4] In 1968, less than a year after East End riders had been conveniently moved off the integrated streetcar system and onto diesel buses, PAT proposed its low-cost busway concept for the east. Citizens were told by PAT, "This is merely the early action part; the time will come when [the east] will get a truly high-speed rapid transit system, and [the MLK-EB] is a sort of stopgap."[5] According to PAT's director at the time, the MLK-EB "should not be considered as the ultimate form of transportation to these areas." Rather, "[s]trategic rights-of-way will be preserved for transit use and [busway] construction...will provide the basis for later improvements using advanced technology."[6]

The East End Corridor, as has been repeatedly acknowledged in regional planning studies for decades, has the region's highest transit demand. According to the adopted 1976 long-range transit plan:

> The corridor east [of downtown Pittsburgh] is the most complex, highly urbanized corridor in southwestern Pennsylvania region...[and it] would support by the far the most significant rapid [rail] transit line in the region... . The [East Rapid Rail Transit Line] is urgently needed, will generate high patronage levels...[A]lthough a part of the current program, [the MLK-EB] was not necessarily a facility that would still be in place in the Year 2000... [but rather] one that which could be upgraded to another technology in later years.[7]

Yet a quarter-century later, PAT is extending the low-cost busway rather than upgrading it to LRT.

LRT Extensions and the MLK-EB Extension

When the MLK-EB was first proposed, eastern residents asked why the east wasn't getting the same system as the south. PAT's representative replied that it was just "trying to get the most out of its dollars."[8] Yet PAT invested nearly five times more in the South Corridor to serve fewer riders than the East End Corridor—hardly a cost-efficient choice. Since completing both systems in the mid 1980s, PAT has continued to accord funding priority to low-ridership transit projects benefiting white communities and commercial development interests patronized primarily by whites.

PAT's South Corridor LRT Extension (South Extension) is a 12.7-mile-long expansion project that includes the construction of a new LRT line on two abandoned trolley alignments and a modernization of the existing Library Line. Scheduled to open in 2004, the first part of the extension will be a crescent-shaped, 5.5-mile segment that will connect at both ends to the LRT Main Line, providing suburban riders with a bypass of slower Main Line sections, at a cost in excess of $400 million to save just two minutes travel time on average.[9]

PAT is also now designing the North Extension—a $389 million, 1.4-mile northern extension of the South Hills LRT to downtown Pittsburgh's two new, professional sports stadiums on the North Shore of the Allegheny River. The stadiums themselves were extremely controversial because voters had rejected the use of public funds to build them and commitments to minority participation in construction were flagrantly violated. The North Extension will use transit dollars owed to the East End, and its chosen path pointedly avoids the predominantly black, dense North Side neighborhoods, which all preceding long-range transit plans had specified serving. With a second .2-mile component of the project, PAT will eliminate the unserviced LRT track that extends to the MLK-EB's terminus from the subway (the tracks had been built for MLK-EB's future conversion), in order to relocate the LRT branch slightly closer to the new convention center.[10] The only "gain" resulting from this $68 million realignment is that the walking distance for South Hills LRT riders will be reduced 400 feet from that which would be available if PAT would simply service the existing branch to the MLK-EB. The hidden cost for the East End is that this wasteful realignment will add $100 million to the cost of the hoped-for upgrade of the MLK-EB.

While PAT has allocated billions of dollars for low-ridership, boondoggle projects, plans for critical rail-based transit investments in the East End Corridor were cut back "because of fiscal constraint."[11]

Even as eastern citizens were being told in 1998 that LRT to the East End couldn't occur before the next ten to fifteen years, PAT allocated funding almost overnight for the low-ridership extension to the stadiums, which, like the funded South Extension, wasn't a part of any long-range plan for an integrated regional LRT system.

Instead of connecting the East End to this growing LRT system as promised, PAT is extending the MLK-EB 2.3 miles. The MLK-EB Extension, when open in 2003, is expected to provide 13,600 passenger trips daily and add three stations.[12] The extended MLK-EB represents a total investment of only $237 million by PAT in the East End Corridor, compared with $1.7 billion in the South Corridor. The annual capital per-rider cost works out to be a $16 per-rider investment in the east compared with $105 per-rider investment in the south. Despite this glaring inequity, in 1998, PAT's board chairman had the following response to eastern residents' demands for LRT:

> Decisions on what fixed guideway systems to build must be responsive to the needs of the region while being responsible to the taxpaying public. Converting the [MLK-EB] to light rail would come at a high cost not just in terms of dollars, but at the cost of other critical transit improvement projects. It is the job of the Port Authority Board to determine the most prudent and practical use of limited public funding for all of Allegheny County.[13]

The MLK-EB was originally built for straightforward upgrade to LRT, with civil structures designed for LRT's heavier loads and higher clearances, and the unused tracks in place to later connect the subway to the MLK-EB's downtown terminus.[14] Since the planning for the MLK-EB Extension in 1988, affected residents and communities repeatedly requested LRT upgrade and extension rather than a busway expansion. Contrary to previous assurances that the MLK-EB was a temporary facility, PAT's steadfast position during extension planning was that an LRT upgrade would not be considered because it would require light rail "installation along the entire 9.1 miles of facility, consisting of the 6.8 mile long existing busway plus the 2.3 mile extension. The length of construction would be four times as long, 9.1 miles compared with 2.3 miles, and thus would be significantly more expensive." [15]

The communities along the MLK-EB Extension are 50.3 percent black. The East End community of Rankin Borough, which is 71 percent black, will bear the brunt of the noise and air pollution from the extension. Over 238 bus trips each day, a 934 percent increase, will use residential streets in Rankin, passing homes, playgrounds, and a public housing complex. Though scientific studies have shown a link between heavy diesel bus and truck traffic on residential streets and increased rates of asthma and other respiratory illnesses, PAT never considered the environmental impacts on Rankin, or the added impacts—from the 50 percent increase in busway traffic—to communities adjoining the existing MLK-EB.

Braddock Borough, further down the East End Corridor and 68.8 percent black, may become the terminus of a second 1.7-mile extension of the MLK-EB that PAT is now considering to connect with the proposed Mon/Fayette toll road. Rankin and Braddock, along with Wilkinsburg, have the three highest percentages of black residents among the county's 130 municipalities. The high concentration of black families in these and other East End communities is the direct result of long-standing discrimination in housing practices and segregation in public housing.

Federal laws require that PAT consider alternative modes for its transit projects. Though an alternative for the MLK-EB Extension was never considered, PAT evaluated both LRT and a cheaper busway alternative for the South Extension. The first two miles of the South Extension's alignment parallels PAT's South Route 51 Busway (South Busway). The 4.5-mile South Busway supports 677 bus trips from sixteen routes that provide a bypass of traffic lights and heavy rush hour traffic on the adjacent four-lane commercial artery. Functionally, and also because it is far removed from residential areas, the South Busway is very different from the MLK-EB. While PAT determined it would have been more than three times cheaper to extend the South Busway than to build an LRT extension, the detriment it would have caused precluded a busway extension.[16] Unlike the existing South Busway's highway setting, its expansion would have passed through the middle of predominantly white suburban residential neighborhoods (communities along the South Extension are only 1.2 percent black). Furthermore, according to PAT, "[B]ecause the Library Line [a part of the South Extension] was made into an interim LRT system, it would be difficult to revert to a lesser alternative."[17] Yet that same "lesser alternative" is all PAT would consider in the East End Corridor.

The Environmental Assessment (EA) for the MLK-EB Extension in 1995 stated that "[t]he 'ease' of converting to light rail is actually a question of money; if sufficient money is available, then the Busway could be converted to light rail."[18] But for more than a decade of planning for the MLK-EB Extension, PAT never prepared nor made public any LRT conversion-cost estimates to justify its position, even though it knew, as evidenced by the South Extension, that cost factors alone weren't a sufficient basis for eliminating alternatives. In 1998,

PAT reluctantly produced an estimate of $401 million for LRT from downtown to Rankin, and quickly advertised that "the construction cost is too expensive when the East Busway Extension will provide virtually the same rapid transit benefits for a fraction of the cost."[19] PAT's flyers didn't mention the environmental and quality-of-service reasons why PAT choose LRT for the south, nor the long-standing discrepancy in per-annual-rider investment between the east and the south. The MLK-EB's LRT upgrade that PAT decided was too expensive would be one-fourth the cost of PAT's South LRT investments, with a $27 per-annual-rider capital cost.

Around the country, many cities that have built LRT lines have witnessed tremendous economic investment along the transit line and around stations. In many cases, cities have used LRT to develop depressed areas and to control land use and growth. As the director of Portland, Oregon's transit agency pointed out, "Light rail provides a strong ability to affect land use. Investors aren't going to spend $1 million or $10 million around a bus shelter, but they will around a permanent light rail station."[20] Pittsburgh's experience is no exception.

In choosing LRT for the South Extension, PAT stated, "The generation of economic benefits in the community is directly related to the amount of capital and operating funds spent on the project."[21] This "more spent the better" attitude is in stark contrast to PAT's policies in the economically devastated East End. PAT, like other transit agencies, is even working on joint transit-oriented developments at LRT stations. One proposed development includes theaters, restaurants, retail stores, office space, apartments, and a parking garage. This is a far cry from the East End Corridor, where PAT's investment is best exemplified by the landmark Wilkinsburg Train Station that has sat abandoned and deteriorating at the MLK-EB's entrance for two decades.

Bypassing the North Side with PAT's North Extension

The North Side is a collection of historic, high-density residential and commercial neighborhoods across the Allegheny River from downtown. Found in every regional transit plan for decades, the North Side, like the East End, has always been included in the plans for a future east to west rapid-rail line.[22] Built to serve the suburbs, an endless wall of highways running parallel to the river cuts the North Side off from the river's North Shore and the shore's publicly financed attractions. The North Extension is planned to run from downtown to the North Shore by crossing under the Allegheny River to a station next to the new Pirates baseball park on the North Shore. But from there, instead of crossing under the highways to also serve North Side neighborhoods, which are 61.1 percent black, PAT's newly chosen alignment turns abruptly left, following the highway to a second station (only 2,000 feet from the original alignment) and terminates next to the new Steelers football field, creating a second station only 2,000 feet from the first.

The North Extension will connect the South Hills to the two stadiums and is further intended to provide a catalyst for trendy North Shore development. The North Extension will also serve a large parking facility at its terminus for use by suburban commuters. Commuters will enjoy parking at a reduced rate, as compared to downtown garages, as well as, a free LRT ride into downtown. Forecast to carry only 10,105 passenger trips daily when it opens in 2008, PAT's North Extension represents a capital investment of $107 per-annual-rider, or seven times that of the MLK-EB.

Early in the planning for the North Extension, LRT alignments that would have provided service to North Side populations were precipitously discarded, because the new alignment would provide development benefits between the new stadiums.[23] North Side residents were dissuaded by PAT that a LRT alignment into North Side would be too expensive, and were shown an arrow on a map promising a future branch. PAT never produced any cost estimate to justify that position, nor mentioned that an LRT expansion west to the Pittsburgh International Airport would likely be built from the North Extension, cutting off the North Side altogether.

Environmental and Health Burdens

In addition to isolation and second-class service provided by the discriminatory allocation of capital funding, PAT's transit decisions have created adverse environmental results impacting the health, welfare, and safety of MLK-EB corridor residents. Unlike the electrically powered, clean and quiet, light rail vehicles (LRV) that PAT has elected to use in the South, the 1,500 diesel bus trips traveling on the extended MLK-EB every day generate high levels of air and noise pollution in the adjacent neighborhoods, particularly at station areas and in terminal communities.

In choosing LRT for the South Extension, PAT acknowledged the environmental benefits of LRVs, despite their costing ten times more than diesel buses. PAT's 1994 EA for the South Extension stated that,

"LRT will enhance air quality, since LRV's do not themselves emit air pollutants and emissions from a single fixed source of electric power can be better controlled than emissions from many buses."[24] The study also pointed out other serious busway environmental problems, yet PAT's 1995 EA for the MLK-EB Extension didn't mention their concerns for operating a busway in the East End Corridor.

The Environmental Protection Agency lists more than forty chemicals in diesel exhaust as toxic air contaminants, known and probable human carcinogens, reproductive toxicants, or endocrine disrupters. PAT's diesel buses further emit very high levels of particulate matter, minute airborne particles coated with the dangerous chemicals, that settle deep in the lungs where the chemicals are absorbed. Exposure causes lung function decrements and symptomatic effects, especially in children and asthmatics; increased cardiopulmonary and lung cancer mortality; and premature death in the elderly.

In response to eastern residents' concerns about the MLK-EB's extension, and in an effort to avoid a complete environmental review and consideration of the LRT alternative, PAT specifically utilized methodologies that intentionally understated the MLK-EB's adverse environmental impacts when it authored its 1995 EA of the extension. Though federal regulations require the more thorough Environmental Impact Statement (EIS) for large projects, PAT has been able to dodge the $100-million-project-cost threshold that automatically triggers an EIS by making incremental short additions to the MLK-EB. While citizens have cited the EA's extensive deficiencies and PAT's own stated environmental concerns for busways in the South Hills, PAT has refused to conduct an EIS.

When PAT compared impacts of busway and LRT alternatives in a 1978 EIS for the South Corridor, it concluded that

> [c]oncentrations of buses at stations and high frequency service along the busways may be expected to create odor problems within immediately adjacent residential areas....Possible odor problems could result from concentrations of express buses and feeder buses at station areas....Noise generated by bus pullaways could be a problem at [busway] stations.[25]

Conversely, for LRT, "No noise impact would be expected since noise levels are low when the [light rail] vehicles accelerate or decelerate at station areas."[26] Yet when it came to the MLK-EB Extension, PAT's 1995 EA stated that "[a] conversion to rail is not under consideration at the present time because there is no reason to do such a conversion."[27] In order to gain support for its low-cost busway plan, PAT withheld from eastern residents its environmental reasons for rejecting busways in the South Corridor that would have allowed an informed comparison of alternatives.

Sitting a few feet from the MLK-EB's new terminus is Mom's House, a nonprofit day-care center for the children of single, low-income students, most of whom are black. Only 20 feet and a soundwall separate them from where nearly 600 bus trips each day will enter and exit the busway, stop and start, turn around, and possibly idle for extended periods of time at the station, generating maximum levels of noise and air pollution. Young children are particularly susceptible to the air pollution that will be generated by PAT's "dirty" diesel buses, but, despite repeated requests, PAT refuses to relocate Mom's House.

Transit Service Disparities

Even if the environmental burden and investment inequities didn't exist, the differences between the LRT and the MLK-EB are not merely a choice of rubber over steel wheels. The MLK-EB—on neither qualitative nor quantitative measures—does not provide East End Corridor residents with the same superior quality transit enjoyed by the South Hills residents. Moreover, East End and North Side communities, by their separation from the growing regional LRT system, are deprived of the economic development, investment, and other opportunities that participation could leverage.

Transit Stations

LRT stations have platforms level with the LRV's floor, allowing for quicker, easier, and safer vehicle boarding along. Level platforms also provide better accessibility for the disabled, the elderly, and small children. LRVs also offer the ability to use multiple doors. LRT stations have amenities such as full canopy coverage over the platform, passenger information systems, and at the largest stations, manned fare-collection booths providing assistance and security. By comparison, MLK-EB stations are little more than curbed, 8-inch-high concrete sidewalks with only partial canopy coverage, no passenger information systems, and no fare-collection booths.

Downtown MLK-EB stops don't have stations at all; rather riders wait on narrow, crowded city sidewalks for their bus, exposed to weather and passing traffic, and pushed by pedestrians moving through the crowd. A continuous line of buses pulling up to the curb makes it difficult to hear, and clouds of diesel exhaust trapped by the buildings descend on waiting riders. By contrast, downtown LRT riders wait in brightly lit, clean, quiet, and beautifully designed multilevel subway stations, with expensive granite walls and terrazzo floors, wide platforms, benches, elevators and escalators, neon artwork, and piped-in classical music. PAT is leasing open space for shops to sell coffee, flowers, and newspapers, and magazines, allowing South Hills riders to enjoy a cappuccino and a paper and listen to the music of Beethoven while waiting for their LRV.

Downtown Access and Service Frequency

The greater reliability and access afforded by the LRT, along with its ability to operate without restriction or delay underground, is another reason why PAT chose LRT for the South Extension. Once downtown, buses exiting the MLK-EB are forced to use regular city streets and some short bus lanes, often being delayed at intersections and in heavy traffic congestion. During downtown events, PAT must reroute MLK-EB buses and even eliminate stops, leaving unwary riders stranded and searching city streets for their bus, while the LRT operates as usual. But even operating at its best, the MLK-EB provides poor downtown access for East Enders, since PAT does not allow local buses providing service on the MLK-EB to travel more than two blocks into the city from its terminus. Thus, the MLK-EB buses that serve End residents provide access to less than 40 percent of downtown within a 5 minute walk of their three curbside stops. By contrast, over 90 percent of downtown is accessible from the four subway stations serving the South Corridor. PAT does allow the predominantly white suburban-express routes served by the MLK-EB to have longer loops covering most of downtown. Furthermore, far fewer buses stop at MLK-EB stations each day as compared with LRVs at LRT stations. Consequently, East End riders wait at MLK-EB stations 50 percent longer on average to board than riders using the LRT.

Vehicles

PAT spends $3 million per LRV, compared with only $250,000 to $300,000 for the standard diesel buses providing service on the MLK-EB. The LRVs have multiple doors and wider aisles, bigger windows, brighter interior lighting, and more comfortable seating. They also provide a much smoother and quieter ride for patrons than PAT's diesel buses. LRV interior noise levels are one hundred times quieter when accelerating and ten times quieter at cruising speed than those of a diesel bus.[28] LRVs are also seven times less likely to have a breakdown.[29] For its predominantly white clientele using express buses on the MLK-EB, PAT goes the extra mile, buying special $400,000 coach-style touring buses with reclining high-back seats, fold-up armrests, individual reading lights and air vents, storage racks, and passenger compartments insulated against road and engine noise.[30]

Despite all the inequities between the South Hills LRT and MLK-EB Busway, and even between urban and suburban bus routes, East End Corridor residents pay the same fare. In arguing against the MLK-EB's upgrade, PAT stated that its busways are more cost effective to operate. It then stands to reason that the black and low-income transit-dependent riders are subsidizing the higher operating and capital costs benefiting white suburban choice riders not only with their health and the livability of their neighborhoods, but with their wallets.

Lost Transportation Opportunities

Since busways require 40 percent more width than LRT, the wider MLK-EB has denied East Enders the opportunity to develop an adjacent bike trail that would connect them to the growing regional trail system. Trails provide a safe place for recreation off crowded city streets, allow commuting alternatives, and their use could help address high rates of obesity and heart disease afflicting blacks. A PAT representative's dismissal of the need to accommodate a bike trail, because East End residents can't afford bikes, is an example of the soft racism affecting transit investments.[31]

Adding Insult to Injury: Maglev and Mon/Fay Toll Road

Before PAT reneged on its commitment to upgrade the MLK-EB, planners envisioned that the urban East End Corridor and eastern suburban communities would be connected to downtown on one single integrated transit line. Early planners determined that the an eastern aligned LRT line was "the most pressing transit need in Allegheny County."[32] Instead of building it, PAT plans to invest billions for a high-tech system, the Pennsylvania High Speed Maglev project, that will serve only suburban commuters. Moreover, the proposed Mon/Fayette toll road will spend billions more to provide suburban commuters a bypass of traffic, at the environmental expense of East End communities and their residents, themselves left segregated to the second-rate MLK-EB.

The Pennsylvania Maglev Project

PAT is part of a consortium of private and public investors developing plans for a $3.4 billion, 52-mile west to east high-speed magnetic levitation train (Maglev) that is being promoted as the start of new high-speed, intracity transportation line. Forecast to carry an optimistic 67,000 passenger trips daily, Maglev, in reality, would provide a very comfortable, very fast, and very expensive, exclusive transit system for suburban commuters to travel downtown and to the airport. Some 42 percent would be the same suburban commuters that could be served by an eastern LRT line that would also serve East End corridor residents. PAT claims that the LRT line is too expensive, yet PAT supports making a $172 per-annual-rider investment for Maglev that would bypass altogether the black and lower-income East End Corridor communities. Maglev is nearly eleven times PAT's $16 capital-cost-per-rider investment for the MLK-EB.

Although Maglev would run directly above part of the MLK-EB downtown, PAT never once considered connecting the multibillion-dollar, high-tech system to it; rather, PAT's plans connect the Maglev to the LRT system. Still, East End Corridor residents would likely pay for Maglev, since potential funding includes a combination of matching state and local sources that could otherwise be used to build a single eastern LRT line serving everyone, not just a privileged few.

Mon/Fayette Toll Road Bypass

Any picture of the inequity in Pittsburgh's transit investments would be incomplete without discussion of the Mon/Fayette toll road (MFT), a proposed four-lane tolled expressway stretching north to Pittsburgh from West Virginia. Its most controversial section is a $2 billion, 24-mile, Y-shaped segment within Allegheny County. Where it crosses the Monongahela River in Allegheny County, the MFT will divide in two arms. One arm will head northeast and the other arm will head west—following the rivers' northern shore. Both arms will then connect to I-376 and provide suburban commuters from the east with a bypass of heavy rush hour congestion—congestion that is the direct consequence of PAT's refusal to upgrade the MLK-EB.[33] The Braddock, Rankin, and Hazelwood neighborhoods will bear the environmental burden of the MFT bypass cutting through the middle of their residential neighborhoods and business districts for the benefit of suburban commuters.

There are two possible alignments for the northeastern arm. One would use the north shore of the Monongahela River and the other would use the south shore. The communities along both shores, who will bear the air pollution and noise impacts of the MFT bypass, have substantially higher black populations than the uniformly white suburban communities that will principally benefit from it. Like PAT, the Pennsylvania Turnpike Commission (PTC), which is building the toll road, has favored the commercial and real estate development interests, owned and primarily patronized by whites, in precipitously dismissing a preferable bypass alignment on the Monongahela's southern shore. The PTC will spend tens of millions of dollars to depress the bypass and cover sections with park space in Hazelwood, which is 35.2 percent black. Yet in Braddock, 68.8 percent black, the MFT will be elevated 25 feet above adjacent residential streets on a built-up earthen mound, requiring the closing of 60 percent of the cross streets and the elimination of more than ten business-district blocks. Braddock residents won't even receive sound barriers, because the PTC won't build multimillion dollar sound barriers to protect $50,000 homes.[33]

Building an eastern LRT line as an alternative to the MFT's bypass component was never even considered by the PTC and PAT, despite federal requirements.[34] In fact, PAT has enthusiastically supported the MFT, citing its ability to allow it to funnel more suburban buses onto the MLK-EB using residential streets in Rankin, and also in Braddock with a proposed second MLK-EB extension. Residents of Rankin and Braddock, sandwiched between the MLK-EB and the MFT, will pay for the MFT not only with their health, but also with taxes as developable property is taken off tax rolls for the expressway and as transportation funds are used for building the MFT, instead of upgrading the MLK-EB.

Summary

The evaluation of PAT's planning decisions, allocations of capital funding, and administration of its fixed-transit guideway facilities—particularly its two major transit corridors, east and south—clearly shows that PAT has knowingly provided superior transit service to white communities and inferior transit service to black communities. PAT has chosen LRT as the backbone of a growing regional transit system for numerous environmental, quality of service, and economic reasons. But despite previous long-range plans, higher priority, and greater cost effectiveness for such investments, black communities are simply not considered by PAT for integration into that growing system.

PAT's actions constitute discrimination based upon race. This discrimination has been implemented by the clear, well-documented practice of PAT to mislead the public and even federal officials by withholding critical information regarding alternatives and environmental concerns. The MLK-EB Extension's 1995 EA did not include any environmental justice and equity analysis, although studies in white transit corridors completed years earlier had included such sections. PAT allows the public only information supporting its project. When PAT's authority is challenged, it uses what has been described as a "gangland style of selling 'community improvements' on a take-it-or-leave-it basis," to strong-arm weak local officials and governments, with a fraction of PAT's resources, into letting the agency do what it wants.[35]

The residents of the East End and North Side deserve no less advocacy or expenditure for their community's environment, economic development, quality of life, health, safety, welfare, and the quality of their transit service than the residents of the South Hills. Ultimately, PAT's discriminatory policies, its squandering of limited transit resources on high-cost, low-ridership projects, and poor planning hurt the entire region. Buses and cars clog streets, billions are wasted for new highways like the MFT, and suburban sprawl continues unchecked, causing untold environmental damage. In the end, urban business districts and neighborhoods will decline, urban schools will fail, and the city will become more and more racially and economically segregated.

Pittsburgh Fights Back

In June 2001, the Environmental Justice Resource Center (EJRC) at Clark Atlanta University received a $100,000 grant from the Heinz Endowments to assist local African American groups in Pittsburgh in addressing the previously outlined transportation disparities. To these ends, the EJRC established the Pittsburgh Transportation Equity Project (PTEP). PTEP employs a multifaceted approach to target, document, and address the equity issues of Pittsburgh's transportation investments, regional planning, decision-making, and public participation. PTEP was designed to encourage African American groups and community leaders to become active players in transportation decision-making.

PTEP had several objectives:

- To inform African American residents in the Pittsburgh-Allegheny area about transportation equity, transit discrimination trends, and citizens' response;

- to organize a core transportation equity network;

- to document the impact of the region's transportation policies on transportation investments and equity;

- to empower African American groups on transportation decision-making;

- to serve as an information clearinghouse on transportation equity policies and practices;

- to impact transportation "visioning," decision-making, and transportation investments in the Pittsburgh area; and

- to inform local African American community-based organizations and leaders on major issues surrounding smart growth, including transportation equity, land-use planning, housing, environmental justice, and community economic-development decision-making.

Special efforts were made to build a transportation equity project that is representative of the diverse African American community, including religious, community development, social service, academia, business, civil rights, media, youth, and transit riders. PTEP's steering committee was recruited to represent different sectors and organizations from Pittsburgh's north, south, east, and west neighborhoods. PTEP laid the foundation for building a strong core transportation-equity network among African Americans and provided opportunities for collaboration and networking among Pittsburgh-area grassroots groups, community organizations, academic institutions, churches, and voluntary associations.

After several meetings, the planning committee identified the following areas to focus their attention on:

- Community Education—Provide information and data to the community, coordinate community forums, develop community surveys, and provide information to the PTEP from the community perspective

- Community Development—Connect transportation to everyday social issues in the African American community

- Research/Policy Analysis—Research transportation issues, trends, and policies nationally and locally

- Evaluation—Develop tools to evaluate and measure PTEP's goals and objectives

- Political Interface—Maintain a relationship with local, state, and federal government officials

- Resource Development—Research grants and foundations for PTEP's operational budget

- Collaboration/Partnerships—Build collaborations with other transportation groups, community organizations, and grassroots groups

- Workforce Development—Connect transportation resources to develop new employment opportunities; research contracts; and make certain that the bidding process is open and minorities have access to the process

- Health/Environmental—Research the environmental impact of transportation policies on the African American community.

PTEP identified the leading decision-makers in transportation planning and projects in Pittsburgh communities and throughout the region. They also identified the leading African American and community organizations. PTEP has also begun building a relationship with the different organizations whose constituents will be impacted by transportation planning and projects. PTEP is working on developing strong media relationships. The future of PTEP depends on strong community relationships and collaborations.

PTEP's staff has been working with the advisory board on how to move PTEP strategically through its first year. Confronting critical public transit issues has been made all the more challenging due to recent budget cuts. PTEP has been working with other transit groups to address the proposed elimination of bus services on weekends and the reduction of weekday service hours. PTEP has taken bus trips to Harrisburg to lobby with state representatives, picketed the appropriation hearings, and spoken to newspapers and television reporters. PTEP has also begun conversations with corporations and banks to address how these eliminations would impact their workforce. In addition to the public transportation factor, PTEP has been working to build bridges in the African American communities through the existing black leadership and to engage the community in talks about transit issues.

As of 2003, PTEP is involved in several projects to address transportation disparities and inequities in black and low-income communities. The Diesel Fuel project studies how diesel fuel emissions impact the East End youth and elderly populations. The Riders' Union project uses transit riders to create awareness through the media about how transportation issues impact the community. The Youth Policy Institute organizes a group of progressive youth selected from pre-existing youth-serving organizations from the community, who will work on understanding transportation issues at the policy level. PTEP also works with the Save Our Transit Project to keep mass transit funding in place or find other alternatives to subsidize PAT's funding cuts. Access to Work mobilizes people in the interest of getting individuals to jobs areas in the region. Finally, the Community Organizing Methodology develops community relations through outreach and canvassing to the faith-based grassroots organizations, institutions, government agencies, and private corporations and communities.

142   HIGHWAY ROBBERY

notes

1.   PAT, "Statistics" and "History," http://www.portauthority.org.

2.   PAT, *Ridership Report* (July 2001).

3.   SPRPC, *TAC Transit Component of the Regional Transportation Plan* (April 1974), B9.

4.   PAT, *Early Action Program for Rapid Transit Draft Environmental Statement* (March 1, 1971), 2.

5.   PAT, *Environmental Hearing on Early Action Program*, vol. II (April 20, 1971), 427.

6.   "Early Action Program explained," *The Gazette*, September 25 1969, 4.

7.   SPRPC, *Cycle II Transportation Planning* (July 1976), 30–34.

8.   "Early Action Program explained," *The Gazette*, September 25, 1969, 4.

9.   PAT, *Stage II Corridor Planning Analysis/EA* (October 1993).

10.   PAT, *North Shore Connector FEIS and Section 4(f) Statement* (April 2002), Summary.

11.   SPRPC, *Revised Transportation Plan for Southwestern Pennsylvania* (1980), 21.

12.   PAT, *Phase I Martin Luther King Jr. East Busway Extension EA*, (October 1995), 1.4.

13.   Holmes, N. H. "The East Busway Extension is the Only Reasonable Option," *Pittsburgh Post-Gazette*, July 8, 1998, letter to the editor.

14.   PAT, *Phase I Martin Luther King, Jr. East Busway Extension EA* (October 1995), 6.13.

15.   Ibid., 1.8.

16.   PAT, *Stage II Corridor Planning Analysis/EA* (October 1993), Table 2.3.

17.   PAT, *Stage II Light Rail Transit Environmental Report* (September 1994), 5.

18.   PAT, *Phase I Martin Luther King, Jr. East Busway Extension EA* (October 1995), 6.24.

19.   PAT, "East Busway Light Rail Conversion to Cost $401 Million," News Release (September 22, 1998).

20.   F. Hansen, *City Club Speech* (March 26, 1999), www.tri-met.org/home.htm.

21.   PAT, *Stage II Corridor Planning Analysis/EA* (October 1993), S–9.

22.   SPRPC, *TAC Transit Component of the Regional Transportation Plan* (April 1974), Fig. B13.

23.   PGH Planning Department/SPRPC, *Phase I Preliminary Alternatives Analysis* (January 1999).

24.   PAT, *Stage II Light Rail Transit Environmental Report* (September 1994), 7.

25.   PAT, *Pittsburgh LRT Reconstruction: FEIS, UMTA #PA-03-0012* (December 1978), III–43.

26.   Ibid., III–31.

27.   PAT, *Phase I Martin Luther King, Jr. East Busway Extension EA* (October 1995), 6.13.

28.   PAT, *Pittsburgh LRT Reconstruction*, III–26, 40, V–40.

29.   PAT Planning Department, *Monthly Performance Indicators* (June 2001).

30.   Grata, J., "Port Authority Buys 40 Buses Fit for Touring," *Pittsburgh Post-Gazette*, March 22, 2001.

31.   Brian Nogrady, meeting notes from PA Main Line Linear Park Task Force meeting quoting a PAT representative on March 18, 1997.

32.   SPRPC, *TAC Transit Component of the Regional Transportation Plan* (April 1974), B14.

33.   R. Feathers, "Looking at the Toll Road...Seven Lenses," *GASP Newsletter* (Fall 2001), 3.

34.   PTC, *CMS/MIS Final Report, Mon/Fayette Transportation Project* (December 1996), 19.

35.   PAT, testimony of Donald Anderson, Bethel Park Jaycees in *Environmental Hearing on Early Action Program* 2 (April 20,1971): 510.

SEVEN

The Baltimore Transit Riders League
Amy Menzer and Caroline Harmon

Over one thousand riders of Baltimore-area public transportation comprise Baltimore's Transit Riders League. Convened in 1999, we are a citizen-led initiative of Citizens Planning and Housing Association, fighting for more and improved transit service through increased funding and better policy. Our members ride Greater Baltimore's seventy-two bus routes, three commuter rail lines serving Washington, DC, a single 30-mile light rail line, several versions of locally operated transit, and a single 15-mile Metro subway route. This chapter examines two of the main tensions that surround our transportation activism: tension between the region's neighborhoods and the region's transit riders as well as tension between our dual roles as allies and adversaries of the Maryland Transit Administration (MTA). Additionally, two Riders League campaign victories (*Fair*box Reform and Sunday Subway Service) are outlined.

For over sixty years, Citizens Planning and Housing Association (CPHA) has been the hub for numerous citizen-led initiatives to improve the quality of life.[1] Initially, CPHA focused on Baltimore city neighborhoods; later they expanded to engage the broader metropolitan region. The central component of CPHA's initiatives is a commitment to grassroots public participation in defining the problems, researching their causes and their possible solutions, crafting policy remedies, advocating for those proposals, and monitoring their implementation. Regional advocacy efforts have included expanding access to housing opportunities and better transit service that can be enjoyed by all races and income groups. It was a logical extension of this tradition when members of CPHA's Transportation Committee and its board of governors, inspired by the example of the Los Angeles Bus Riders Union, decided to pursue the formation of the Transit Riders League of Metropolitan Baltimore.[2]

With generous funding from the Open Society Institute, CPHA began organizing to form the League in the summer of 1999.

As part of CPHA's ongoing Campaign for Regional Solutions, the Transportation Committee had been focusing on the patterns of investment by the Baltimore Regional Transportation Board (BRTB), Baltimore's regional metropolitan planning organization (MPO). The BRTB, whose members include the mayors of Baltimore and Annapolis and the five county executives of the suburban jurisdictions surrounding Baltimore, operates in relative obscurity from most residents of the region, although the Board's decisions dictate how federal transportation dollars will be spent. Despite the city of Baltimore's larger population, only one of the seven members on the BRTB represents Baltimore. Each member has one vote on how federal transportation dollars are spent. Consequently, this arrangement favors outer suburban jurisdictions and road expansions. In addition, CPHA's Transportation Committee was concerned that the BRTB's decisions were fueling the sprawling development of houses, fast food restaurants, and office parks. BRTB's decisions were making the task of advocating for expanded transit, improved job access, and reinvestment in existing communities harder by the minute.[3]

Everyday transit users have remained fairly marginal in the decision-making process at the BRTB and in other arenas CPHA sought to influence. CPHA had publicly called for involvement by riders as early as 1974, when they criticized the MTA (which operates the Baltimore region's public bus and rail lines) for its lack of citizen involvement in their plan for new rail lines.[4] Well-intentioned transportation planners and citizens supportive of more transportation choices play important roles in transit development, but they are not a substitute for hearing from transit riders themselves.[5] Furthermore, the ongoing lack of a vocal and organized group of transit users tended to reinforce their invisibility and make it easier to dismiss or de-prioritize their needs. Transit users seemed to be viewed as part of a burdensome welfare program, implying that highway use is not subsidized. Where transit riders' input was given, such as through a Citizens' Advisory Committee of the MTA, it was limited to a small appointed body rather than a broad-based, independent interest group. Their work, however dedicated, was not leading to major shifts in transportation policy or funding, and it was not leading to broader participation of transit riders in the decision-making process.

The Transit Riders League of Metropolitan Baltimore has begun to make those shifts happen. The Transit Riders League is dedicated to improving and expanding public transit in the Baltimore region through informed citizen action.[6] We demand equity and justice in transportation policy and funding; we demand a public transportation system that serves the needs of all people; and we demand full access to and involvement in decisions affecting users of public transit.[7] Transit Riders League members engage in an ongoing process of sharing grievances with each other about the transit system, identifying common concerns and broader policy issues that speak to these grievances, researching possible solutions and strategies for success, and pursuing those solutions. Riders learn that their perceptions and intuition about problems are important, and that further research can help the group determine how best to frame an issue, how widespread an issue's appeal may be, and whether the group should make the issue a priority. The first step for the Transit Riders League was to gain a better understanding of the Baltimore region's transit system and how its various pieces fit together.

Mass Transit in the Baltimore Region

Like the old East Coast city that it is, Baltimore depends on public transit. Bus ridership is very high, while service is bare-bones.[8] Rapid transit is an option for only a very small percentage of area residents, and many of those with the rapid transit option choose not to use it. Paratransit service often fails its thousands of disabled passengers. The MTA and the BRTB lack a comprehensive vision and continue to fail to invest in mass transit.

The MTA operates a single-line Metro subway system, one light rail line, a seventy-two-route bus network, and a three-line commuter rail system called MARC. In addition, the MTA subsidizes suburban Locally Operated Transit Systems (LOTS), such as the highly successful Annapolis Transit and Howard Transit.

Overall ridership increased by 15 percent between 1990 and 1998, after having decreased by 21 percent in the 1980s.[9] Following fare increases in the summer of 2003, fares are currently $1.60 on buses, light rail, and Metro, and users can purchase a $64 monthly pass for these three modes. Although the MTA estimates that 50 percent of bus riders transfer, free transfers are not offered to riders using single-line tickets. For riders, who need to transfer and are not using a monthly pass, must instead purchase a $3.00 day pass.[10] The monthly MARC pass is honored on all modes of transit, except the MARC commuter trains, which operate under a separate fare structure with prices varying by location.

In good economic times and under pro-transit state government, a reduction in transit fares was planned to encourage more ridership. In 2002, it became clear that Maryland was experiencing a fiscal crisis along with many other states, and the planned fare reduction was swiftly abandoned. During the same year, the state saw the election of its first Republican governor in nearly 30 years. In this new fiscal and political context, many of the modest gains that pro-transit advocates had made are at risk. Transportation funds are being diverted and used to close general budget gaps. Extensive cutbacks in transit funding and the reallocation of these funds for the construction and widening of highways are planned. The Transit Riders League continues to fight all these proposals.

MTA RIDERSHIP AND BUDGET BY MODE

Mode*	Unlinked riders	Percent of all riders	Annual MTA operating budget**	Annual MTA capital budget**
MARC	21,577	6.3%	45.7	51.0
Metro	48,496	14.2%	27.5	3.4
Light Rail	26,610	7.8%	37.7	30.5
Bus	245,314	71.7%	151.1	31.8
Other***			22.5	27.5
Total	341,997	100.0%	284.50	144.2

*FY2000; Figures average weekly boardings **In millions ***Freight, grants, paratransit, etc. Table Sources: Christensen, 2001; Maryland Mass Transit Administration, 2001

Buses

Most Baltimore-area transit riders take the bus. Of the 341,997 boardings that the MTA saw on an average weekday in 2000, 245,314 of those, or 71.7 percent of all riders, were on the bus. Bus service includes fifty-two core lines, including twenty long-haul commuter bus routes in the Greater Baltimore region and Greater Washington, DC region. MTA operates 787 buses, of which 509 (64.7 percent) are wheelchair-lift equipped.[11] Excluded from this data are the 38,000 average daily boardings of four school service routes that the MTA operates through a contract with the Baltimore City School District.

Metro

The Metro subway system consists of a single 15-mile line spanning fourteen stations from eastern Baltimore to the Northwestern Baltimore County suburb of Owings Mills. The route connects a major shopping center (Owings Mills Mall) to Maryland's largest private employer, the renowned research and health-care facilities of the Johns Hopkins Medical Institution. In 2000, the Metro saw 48,496 boardings on an average weekday.

Opened in November 1983, the Metro was extended in May 1995 from downtown to Johns Hopkins. The subway route was designed as part of the MTA's six-line, sixty-three-station 1968 rail plan.[12] Three years later a 28-mile version of the current route was prioritized in their "Phase I Plan"[13] which was later cut to the short 15-mile existing route in the 1980 Phase II Plan. When construction was slated to begin in the mid 1970s, "a dearth of comprehensive policy and coordinated decision-making" stood in the way.[14] In 1974, a major source of funding dried up, as costs were escalating. *The Baltimore Sun* wrote: "What once was considered a bottomless source of revenue for transportation, the gasoline tax, had become a less-than-dependable vehicle for raising money, thanks to the gasoline crisis." The southern half of the line was cut amid racially-based protest in suburban Anne Arundel County to the south. At the center of the protest, "Bob Pascal, the new Anne Arundel County Executive, listened closely to a vocal group of [suburban] residents when they complained that the Metro would enable poor, inner-city blacks to travel to the suburbs, steal residents' TVs and then return to their ghettos in Baltimore."[15]

Original ridership projections for the first 4.5-mile section of the Metro were 83,000. This goal has never been met, with current ridership standing at 48,000. With weekend ridership very low, Sunday service on the Metro was retracted in the early 1990s but finally reinstated in September 2001—a major victory of the Transit Riders League, as part of a two-year campaign for seven-day rail service in the Baltimore region.

Light Rail

Baltimore's 30-mile, thirty-three-station light rail system handles 26,610 boardings on an average weekday. Destinations include the area's two major stadiums, as well as the Baltimore-Washington airport. Weekend ridership increased sharply in 2000, with a 24.1 percent increase on Saturdays and a 13.4 percent increase on

Sundays.[16] Currently, the light rail line operates on Sundays from approximately 10 a.m. to 9 p.m.

Opening in 1992 amid controversy, the light rail line was built at the urging of powerful Maryland Governor William Donald Schaeffer, whose "controversial 'do it now' credo" forced the MTA to surmount numerous obstacles and speed up their typical planning process.[17] The current light rail line closely resembles the north and south Metro lines envisioned in the 1968 Baltimore Region Rapid Transit System plan.[18] Protests this time included a "declaration of war from the north," in which the wealthy neighborhoods "feared for their own environments," with one neighborhood filing a failed lawsuit to delay the process.[19] In addition, the initial path was rerouted to skirt the building used by the Baltimore Symphony Orchestra, who "feared noise and vibration during its concerts," and in the end "pure music prevailed."[20]

As it stands, the light rail line misses major population centers like Towson, which is the county seat and an older suburb in Baltimore County. To the south, the light rail line stops just short of an older suburban population center due to resident opposition.

MARC

The MARC commuter rail system is a 187-mile network of three routes covering forty stations, including Baltimore's Pennsylvania Station and Washington, DC's Union Station. Service extends through seven Maryland counties and northeastern West Virginia, handling 21,577 boardings on an average weekday.[21] Weekday fares are $11.50 round-trip from Baltimore to Washington's Union Station. No weekend MARC hours are offered. Weekend Amtrak fares between Baltimore and Washington, DC are $46 round-trip. MARC service uses 20 percent of the MTA's operational budget for 6.3 percent of the MTA's riders.

Paratransit

For the last two years, paratransit service to physically disabled riders has been offered through a contract with privately owned Yellow Transportation, and serves an average of 1590 passengers a day. Service is twenty-four hours a day, seven days a week, and must be ordered by 4 p.m. on the preceding day.[22] Yellow Transportation stepped in on thirty-days notice to fill a gap left by a previous contractor who underbid and couldn't fulfill the demand. Since then, the MTA has been indebted to Yellow Transportation and has neglected to demand adequate service from them.

Regional Transit Oversight

Baltimore's long-term regional transportation plan (RTP) is a twenty-year plan that must be updated every three years by the BRTB. Traditionally, the plan lacks a regional vision, pays little attention to public input, and spends its money on highway projects. In the end, it's been hard for the Transit Riders League to distinguish the RTP from a stapled-together pile of each county's pet highway projects. In 1998, a year before the launch of the Transit Riders League, CPHA took on the BRTB, asking that the group drastically increase the access of the region's citizens to the planning process. Faced with indifference, CPHA asked the US Department of Transportation to withhold the BRTB's federal MPO recertification pending improvements in public access to decision-making. Because of the public input process that the BRTB was forced to devise, Baltimore's 2001 RTP showed some improvements over the 1998 version.

Despite improvements in the plan, the BRTB committed around $3.2 billion on eighty highway widenings and extensions in 2002. By contrast, $1.8 billion was committed to five relatively small transit projects, each with a start date of 2010 or 2020. The Transit Riders League testified against this de-prioritization of transit, against the distant horizons for the transit projects that were included, and against the removal of a proposed extension of the Metro subway to Johns Hopkins' Bayview Campus, which could have increased access to an area of high job growth and paved the way for a better connection between the MARC train line and the Metro.

In response to pressure from CPHA, the Transit Riders League and other advocacy groups, the BRTB launched an 18-month visioning process called Vision 2030 in May 2001 that presented an opportunity to formulate a preferred direction for future development patterns and the economic well-being of the region. CPHA made successful efforts to convince the BRTB to hold a more extensive series of public meetings and include stakeholders such as the Transit Riders League on the Vision 2030 oversight committee. Survey results from seventeen public meetings overwhelmingly favored planning scenarios that emphasized public transportation and redevelopment. However, results of a random telephone poll were less positive, with 12 percent of those polled citing traffic congestion as a primary concern (compared to 5 percent nationally), but only 31 percent viewing the lack of public transportation as part of the problem.[23]

It is uncertain whether Vision 2030 can have the impact that advocates, including CPHA, seek. The final advisory report to the

BRTB contains fifteen vision statements for the region and over one hundred strategies for the region's leaders to pursue. As a result of Vision 2030, the BRTB is doing much more extensive public outreach for the plan, through a process the BRTB has dubbed "Transportation 2030." CPHA remains active in monitoring the implementation of Vision 2030 and continues to involve transit riders in the BRTB planning process.

Organizing Tensions

The Transit Riders League must grapple with various tensions when deciding how to pursue our agenda. While everyday users of the transit system have plenty of complaints about how it is operated and managed, the Tranist Riders League has also learned how marginalized transit itself is within the Baltimore region's political and fiscal agenda. Opposition to new and existing bus and rail lines among neighborhood associations is widespread. Efforts by some citizens to curtail or relocate bus routes are ongoing, because they view transit as a threat to their property values and safety. In contrast, transit riders argue for the right to mobility throughout the region, which necessarily involves moving through and within neighborhoods with greater freedom.

Fundamentally, the existence of an organized group of transit riders poses the following questions: Who gets to define justice? Who gets to define community? Rather than allowing neighborhood associations to define what community is, the Transit Riders League contends that because neighborhood associations and transit riders are both interest groups, they are both communities. And transit riders, of course, are also residents of neighborhoods. How the tensions and misunderstandings between these interests are negotiated affects the prospects for expanding transit service.

We also must determine how and where the Transit Riders League should criticize the MTA? An ongoing fear has been that legislators or neighborhood associations would use League criticism of the MTA to argue against more transit funding. The Transit Riders League has attempted to balance demands for better service from the MTA with advocacy in the state legislature for more MTA funding. In its early work, the League focused more on increasing funding for transit and less on challenging the MTA on basic service quality issues.

Finally, while the Transit Riders League has consciously chosen to build partnerships with other groups across the state in advocating for more transit funding, we also seek to build a larger constituency that can advocate on behalf of the Baltimore region to increase the proportion of state funding for transit allocated for the Baltimore area.

Baltimore and Washington Funding Feud

Baltimore funding and services are a shadow of what is offered in Washington, DC. The Washington, DC, Metro system is a fully elaborated subway with five different lines spanning various parts of the city and its surrounding Virginia and Maryland suburbs. There are plans to integrate a suburb-to-suburb light rail line in Maryland into the DC Metro system, creating a sixth DC line. Among the DC Metro's built-in ridership are 500,000 federal employees, as well as the many tourists to the nation's capital. Maryland's DC suburbs have a much higher concentration of wealth, and experience much higher levels of traffic congestion than does the Baltimore metropolitan area. One third of the MTA's budget goes directly to the Washington Metropolitan Area Transit Authority which administers the Washington, DC, area system. In 2000, more than $1 billion was added to the state's capital transportation program for transit projects; however, $600 million was allocated to improve Washington, DC–area service, as compared to $300 million for the Baltimore region.

This pattern of Baltimore's lower transit ridership levels translating into fewer state dollars to expand service came to a head in the spring of 2003, when Maryland's new Republican governor announced that he intended to seek federal support for just two major transportation projects as part of the reauthorization of federal transportation legislation. Both projects, one for highway construction and the other for light rail train expansion, would benefit Maryland residents in the Washington, DC, suburbs, who represent a key voting block in statewide elections. All of the Baltimore region's elected leaders swiftly and decisively mobilized to denounce the new governor's choices, and demanded planning and funding for two lines proposed in the freshly minted Baltimore Regional Rail Plan. The Transit Riders League was called on to be part of this unified stance. The League believes its existence played an important role in raising leaders' and the public's consciousness and making unification possible. The governor subsequently changed his position and agreed to include the Baltimore Regional Rail Plan in his federal funding request, but his new transportation secretary dubbed it a "transit plan," increasing the chances that Baltimore residents will probably see a low-budget, knock-off, non-rail version of what they were told they would receive and what Washington-region residents have come to feel entitled to.

The Fight for *Fair*box Reform

Unbeknownst to most transit riders, the Maryland State legislature mandates certain performance measures for the MTA to ensure efficiency. A common efficiency measure is the "farebox recovery requirement," which obligates a certain share of transportation funding to come from the farebox. In Maryland, prior to 2000, the farebox recovery was 50 percent, meaning that 50 percent of the costs involved in operating the transit system had to come from passenger fares.[24] Transit Riders League members learned how to convince people, and remind themselves, that this technical-sounding efficiency measure got in the way of improving service.

Confronting the farebox requirement was a challenging issue for transit riders to take on as their first major campaign. On the surface, the idea of holding the MTA to a certain performance standard made sense. However, concern was raised that giving the MTA more flexibility in how it funds operating costs would lead to even less reliable service since passenger fares would matter less. Some were so exasperated with the MTA over bad service that the idea of advocating for anything that benefited the MTA seemed counterintuitive. Though there was some reservation, the case was clear that the MTA's farebox recovery ratio, which was among the highest in the country, interfered with the expansion required to attract new riders.[25] A number of the service-quality issues the Transit Riders League sought to address with the MTA, from bus overcrowding to bus maintenance to on-time performance, were all constrained in some ways by the farebox recovery requirement. The Transit Riders League determined it was unlikely to get very far in working with the MTA to address these issues unless some of the basic ways the MTA's funding was constrained were addressed first.

The farebox recovery performance standard was so rigid that it was actually undermining the MTA's ability to be more innovative— some risky efforts would not meet a 50 percent farebox requirement— which in turn was undermining their ability to attract new riders and generate more revenue. Typically, performance is measured by how inexpensively the service could be provided. Another way to measure performance, and a more equitable way from the perspective of the Riders League, would be to measure customer satisfaction or increases in ridership, both of which might be more costly ways to operate.

The *Fare*box Reform Coalition, spearheaded by CPHA and the Transit Riders League, along with various other groups, lobbied elected officials, generated media attention, and ultimately convinced the legislature to lower the required farebox recovery to 40 percent of operating costs.[26] Transit riders brought a face and a voice to the need for improved service quality and transit expansion. The farebox requirement reflects the public transit system's historically marginalized place in state policy and funding priorities. Its reduction by Maryland's 2000 general assembly reflected a shift in consciousness regarding the importance of decent transit service. However, the state's overall fiscal constraints continue to place transit funding on the chopping block.

Sunday Subway Service and Transportation Equity

Something that unites virtually all Transit Riders League members regardless of their race, age, income, ability, or location, is the way their time is restricted and regulated by the availability, frequency, and reliability of transit service. Car users do not experience similar constraints, but would undoubtedly be outraged were they to find that a major highway route between downtown Baltimore and the outer suburbs was simply closed on Sundays. Or that the only times the highway could be used was during morning and evening rush hours. The inequity of how transit riders' time is valued and their mobility limited informed the Transit Riders League's Seven-Day Rail proposal as part of CPHA's Rally for the Region in October 2000.

Under the league's proposal, riders would have been able to take MARC commuter trains to recreation and jobs in suburban Harford County on the weekends. More jobs at Baltimore-Washington International Airport and its business center would have been accessible through extended light rail hours, and Baltimore County residents would have been able to go to church or to the city's Inner Harbor on Sundays by riding the subway. Additionally, residents of Baltimore's historically African American Sharp-Leadenhall community would have been able to use their shiny new light rail station more than eight times a year, the only times the station is open, when it serves fans from throughout the region who converge on the community to attend the Superbowl champion Baltimore Ravens home football games.

In response to such gross inequities as Sharp-Leadenhall's situation, the strategy of the Transit Riders League's Seven-Day Rail proposal was to advocate for better transit for the benefit of both current and potential transit riders, with the recognition that attracting more people to use transit would help strengthen its constituency of supporters, increase funding, and improve its quality for all users. Its focus on supporting expanded rail service, despite low farebox recovery ratios on the light rail line, Metro, and MARC, was based on an interpretation of equity issues in Baltimore that, rather than pitting certain transit users against others, sought expansion for all. Expanding Baltimore's rail network and operating hours was an important element in making it a more viable mode for riders to regularly use.

The Transit Riders League employed many tactics in pursuit of its proposal and worked with other organizations to strengthen its case. Again the league met with MTA officials and elected officials. The league participated heavily in CPHA's Rally for the Region, which brought together over 1,000 people from throughout metropolitan Baltimore to support a number of policy proposals, including Seven-Day Rail, that strengthened existing communities in the city and surrounding counties and helped build collaborations across jurisdictional lines. We linked our proposal to the then-governor's much broader proposed $750 million transit initiative for improvements over the next six years.[27] We also attended CPHA's Regional Lobby Day in Annapolis to follow up with legislators on the proposals put forward in the Rally for the Region. In the height of the legislative session, to ensure passage of the Governor's Transit Initiative and the funding of our proposal, the Riders League spearheaded the organization of the first statewide rally for public transit, at which transit advocates from all over the state came together to support the Governor's Transit Initiative and save it from legislators' cuts.

The Transit Riders League was ultimately successful in getting a central element of its Seven-Day Rail proposal implemented. In September 2001, Baltimore's Metro subway began operating on Sundays again. When the opening date was announced at a press conference, the governor himself pointed out that he knew of no other subway system in the nation that did not operate on Sundays.[28] The Transit Initiative, with Transit Riders League support, also succeeded in securing $500 million in new funding for transit over the next six years. However, since its initial passage, this broad increase in funding for transit has been reversed, with funding for neighborhood shuttles and existing bus lines cut and fares increased, to plug gaps in the state's general revenues.

Conclusion

Not much in the content of the Transit Riders League's priorities has changed since it was first founded. What has changed is that the league has established itself as an important force in shaping the politics and economics of transit funding in the Baltimore region and across the state. The Transit Riders League, along with CPHA's Transportation Committee, enjoyed a close and relatively positive relationship with the MTA and with the governor's office through 2002. Through this relationship, the league, the MTA, and the governor all achieved more than they might have otherwise. A new fiscal climate and a new governor, since 2002, have presented new challenges for the league. They have also presented the opportunity to the league to deepen its base and refine its message with a constituency that has good reason to be outraged.

Organizing tensions affect each level of analysis. Defining what equity means—or which definition of equity matters most in a given situation—is sometimes as difficult as achieving it, even amongst a constituency that agrees on the basic mission of improving transit. Internal tensions must be balanced and considered along with external events and opportunities. At the same time that transit cuts were announced and a new governor was elected, the Transit Riders League had hoped to shift its attentions to address the service-quality issues that spur most of the league's members into action. How much power the Transit Riders League will be able to wield and in which arenas is uncertain. What is certain, however, is that an abundance of transportation inequities remain to be addressed in the Baltimore region. The Transit Riders League's voice is only beginning to be heard.

notes

1. Anna Karni, "Community, Religious, Business, Environmental Groups explore New Decision-making Strategies," *Baltimore Afro-American* 108, no. 40 (May 20–26, 2000).

2. "Baltimore Region Trails in State Transit Funding," *The Sun*, January 23, 2000, 2C.

3. John Murphy, "Outer Areas Get Wealth of Residents," *The Sun*, September 26, 1999, A1 and A10; Marcia Myers and Gady A. Epstein, "$7.8 Billion Sought for MD Transit," *The Sun*, January 18, 2000.

4. Metropolitan Department of Transportation, *Phase II Transit Study, Final Report* (Baltimore, MD: Metropolitan Department of Transportation,1980).

5. Marcia Myers, "Billions in Transportation Funds at Risk," *The Sun*, July 27, 1999.

6. "Rally to Urge United Problem-solving Push," *The Sun*, November 8, 2000; "Region Beginning to Rally," *The Sun*, November 8, 2000; "CPHA 'Rally for the Region' Draws Crowd," *The Sun*, November 8, 2000; "Glendening, O'Malley Highlight Regional Plans at Citizens Rally," *The Sun*, November 8, 2000.

7. Paul D. Samuel, "Making Sense of Baltimore's Transit Mess," *The Statewide Daily Record* 110, no. 133 (March 13, 1999); Deborah Walike, "Come Together," *The Sun*, November 8, 2000.

8. "Improving Mass Transit," *The Sun*, April 7, 2000.

9. Baltimore Metropolitan Council, "Table I-7" in *Regional Economic Indicators* (Baltimore, MD: BMC, 2001).

10. URS Corporation, *Mode Choice Model Validation* (Baltimore, MD: BMC, 2001), 36.

11. Maryland Mass Transit Administration, *Transit Route Profiles 2000: System Over* (Baltimore, MD: Maryland MTA, 2001), 2.

12. Mass Transit Steering Committee, *Baltimore Region Rapid Transit System: Feasibility and Preliminary Engineering* (Baltimore, MD: Regional Planning Council, 1968), 33.

13. Metropolitan Transit Authority, *Baltimore Region Rapid Transit System: Phase I Plan* (Baltimore, MD: Metropolitan Transit Authority, 1971), 1.

14. Maryland Department of Transportation, *Phase II Transit Study: Final Report* (Baltimore, MD: MD DOT, 1980), 175.

15. R. Gutierrez, R. Lewis, R. Promisel, and A. Qayyum, *Baltimore Metro: An Initiative and Outcome in Rapid Public Transportation* (Baltimore, MD: Johns Hopkins University, 1990): 29.

16. Ibid., 30.

17. Maryland Mass Transit Administration, *National Transit Database: Annual Report* (Baltimore, MD: Maryland MTA, 2000), 7.

18. H. H. Harwood, *Baltimore's Light Rail: Then and Now* (New York: Quadrant Press, Inc., 1995), 37.

19. Mass Transit Steering Committee, *Baltimore Region Rapid Transit System*, 3.

20. Ibid., 41.

21. Ibid., 40–41.

22. Maryland Mass Transit Administration, *National Transit Database*, 7.

23. Baltimore Regional Transportation Board, *Vision 2030: Shaping the Region's Future Together*, (Baltimore, MD: BRTB, 2003), 3, www.baltometro.org/vision2030.html.

24. John W. Croft. "Transit Riders Rally for Funds," *The Montgomery Journal*, March 2, 2000, A7.

25. "Lower Fare Box Rule Gives Transit A Chance," *The Sun*, March 4, 2000, A10.

26. Ibid.

27. Marcia Myers and Gady A. Epstein, "$7.8 Billion Sought for MD Transit," *The Sun*, January 18, 2000.

28. Gerard Shields, "Subway Riders Praise Glendening for Plan to Restart Sunday Service," *The Sun*, August 21, 2001.

EIGHT
Just Transportation
Nancy Jakowitsch and Michelle Ernst

The national transportation system should be socially equitable and strengthen civil rights; enabling all people to gain access to good jobs, education and training, and needed services. Where possible, personal transportation expenses should be minimized in ways that support wealth creation. Integrated with land use planning, transportation should also enhance the quality, livability, and character of communities and support revitalization without displacement. The transportation system should allow every American to participate fully in society whether or not they own a car and regardless of age, ability, ethnicity, or income.

—New Transportation Charter [1]

The transportation and urban development policies of the Interstate Era (1956–1991) erected major barriers to mobility for the more than 30 percent of Americans who cannot or do not drive automobiles. These policies tended to promote a "one-size-fits-all" approach to highways and transportation planning, which has separated jobs and workplaces from housing and services and turned the car into the link between them. This development pattern has made the car a basic necessity in most cities and communities across the country. This has happened in part from land-use practices, transportation policies that focused roadway investment in growing areas, and the huge attraction of highway access for development opportunities at the expense of access by transit. The resulting exodus of the population to suburban areas and beyond shifted tax bases to the exurbs, leaving a pattern of urban disinvestment nearly uniform throughout the United States. In this environment, the voices and concerns of the affected communities and their allies have largely been ignored.

This spatial mismatch between jobs, services, and housing has created serious environmental justice challenges in today's cities. Foremost among these dilemmas—although not necessarily most prominent in the public eye—is the nationwide shortage of affordable transportation choices. Inadequate transit funding reinforces the lack of access to job opportunities in many low-income and people of color communities. "Transportation racism" was also perpetuated by transportation-related health burdens disproportionately affecting specific socioeconomic groups and the limited availability of federal transportation resources at the metropolitan level, where 80 percent of people of color reside.

Increased investment in transit and related development can begin the tasks of knitting ill-affected communities back together, curbing environmental impacts, and addressing past environmental injustices. However, ensuring mobility and equal access to jobs for low-income and communities of color will require massive systemic changes. Effectively addressing the interrelated challenges facing African American, Latino, and other communities of color will require decision-makers to begin to take comprehensive approaches to transportation, housing, and economic development. It is equally important that government agencies and urban planners openly engage transportation justice concerns by enabling meaningful public involvement, collecting and reporting data on projects, requiring performance measures, and invoking alternative dispute resolution when needed. Although numerous states and metropolitan areas have efforts underway that begin to advance more comprehensive planning approaches, additional collaboration is needed between multiple agencies and stakeholders to maximize what would otherwise result in isolated strategies.

One of the key challenges to implementing transportation policy "for the people" is the practice of public institutions which do not necessarily share or prioritize environmental and social justice goals. The Federal Highway Administration (FHWA), for instance, recently de-emphasized environmental justice as a policy goal. The US Department of Transportation (US DOT) does not hold civil rights as a "shared responsibility."[2] This has significant ramifications, since the department has oversight over other federal-aid recipients in the transportation sector.

A number of municipal and state agencies have already begun to rethink transportation planning approaches—requiring community-defined performance measures, making investments in multiple modes of transportation, and planning land-use connectivity. But significant obstacles still block the way to a more just and sustainable nationwide transportation system. Addressing those obstacles will require a dialog between active community stakeholders, innovative transportation agencies and related agencies, and visionary decision-makers. This chapter outlines the nation's leading transportation law, evidence of transportation discrimination, and policy recommendations that can facilitate changes to a more equitable and sustainable transportation system.

ISTEA: A Tool for Environmental Justice

The landmark transportation laws of the past twelve years—the Intermodal Surface Transportation Efficiency Act of 1991 (ISTEA) and the Transportation Equity Act for the 21st Century of 1998 (TEA-21)—adhered to civil rights statutes and affirmed the principles of environmental justice. ISTEA and TEA-21 created a bold new vision for transportation in the post-interstate era, enabling transportation to make other public goals happen. They reflect much of the thinking of the late Senator Daniel Patrick Moynihan, who was among the first to express public alarm at the impact of the interstate highway program on urban communities and the American landscape.[3] Working closely with the Surface Transportation Policy Project—a broad coalition of urban, environmental, and multimodal transportation advocates—Senator Moynihan created pioneering reforms that required meaningful public participation, greater investment in the maintenance and diversity of the nation's transportation system, stronger protections for the environment, and the preservation of historic and cultural resources.[4]

ISTEA attempted to level the playing field between highway and transit investments, overturning a historic bias whereby the federal government covered a greater percentage of costs for highways than transit and thus deterred localities and states from investing in transit. Prior to ISTEA, federal funds would cover 90 percent of the costs for highway projects but only 75 percent of costs for transit projects. This transportation inequity prompted states and localities to invest their own dollars where the federal share was the greatest.

The law also introduced the option of flexing highway funds to transit and other alternatives, and dedicated resources specifically for community enhancements and air quality. The flexibility provision allowed state transportation departments and Metropolitan Planning Organizations (MPOs) to move away from a one-size-fits-all approach to highway building to a systems approach where approximately 75 percent of "highway" funds are directly eligible for transit, bicycle, pedestrian, and other community projects—such as building child care and health care facilities at transit stations. Few agencies have used this provision, adhering to pre-ISTEA priorities.

ISTEA and TEA-21 expanded transportation policy, leading to increased investment in transit and locally-initiated projects in particular through the following programs. For example, the Transportation Enhancements program (TE) has enabled communities to fund bike and pedestrian facilities; public art and streetscape improvements; the purchase and restoration of historic buildings, including railroad stations and cultural heritage trails; and other forms of community development. The program has funded more than 15,000 projects nationwide, providing more transportation choices for all people, including bicyclists, pedestrians, and persons with disabilities.

The Congestion Mitigation and Air Quality (CMAQ) program is another hallmark of ISTEA, and is eligible for transit capital and operations, clean-fuel buses, bicycle programs, transit-oriented development (TOD) and other investments that reduce air pollution. ISTEA also required that transportation plans conform to federal air quality goals to help stabilize transportation emissions in nonattainment and maintenance areas. Created immediately after the Clean Air Act Amendments of 1990 (CAAA), CMAQ remains the only federally funded transportation program explicitly targeting air quality improvement. [5]

In a move to link transportation investment with other federal priorities, TEA-21 established the Job Access and Reverse Commute (JARC) program in 1998 as a response to the 1996 welfare reform law, known as the Temporary Assistance for Needy Families (TANF) program, and the evidence that jobs were increasingly located in suburban areas, where reliable transit service was not available. JARC funds are used to improve transit services and help a growing workforce of TANF recipients and low-income workers overcome the basic challenge of commuting to work. A component of the federal transit program, JARC requires coordination between transit and human service agencies and stakeholder input. The program gives transit riders, service providers, employers, and multiple agencies a chance to make decisions collaboratively.

The Transportation and Community and System Preservation (TCSP) program helps diverse stakeholders plan and implement strategies that address the complex links between land use, community, quality of life, and transportation. Heavily earmarked by Congress, the program also seeks to ensure efficient access to jobs, services, and commercial centers; reduce the need for costly infrastructure investments with smart development practices; and improve the efficiency of transportation systems.

While ISTEA established both balance and policy direction via core highway programs (such as CMAQ and TE) and discretionary programs (such as JARC and TCSP), these programs make up a very small portion of the $32 billion highway program and the $7.2 billion transit program. Underpinning the ability for the entire federal surface transportation program to support environmental justice is an outcome-oriented framework that emphasizes accessibility and mobility as planning factors, relates to the National Environmental Policy Act (NEPA) and CAAA, and requires "continuous, cooperative, and comprehensive" public involvement. These laws challenged the one-size-fits-all approach to transportation perfected during the Interstate Era, calling for agencies to address concerns that had been overlooked for too long.

Although ISTEA and TEA-21 have allowed the public to play a stronger role in the decision-making process, transforming the vision into reality largely depends on public resources and institutions for policy implementation. One barrier to advancing environmental justice is the lack of coordination between state transportation departments, which program 94 percent of federal transportation funds, and local governments, which dominate land use decisions.[6] MPOs, which are governed by local elected officials, have directly controlled only 6 percent of federal transportation funds over the past twelve years and do not have authority over land use.

Both ISTEA and TEA-21 were designed to expire within six years unless they were updated and reauthorized. The landmark ISTEA law of 1991 was reauthorized as TEA-21 in 1998. Currently, TEA-21 is being reviewed for reauthorization. Through the next law, which is informally called TEA-3, Congress will determine key funding and programmatic decisions for the federal surface transportation program. Lawmakers will decide whether to defend and build upon the ISTEA and TEA-21 framework, potentially strengthening provisions for environmental justice, or to unravel key reforms still in their infancy. As TEA-21 reauthorization moves forward and after its passage, larger questions remain that are fundamental to transportation reform and environmental justice: What are "we the people" getting in return for public investment? Who benefits and who pays? And what policies can leverage transportation justice efforts at the national, state, and local levels?

Growing Evidence of Transportation Discrimination

Despite the progress made under ISTEA and TEA-21, transportation choices that are affordable, competitive, and healthy for the public and environment remain an exception instead of the normal practice of transportation decision-makers. Our current transportation system continues to place a significant burden on communities, and minorities and the poor are the socioeconomic groups most adversely impacted. Low-income families spend a higher portion of their income to get around than do wealthy families. Moreover, communities of color bear a disproportionate share of asthma cases, pedestrian fatalities, and other health impacts. Both low-income and communities of color are also finding transportation to be a top barrier to access employment in suburban areas and urban and rural communities.

Driven to Poverty

With few alternatives to driving available to most Americans, families have no choice but to spend heavily on car ownership. US households are now spending nearly one-fifth of their family budgets on transportation.[7] The poorest families, those earning less than $14,000 per year after taxes, spend approximately 40 percent of their take-home pay on transportation expenditures. This compares to 22 percent for families earning between $27,177 and $44,461 annually, and 13 percent per year for families making more than $71,900 per year.[8]

This trend coincides with the Interstate Era and the advent of the private automobile. In 1935, families expended just 10 percent of their budgets on transportation. By 1960, that figure had risen to 14 percent. From 1972 through today, the portion of the family budget devoted to getting around increased to 20 percent.[9] The vast majority (nearly 95 percent) of expenditures on transportation go toward owning and operating a private automobile. Even for the poorest families, almost 95 percent of the $3,178 spent on transportation annually goes to down-payments and monthly payments, insurance, gasoline, repairs, and other vehicle-related expenses.[10]

Unfortunately, the investment in a private vehicle yields little financial return. A new $20,000 car will lose 25 percent of its value in just the first year, and almost 80 percent of its value over ten years.[11] And the almost obligatory expenditures on car ownership leave less of the family budget for other necessities like housing, food, health care, and education. An analysis of the Census 2000 Supplementary Survey by the Center for Neighborhood Technology estimated that excessive auto expenditures by low-income families suppress home ownership by between 5 and 10 percent of what it would be if households could reduce transportation expenditures to average levels and invest these cost savings in home ownership instead.

In places which offer more transportation choices, the burden of transportation expenditures is far lower. Families living in auto-dependent Tampa–St. Petersburg, Florida spend almost 25 percent of their household budgets on transportation. In contrast, households living in cities with good transit service and walkable neighborhoods spend far less. Residents of San Francisco, Boston, Portland, and New York spend, respectively, 16.9 percent, 16.8 percent, 16.2 percent, and 15.1 percent of their budgets on transportation expenses.

Shifting government priorities to increase public investment in transit and manage growth to better accommodate more transportation choices can greatly reduce the household costs of transportation. A recent Bureau of Transportation Statistics study found that, for the 66 percent of the working poor who commuted by private vehicle, individuals spent fully 21 percent of their income to get to and from work. In contrast, the working poor who were able to take public transportation, bicycle, carpool, or walk to work spent far less, leaving more for housing, health care, food, and education.[12] Adequate funding for transportation alternatives is more than just good transportation policy; it is good fiscal policy, helping families invest in real opportunities for financial security such as home ownership and education.

Clean Air and Public Health Disparities

Our auto-dependent transportation system is also a major contributor to the United States's unhealthy air quality. Despite progress made since the 1970 Clean Air Act, nearly half of all Americans (133 million) breathe unhealthy air. Medical research has demonstrated that air pollution exacerbates and may even cause the onset of asthma. Researchers have also linked air pollution to heart disease, lung cancer, birth defects, brain damage, and even premature mortality.[13]

African Americans and Latinos are disproportionately exposed to harmful air pollutants partly as a result of the Interstate Era when urban freeways were often routed through communities of color in cities across the country. A recent study in the Los Angeles region found that the cancer risk along highway corridors with significant big truck traffic was 1,700 per million residents, the highest in region, and much higher than the regional average of 1,200 to 1,400 per million residents.[14]

While 33 percent of whites have been found to live in metropolitan areas failing to meet national air quality standards for two or more pollutants, 50 percent of African Americans and 60 percent of Latinos lived in these areas. Even greater differences were found for areas that violate air quality standards for three and four pollutants.[15] The higher rate of exposure to air pollution is also resulting in disproportionately high rates of cancer and asthma among people of color.

A new study by the American Cancer Society found that, compared to white men, African American men are 20 percent more likely to have cancer and 40 percent more likely to die from cancer.[16] Asthma is almost twice as common among African Americans as whites, even when controlling for income levels. African American children are three times as likely to be hospitalized for treatment of asthma as white children. Asthma attacks send more than four times as many African Americans (22.9 visits per 1,000 people) to the emergency room as whites (4.9 visits per 1,000 people).[17]

Even more troubling is the disparity in asthma-related deaths among African Americans and whites. Though African Americans make up 12 percent of the US population, they account for 23.7 percent of all deaths due to asthma. In 1998, the age-adjusted mortality rate for asthma was more than three times as high for African Americans (3.7 deaths per 100,000 people) as for whites (1.1 deaths per 100,000 people).[18]

Pedestrian Fatalities and Environmental Justice

Similarly, people of color are also disproportionately the victims of pedestrian fatalities. While the data on race and ethnicity for pedestrian deaths is far from complete (records for 37 percent of pedestrian fatalities did not record ethnicity data), the available data does offer important findings. It is also a reminder that a legacy of the Interstate Era is greater exposure to traffic in low-income and communities of color.

Whites comprise 69 percent of the US population, but account for 60 percent of pedestrian deaths for which ethnicity is known. In contrast, African Americans are 12 percent of the population, but make up 20 percent of pedestrian deaths. Similarly, Latinos comprise 13.5 percent of pedestrian deaths, but only 12.5 percent of the total US population.[19] The same pattern holds true for bicyclist fatalities where race and ethnicity was recorded, with whites accounting for 63 percent of bicyclist deaths, African Americans for 18.1 percent and Latinos for 16 percent of premature deaths.[20]

Surveys from specific places in the US produced similar findings in recent years. The Centers for Disease Control and Prevention reported that Latinos in Atlanta were six times more likely to be hit and killed while walking than whites. Latinos in suburban Washington, DC were three times more likely to be hit and killed. An analysis of pedestrian fatalities in Orange County, California determined that while Latinos make up 28 percent of the county's population, they accounted for 40 percent of all pedestrian injuries and 43 percent of all pedestrian deaths.[21] In New Mexico, Native American children had a death rate 2.5 times that of other ethnic and racial groups.[22]

The link between pedestrian and bicyclist deaths and race and ethnicity may be due to the lower rates of car ownership among Latinos and African Americans, and higher rates of walking, bicycling, and transit use. Indeed, an analysis of the 2000 census shows that people of color are much more likely than whites to walk to work. While 2.9 percent of all American workers walked to work in 2000, 3.2 percent of African American workers, and 4.0 percent of Latino workers walked to work.[23]

Access to Employment

Beyond the financial burden and disparate health impacts placed on communities of color and low-income communities, the auto-oriented transportation system also makes it more difficult to find and keep a good job. State and regional transportation priorities typically favor highway development over public transit, contributing to sprawling development at the expense of the urban core and leaving less funding available for transit. The lack of coordination between transportation, economic development, and housing decisions increases the costs of transit service delivery, making transit more difficult to finance. These costs are typically absorbed by local governments, despite shrinking tax bases, due to the restrictions more than thirty states have on state-gas-taxes, which can only be used on highway programs.

Congestion relief and economic development goals drive most infrastructure investments. Research on induced travel, however, finds that new roadways attract almost equal levels of traffic growth due to building booms along new traffic corridors. A Maryland study on the relationship between highway investment and sprawl recently found that more than 90 percent of developed properties within five miles of a major interstate highway were built after the adjacent section of the highway was completed.[24]

As a result of this pattern, sprawl development has become the status quo in many parts of the country. The resulting "spatial mismatch" between jobs and housing concentrates high rates of poverty in the urban core and makes residential and economic development generated by new roads in outer suburbs virtually inaccessible by transit, foot, or bicycle. That lack of coordination between agencies compounds challenges facing transit-dependent communities. According to a recent survey, none of the fifty states consider public transportation availability when allocating state economic development subsidies. In fact, states encouraged the relocation of corporations from transit-accessible urban areas to auto-dependent exurbs.[25]

The combination of policies that favor highway building and auto-dependent, single-use development is especially detrimental because less funding is available for transit and transit becomes a more expensive service. Low-income and minority families are disproportionately affected by inadequate investment in transit since they are more likely to reside in urban communities and depend on transit to get around. Not only have the jobs left the urban core where they live, but environmental justice communities in some instances have no way to get to the jobs in the exurbs.

Toward a Just and Comprehensive Transportation System

Just as short-sighted transportation policies and practices can compound the economic and environmental barriers facing low-income communities, equitable policies—such as fully funding transportation choices and involving communities in planning processes—can help disassemble those barriers. Much of the previously mentioned research indicates that minority and low-income communities will continue to suffer unless transportation decision-makers actively address environmental justice concerns.

ISTEA and TEA-21 sought to reconcile the practices of national agencies with public goals articulated by NEPA and CAAA. Similar provisions are now needed in TEA-3 or future reauthorizations to hardwire transportation policy to Title VI of the Civil Rights Act (Title VI) and the 1994 Executive Order on Environmental Justice. Currently the certification review process provides a regulatory "hammer" for the FHWA and the Federal Transit Administration (FTA), which must certify that transit agencies, MPOs, and state DOTs are in compliance with Title VI. Rewards based on principles common to both transportation reform and environmental justice are also worth developing in TEA-21 reauthorization and related efforts at the state and local levels. These include, but are not limited to, adequate funding for transit, better data collection and analysis, and opportunities for collaborative decision-making.

Transit as a Vehicle for Community Reinvestment

For communities that depend heavily on public transportation, the level and quality of transit service in urban neighborhoods compared to that in more affluent suburban areas is often the definitive transportation justice issue.[26] Federal support for transit capital, but none for operating assistance, may be considered another form of transportation inequity. While measures such as transit service equity and parity between capital and operating expenditures address environmental justice directly, they may preclude a broader discussion on the potential for new projects to address the interrelated challenges facing low-income and minority communities.

Rail transit is not an appropriate investment for many communities. Nonetheless, new rail investments are being planned, designed, or constructed in nearly all of the fifty largest metropolitan areas in the US. These projects may initiate rail service in a community or extend existing systems, including new lines to downtown and regional employment centers, airports, intermodal facilities, and other destinations. While environmental justice is usually absent from these discussions, questions regarding what the infrastructure investment is intended to accomplish and which decisions will most effectively advance these goals can help guide the community interest.

Transportation justice should therefore also advocate for rail alignments that serve communities of color to ensure better access to major employers and destinations such as universities and community colleges. TOD can also help leverage neighborhood amenities such as grocery stores, child care and job-training facilities, banks, affordable housing, and home ownership opportunities—many of which are underrepresented in low-income and minority neighborhoods. When introduced throughout a regional transit network, such transportation and land use policies can also help reduce poverty, especially among working families who spend between 20 and 40 percent of their income on transportation.

Performance Measures for Transportation Justice

Increasing evidence indicates that minority and low-income communities are disproportionately burdened by the shortage of transportation choices that are affordable, environmentally clean, and competitive. The impacts of highway construction on land use patterns, including widespread disinvestment in urban areas, are also well known. Despite numerous statutes and regulations requiring federal, state, and metropolitan transportation agencies to determine and avoid adverse direct and cumulative impacts on socioeconomic groups, agencies do not systematically consider whether new highway investments and rail investments exclusive to affluent neighborhoods will worsen conditions in environmental justice communities.[27]

Greater transparency in transportation policy and finance is needed to ensure that all communities benefit. Environmental justice performance measures related to mobility, accessibility, public health, and economic development can better hardwire Title VI to the federal transportation program. One challenge, however, is that although federal law calls for the strongest data and science to be used to determine disparate impact, US DOT does not collect, maintain, and analyze the information required to determine adverse impacts.[28] And while the Supreme Court's decision in *Alexander v. Sandoval* places a greater emphasis on intentional discrimination, to substantiate a Title VI complaint will still require statistical or anecdotal evidence of disparities.

Data quality is a challenge at the federal, state, and local levels. Federal transportation spending data is not available below the county level, a level too coarse to be useful in comparing socioeconomic data. Similarly, national travel behavior surveys have not disaggregated socioeconomic data below the metropolitan level. These discrepancies prevent cumulative impact analysis in the transportation planning process. Similarly, the NEPA review process only analyzes socioeconomic impacts that are closely associated with environmental factors, making it a poor substitute for Title VI analysis. Transportation data related to demographic characteristics such as race, income, age, gender, disability, ethnicity, and factors like employment and housing are necessary to gauge and mitigate adverse impacts.

As such, the US Commission on Civil Rights recently reported that the US DOT has failed to incorporate the 1994 Executive Order on Environmental Justice into core program activities, although it made progress in public participation.[29] Socioeconomic data applied to state-of-the-art transportation modeling tools that can forecast the impacts of different transportation and land use scenarios that can help mainstream cumulative and disparate impact analysis into the transportation planning process. Such tools can also reinforce the on-going dialog need between agencies and community groups to pursue investments that benefit environmental justice communities.

Collaborative Decision-Making at the Regional Level

Transportation justice also depends on collaborative decision-making between local elected officials, transportation bureaucracies, related agencies, community stakeholders, and the private sector. Such partnerships are best demonstrated by TEA-21's JARC, which enabled transit and human service agencies, community stakeholders, and employers to identify the transit services needed by welfare recipients and low-income workers, and to formalize coordination between transportation, health and human service, and workforce development agencies, and to provide resources for needed improvements.

In the 1991 ISTEA law, Congress established an "early and on-going" role for public participation in the metropolitan transportation planning process, which was later improved in TEA-21 in 1998 to specify consultation with low-income and minority communities. In TEA-21 reauthorization, transportation equity advocates are seeking to build on this foundation by requiring non-governmental participation on the decision-making boards of MPOs and enhancing the role of central-city elected officials by matching population size with voting power. These recommendations seek to make regional transportation investments more accountable to community priorities, especially those of urban residents who are typically underrepresented in the decision-making process.

A more just transportation system also depends on equity within a state, since state transportation agencies program 94 percent of federal transportation funds with "equity" often being defined by disparities within a metropolitan level. However, regional transportation agencies control only 6 percent of the transportation funds, despite serving 80 percent of the US population, who presumably generate 80 percent of the Federal Highway Trust Fund. For instance, although the Atlanta region represents 33.3 percent of the population of the state of Georgia, the metropolitan area only has direct control over 4.4 percent of the federal dollars apportioned to states. This inequity may be blocking funding for community-oriented transportation projects.

The importance of regional financial control may become clearer when considering that 80 percent of the federal "highway" dollars flexed to transit during the ISTEA–TEA-21 period were initiated at the metropolitan level. Half of the use of the flexibility provision took place in California, where metropolitan areas receive the majority of the state's highway account as a result of state legislation implementing ISTEA in 1992 and a more far-reaching bill passed in 1997.[30] In addition, state constitutional or statutory language disallows transit funding through the use of state gas taxes in more than thirty states.

Increased equity within a state would also allow MPOs to facilitate a more collaborative decision-making process with related agencies to address the concomitant challenges facing metropolitan areas and environmental justice communities. Specifically, these changes could lead regional transportation agencies to invest more heavily in transit and provide incentives for land use decisions that spur housing and economic development near transit. For example, in the San Francisco bay area, the MPO prioritizes transportation funds for local governments that zone for higher density housing near transit, and even more funding for units below market rate. Such programs seek to generate multiple benefits with transportation funding, including job and child care access, affordable housing, air quality, and congestion relief.

Conclusion

In recent years federal transportation laws have enabled many communities to pursue transportation investments that reinforce environmental justice. While the ISTEA and TEA-21 policy framework has created new funding sources for local transportation priorities, analysis of transportation spending over the past decade indicates that innovation is happening, although at a much slower pace than expected. A growing body of evidence shows that low-income and minority communities are the most transit-dependent and vulnerable to transportation burdens. These findings signal that additional policy, market, and advocacy tools are needed to ensure that disadvantaged communities get their fair share of benefits.

Such tools should hold federal, state, and metropolitan transportation agencies accountable to legal statutes and regulations that protect people of color and economically disadvantaged communities from discrimination related to transportation. TEA-3 or future transportation reform efforts at the federal, state or local level can further comply with Title VI and the 1994 Executive Order on Environmental Justice by requiring additional performance measures, better data collection and analysis, and resources for environmental justice technical assistance. These efforts should not only help identify disparities but support a dialogue between transportation agencies and community stakeholders to create new models for transportation and social justice.

Communities have much to gain by defending and refining policy initiatives that support transportation justice. Efforts are underway in TEA-21 reauthorization and at the state and local levels to increase funding for affordable transportation choices, target mitigation resources and prevent injustices in communities of color, and increase authority over transportation decisions at the metropolitan level. These changes can help expand the reach of citizen involvement and forge the political will needed for the United States to embrace a more just and sustainable transportation system.

notes

1. Surface Transportation Policy Project, "New Transportation Charter," adopted on December 11, 2001 with over 700 endorsements as of September 2003, http://www.antc.net/charter/default.asp.

2. Jeremy S. Wu, *A White Paper on the Civil Rights Functions and Operations at the US Department of Transportation* (Washington, DC: Departmental Office of Civil Rights, US Department of Transportation, August 2002).

3. Daniel Patrick Moynihan, "New Roads and Urban Chaos," *The Reporter* 22, no. 8 (April 14, 1960).

4. Elizabeth Thompson and Roy Kienitz, *TEA-21 User's Guide: Making the Most of the New Transportation Bill* (Washington, DC: Surface Transportation Policy Project, June 1998), 1.

5. Transportation Research Board, *Special Report 264: The Congestion Mitigation and Air Quality Improvement Program: Assessing 10 Years of Experience* (Washington, DC: National Academy of Sciences, 2002).

6. Sarah Campbell, "TEA-21 and Local Control: The Final Frontier," *Progress* 13, no. 2 (March 2003): 1.

7. Bureau of Labor Statistics, "Table 8 Region of Residence: Average Annual Expenditures and Characteristics" from *Consumer Expenditure Survey*, 2001. http://www.bls.gov/cex/2001/Standard/region.pdf.

8. Bureau of Labor Statistics, "Table 1: Quintiles of Income before Taxes: Average Annual Expenditures and Characteristics" from *Consumer Expenditure Survey*, 2001. http://www.bls.gov/cex/2001/Standard/quintile.pdf.

9. Bureau of Labor Statistic, "At Issue: Tracking Changes in Consumer Spending Habits," *Monthly Labor Review* 122, no. 9 (September 1999), http://www.bls.gov/opub/mlr/1999/09/atissue.htm.

10. Bureau of Labor Statistics, Table 1, *op. cit.*

11. Barbara McCann, et al., *Driven to Spend: The Impact of Sprawl on Household Transportation Expenses* (Washington, DC: Surface Transportation Policy Project and the Center for Neighborhood Technology, 2000), http://www.transact.org/PDFs/DriventoSpend.pdf.

12. Bureau of Transportation Statistics, "Commuting Expenses: Disparity for the Working Poor," Bureau of Transportation Statistics Issue Brief No 1, March 2003.

13. Michelle Ernst, James Corless, and Ryan Greene-Roesel, *Clearing the Air: Public Health Threats from Cars and Heavy Duty Vehicles—Why We Need to Protect Federal Clean Air Laws* (Washington, DC; Surface Transportation Policy Project, 2003), www.transact.org/library/reports_pdfs/Clean_Air/report.pdf.

14. Southern California Air Quality Management District, *Multiple Air Toxics Exposure Study in the South Coast Air Basin: MATES-II (Final Report)*, http://www.aqmd.gov/matesiidf/matestoc.htm.

15. American Lung Association, *Minority Lung Disease Data 2000*, http://www.lungusa.org/pub/minority/mldd_00.html.

16. American Cancer Society, *Cancer Facts and Figures for African Americans, 2000-2004*, http://www.cancer.org/downloads/STT/861403.pdf.

17. American Lung Association, *op. cit.*

18. Ibid.

19. Michelle Ernst and Barbara McCann, *Mean Streets 2002: Pedestrian Safety, Health and Federal Transportation Spending* (Washington, DC: Surface Transportation Policy Project, 2002), http://www.transact.org/PDFs/ms2002/MeanStreets2002.pdf.

20. Surface Transportation Policy Project, *Analysis of the National Highway Traffic Safety Administration's Fatality Analysis Recording System Database 2000-2001* (2002).

21. Ernst and McCann, *op. cit.*

22. Ibid.

23. Ibid.

24. Brad Heavner, *Paving the Way: How Highway Construction Has Contributed to Sprawl in Maryland* (Baltimore: MaryPIRG Foundation, 2000), http://www.marypirg.org/sprawl/Paving.pdf.

25. Mafruza Khan and Greg LeRoy, *Missing the Bus: How States Fail to Connect Economic Development with Public Transit* (Washington, DC: Good Jobs First, 2003), http://www.ctj.org/gjf/pdf/bus.pdf.

26. Federal Transit Administration, "Chapter 12—Title VI," in *Grants Management Seminars Workbook FY2003*, (Washington, DC: General Printing Office, 2002), http://www.fta.dot.gov/office/program/gmw/12titlVI.doc.

27. US Department of Transportation, *Transportation and Environmental Justice Case Studies* (Washington, DC: Government Printing Office, December 2000), i-ii, www.fhwa.dot.gov/environment/ejustice/facts/index.htm.

28. US Commission on Civil Rights, "Not In My Backyard: Executive Order 12,898 and Title VI as Tools for Achieving Environmental Justice" *Draft Report* (Washington, DC, 2003), http://www.usccr.gov/pubs/envjust/ej091103.pdf.

29. Ibid.

30. Senator Koop, Senate Bill 45 of 1997, California law, 1997.

NINE

Building Transportation Equity into Smart Growth

Robert D. Bullard, Glenn S. Johnson, and Angel O. Torres

Unfortunately, when many people think of public transit they think of rickety, smelly diesel buses crowded with poor people. To them, public transit is for losers. On the other hand, thinking about suburbanites, or "choice riders" as they are called by transit planners, getting out of their cars and into public transit, calls to mind a different image: brand-new buses or rail cars equipped with reclining seats, reading lights, and, of course, air conditioning. These perceptions are not too far from reality. Transportation dollars follow power, and power is not in the hands of the poor. In fact, the radically disparate spending of tax dollars has affected land-use decisions nationwide and subsidized the uneven development between central cities and suburbs—literally laying the pavement for suburban sprawl.

Highway funding is the federal government's "hidden urban policy program."[1] Buttressing the asphalt and construction industry, state departments of transportation (DOTs) are basically road-building programs that respond to the highway lobby, a lobby that fills the coffers of many politicians. Few could argue that transportation dollars are dispensed on a level playing field. While political leaders would never think of cutting off their "pork barrel" home-district road-building programs, efficient, clean urban mass transportation systems have few powerful lobbies or political allies.

Transportation decision-making—whether at the federal, regional, state, or local level—often mirrors the power arrangements of the dominant society and its institutions. Money and political power have shifted to the suburbs. In general, suburban America gets what it wants. Affluent suburbanites do not want inner-city bus riders "invading" their communities. Bus riders are equated with crime, drugs, and other "undesirable" elements. Although there is little or no empirical evidence to support these stereotypes, they linger anyway and influence people's beliefs, including those of some planners, about regional transit.

Numerous examples abound in which government subsidies target suburban regions for infrastructure improvements and amenities such as water irrigation systems, ship channels, road and bridge projects, and even shopping malls, while neglecting urban development. For example, the Georgia Department of Transportation committed $46 million in taxpayer money to make Gwinnett County's "Mall of Georgia" possible.[2] The 1.7-million-square-foot, 100-acre mall, located in Atlanta's northern suburbs, opened in the fall of 1999 with parking spaces for 8,600 cars and no transit access.[3]

As black Americans moved to the cities, millions of white Americans voted with their feet, moving to the 'burbs, shifting political power. In 1960, sociologist Daniel Patrick Moynihan, in his article "New Roads to Chaos," predicted many of the urban problems we are grappling with today. Moynihan wrote:

> It is becoming increasingly obvious that American government, both national and local, can no longer ignore what is happening as the suburbs eat endlessly into the countryside. Since the spreading pollution of land follows the roads, those who build the roads must also recognize the responsibility of the consequences.[4]

Thirty years later in 1990, US Senator Moynihan, as Chairman of the Environment and Public Works Subcommittee on Transportation, became the chief architect of the groundbreaking Intermodal Surface Transportation Efficiency Act (ISTEA). ISTEA attempted to change the way transportation planning was conducted and how resources were allocated.

ISTEA recognized that central cities and suburbs are not equal and often compete for scarce resources. One need not be a rocket scientist to predict the outcome of a competition between affluent suburbs and their less affluent central-city competitors. Megabucks are spent on freeways to move suburbanites around, while central-city residents fight for pennies to keep transit services running and fares affordable. These problems appear to be more severe in urban areas with large concentrations of poor people and people of color.

Highways are the lifelines for suburban commuters—connecting them to home, work, shopping, recreation, and other activities. Millions of central-city residents have no options except public transit. Transit providers know this and are not inclined to pamper their low-income, people of color, urban transit-dependent riders as they do their white suburban "choice riders." These double standards persist in the face of budget shortfalls and service cuts. Recent cuts in mass transit subsidies and fare hikes have restricted access to essential social services and economic activities. The money spent on building roads is more about mobility for the rich than equity for all. More roads on the urban edge translate into more cars and more land-use patterns that can only be served by highways. Sprawl-driven transportation also fuels political campaign contributions for those elected officials who promote sprawl as "good business."

Economic development policies flow from forces of production and are often dominated by federal, state, and local government actors. The absence of a coherent urban agenda in the 1990s allowed many of our cities to become forgotten and invisible places. The quality of life for millions of urban Americans is worse today than it was during the turbulent 1960s. A 1999 *USA Today* survey of experts singled out "wealth disparity" as the biggest issue in cities' development for the next fifty years.[5] The growing economic disparity between racial and ethnic groups as compared to whites has a direct correlation to institutional barriers in housing, lending, employment, education, health, and transportation.

The Price of Gridlock

A 1999 headline-grabbing story in *USA Today* reported that "traffic is worse than ever" and that "congestion on US roads is outpacing population growth."[6] While the nation's largest metropolitan areas grew by 22 percent over the past fifteen years, congestion grew by a staggering 235 percent. Daily congestion on the nation's highways continues to plague most cities across the country. The *2002 Urban Mobility Study* from the Texas Transportation Institute revealed that for peak-period travelers the time penalty for traveling during rush-hours jumped from 16 hours per year in 1982 to 62 hours in 2000.[7] The study also found that congestion on the roads during rush hour had increased from 4.5 hours a day in 1982 to 7 hours in 2000 in seventy-five US cities.

In addition to more cars on the road, people are driving more miles and using more gas.[8] According to the Federal Highway Administration (FHWA) report, *Highway Statistics*, total vehicle miles traveled in the United States increased by 59 percent from 1980 to 1995.[9] On fuel alone, American drivers spent over $67.5 billion in 2000, about $1,160 per person. Approximately 5.7 billion gallons of fuel are wasted in the seventy-five urban areas each year. That equates to about 99 gallons of fuel used per person each year.[10]

A 2001 Surface Transportation Policy Project (STPP) and Center for Neighborhood Technology (CNT) report, *Driven to Spend*, found that sprawl drives up transportation costs for American families.[11] The study analyzed government data on consumer expenditures, ranking twenty-eight major metro areas by the portion of the family budget devoted to daily transportation costs, and discovered that the metropolitan areas where transportation takes the biggest bite out of the household budget are Houston, Atlanta, Dallas–Fort Worth, Miami, and Detroit. The average Houstonian used 22 cents out of every dollar spent on transportation—or $8,840 each year on transportation. Essentially, heavy government investment in road infrastructure is contributing to an increase in household transportation costs. This is especially harmful to low-income households—especially African Americans and Latinos, who are disproportionately represented in the lower income category—who spend more of their income on transportation costs than whites.

More cars and increased traffic congestion mean more air pollution. Automobile exhaust combines with heat and sunlight to create ozone, an airborne gas harmful to individuals, particularly those with breathing difficulties. Air pollution from vehicle emissions causes significant amounts of illness, hospitalization, and premature death. A 2001 Center for Disease Control report, *Creating a Healthy Environment: The Impact of the Built Environment on Health*, points a finger at transportation and sprawl as major health threats.

> Bad air makes lung diseases, especially asthma, worse. The more hours [spent] in automobiles, driving over impervious highways that generate massive tree-removal, clearly degrade air quality. When the Atlanta Olympic Games in 1996 brought about a reduction in auto use by 22.5 percent, asthma admissions to [emergency rooms] and hospitals also decreased by 41.6 percent. Less driving, better public transport, well-designed landscape, and residential density will improve air quality more than will additional roadways.[12]

Although it is difficult to put a single price tag on the cost of air pollution, estimates range from $10 billion to $200 billion a year.[13] Inner-city children have the highest rates for asthma prevalence, hospitalization, and mortality.[14] Asthma is the number one reason for childhood emergency room visits in most major cities in the country. The hospitalization rate for African Americans is three to four times the rate for whites. African Americans are almost three times more likely than whites to die from asthma.[15]

Representatives from the grassroots environmental justice organizations and networks have begun to mobilize around clean air as a basic civil right. They are demanding clean air, transportation equity, and fair distribution of regional spending.[16] Groups have called for new interagency approaches to foster greater public participation of impacted populations to create healthy and sustainable communities through wise transportation investments. They want an end to transportation racism that is siphoning off needed funds from communities of color, isolating them from jobs and economic activity centers, and making them sick from breathing other people's automobile pollution. These transportation equity advocates are demanding fair and smart growth.

Is Smart Growth Fair?

The President's Council on Sustainable Development, in *Sustainable America*, outlined a vision statement that emphasizes three major pillars: economic prosperity, environmental protection, and social equity. The vision statement reads:

> Our vision is of a life-sustaining Earth. We are committed to the achievement of a dignified, peaceful, and equitable existence. A sustainable United States will have a growing economy that provides equitable opportunities for satisfying livelihoods and a safe, healthy, high quality of life for current and future generations. Our nation will protect its environment, its natural resource base, and the functions and viability of natural systems on which all life depends.[17]

It is doubtful that this vision of a sustainable America can be achieved without addressing race and social equity, especially in the nation's central cities and metropolitan regions. Social equity has not received much attention in the sustainable development movement or smart growth dialogue. In fact, much of the smart growth dialogue, meetings, and action agendas have only marginally involved people of color, the working class, and low-income persons. In short, the emerging smart growth movement is missing the rich ethnic and economic diversity that characterizes many central cities, suburbs, metropolitan regions, and the nation.

The American Planning Association (APA), in it's *Policy Guide on Smart Growth*, writes:

> Smart growth means using comprehensive planning to guide, design, develop, revitalize and build communities for all that: have a unique sense of community and place; preserve and enhance valuable natural and cultural resources; equitably distribute the costs and benefits of development; expand the range of transportation, employment and housing choices in a fiscally responsible manner; value long-range, regional considerations of

sustainability over short term incremental geographically isolated actions; and promote public health and healthy communities.[18]

The APA also reports that smart growth should not be limited to combating the symptoms of sprawl, but should "promote fairness in rebuilding inner city and inner suburban areas, in the development of suburban communities, and in the growth of small towns and rural areas."[19]

The smart growth movement is built on anti-sprawl rhetoric. But talking about smart growth is much easier than practicing smart growth. Since smart growth leaders have deep ties to the environmental justice and conservation movements, each have their own perspectives and agendas. Consequently, "sprawl" means different things to different people.[20] In the most basic sense, sprawl is random, unplanned growth characterized by inadequate accessibility to essential land uses such as housing, jobs, and public services, including schools, parks, green space, and public transportation. Suburbia is an extension of established patterns of decentralization and low-density development.[21] Sprawl-driven development has "literally sucked population, jobs, investment capital, and tax base from the urban core."[22]

Sprawl is fueled by the "iron triangle" of finance, land-use planning, and transportation service delivery. Typically, strip malls, low-density residential housing, and other isolated, scattered developments leapfrog over the landscape without any rhyme or reason, with urban-suburban sprawl consuming land faster than the population growth in many cities across the country. In order to access these new suburban developments, one must have access to an automobile—since public transit is usually inadequate or nonexistent—thus creating a car-dependent citizenry.

Growth and sprawl are not synonymous. Nevertheless, suburban sprawl has been the dominant growth pattern for nearly all metropolitan regions in the United States for the past five decades.[23] Historically, the decentralization of employment centers has had a major role in shaping metropolitan growth patterns and the location of people, housing, and jobs. Government policies fortified and tax dollars subsidized suburban sprawl through new roads and highways at the expense of public transit.[24] Tax subsidies made it possible for new suburban employment centers to become dominant outside of cities, and to pull middle-income workers and homeowners away from the urban core.[25]

From New York to Los Angeles and a host of cities and metropolitan regions in between, smart growth advocates are gradually moving their plans into action. Unfortunately, social equity issues are often marginalized or are left out altogether. Even in Atlanta, tagged "Sprawlanta," race and equity issues are largely skirted in the emerging smart growth partnerships.[26] Not addressing transportation racism in Atlanta's sprawl problem is tantamount to the Braves playing without a baseball. Atlanta's African American community—which comprises 68 percent of the city's population—and other people of color communities are invisible in the local smart growth initiative.[27]

Race and equity issues routinely get left out of national transportation and smart growth dialogue or are tagged on as an afterthought. Smart growth discussions take place as if America was a colorblind or race-neutral nation. Not talking about the racism in regional planning will not make the problem go away. Many of the smart growth proponents—who have the power and purse strings—need to shed their biases and stereotypes of low-income people and people of color if the nation is to have a fair and equitable smart growth movement.

The State of Race in America

In April 2000, the United States population stood at 281 million. The recent census shows that black and Hispanic populations far outgrew that of whites over the 1990s. There were 211 million whites, 35 million blacks, and 35 million Hispanics in 2000. (The federal government considers race and Hispanic origin to be two distinct categories. Thus, Hispanic Americans can be of any race.) Whites comprised approximately 70 percent of the total US population in 2000.[28]

Three-fifths of all black Americans lived in ten states: New York, California, Texas, Florida, Georgia, Illinois, North Carolina, Maryland, Michigan, and Louisiana, with almost 55 percent of the nation's 35 million blacks living in the South.[29] The Northeast and Midwest were each home to 19 percent of the black population in 2000, and the West home to about 10 percent. Over 88 percent of blacks lived in metropolitan areas, with about 60 percent concentrated in ten metropolitan areas, New York (2.3 million), Chicago (1 million), Detroit (0.7 million), Philadelphia (0.6 million), Houston (0.5 million), Baltimore (0.4 million), Los Angeles (0.4 million), Memphis (0.4 million), Washington, DC (0.3 million), and New Orleans (0.3 million).[30]

While 98 percent of blacks living outside of the South resided in metropolitan areas, over 79 percent of blacks living in the South lived in metropolitan areas. The Southeast is especially attractive to middle-class, post–baby-boomer blacks. A little over one-third (34.9 percent) of blacks live in the suburbs compared with 56.2 percent of whites. Black migrants to the South tend to reside in the suburbs or metropolitan areas. Seven of the ten fastest growing counties for blacks are in the suburbs of metro Atlanta.[31] Black suburbanization has often meant re-segregation. Separate still translates to unequal, even for the most successful and affluent black Americans.

In 2000, 35 million Hispanics of all races lived in the United States with over 91 percent of all Hispanics located in a metropolitan area.[32] Over half of the Latinos of Mexican origin lived in the West and one-third (32.6 percent) lived in the South. Puerto Ricans were found largely in the Northeast (63.9 percent) and Cubans were highly concentrated in the South (80.1 percent). Central Americans were concentrated in the Northeast (32.3 percent), the South (32.3 percent), and West (28.2 percent).

Within the South, Texas and Florida comprise the lion's share of the Hispanic population growth (71 percent). University of Michigan demographer and sociologist William H. Frey contends that, "despite high rates of growth for the Hispanic population in the South, recent redistribution shifts tend to reinforce the South's historic racial profile as primarily a white-black region."[33]

Blacks and Latinos made inroads into the nation's suburbs during the 1990s. In 2000, of the 88 percent of black Americans who resided in metropolitan areas, 34.9 percent lived in the suburbs and 53.1 percent lived in the central cities. Similarly, Latinos accounted for 11 percent suburban population and 19 percent of the population in central cities. Meanwhile, non-Hispanic whites accounted for 77.4 percent of the metropolitan populations, with 56.2 percent living in the suburbs and 22 percent living in the central city.

Blacks, Latinos, and whites have different ratings on the "best places to live." For example, *Black Enterprise's* "Top Ten Cities for African Americans to Live, Work, and Play" listed the following city ranking: (1) Houston, (2) Washington, DC, (3) Atlanta, (4) Charlotte, (5) Memphis, (6) Detroit, (7) Baltimore, (8) Dallas, (9) Chicago, and (10) Philadelphia.[34] Seven of the ten cities are located in the South and five have black majority populations.

Similarly, *Hispanic Magazine's* "Top 10 Cities for Latinos" included: (1) Tampa, (2) Denver, (3) San Jose, (4) Santa Ana, (5) Phoenix, (6) San Antonio, (7) Washington, DC, (8) Chicago,

(9) Miami, and (10) San Diego.[35] Over three-fourths of the "best" cities for Latinos were located in the West and Florida. Latinos tended to favor metropolitan regions with substantial Hispanic populations.

Money magazine also picked its "Ten Best Places to Live in America."[36] *Money's* 2002 "Ten Best Places" (not ranked) were: Los Angeles, Seattle, San Francisco's Bay Area, Las Vegas, Phoenix, Denver, Austin, Chicago, Charlotte, and New York. The magazine selected cities to which people are moving and in which real estate has been booming. Its top picks were rated as "economic and cultural magnets" where people have "voted with their feet and their wallets."[37]

The politics of race and metropolitan development are intertwined.[38] Blacks, Latinos, and whites view the world through very different lenses. There was very little overlap between the ratings of the "best cities" by blacks, Latinos, and whites. For example, Chicago was the only city that made the rating by all three groups. Other than Chicago, the only city that both blacks and Latinos ranked as one of their top-ten cities was Washington, DC.

A large share of the black and Hispanic populations are concentrated in sprawl-threatened cities. In 1998, the Sierra Club rated Atlanta as the "most sprawl threatened" large city (over one million) in the nation.[39] Other sprawled-threatened big cities that made the Sierra Club's "top ten" sprawl list included St. Louis, Washington, DC, Cincinnati, Kansas City, Denver, Seattle, Minneapolis-St. Paul, Fort Lauderdale, and Chicago. The criteria for the ranking included such factors as population trends, land use, traffic congestion, and open space.[40]

Growing Apart

The US is becoming increasingly diverse. However, America's neighborhoods continue to be highly segregated along racial and ethnic lines. While some progress has been eked out over the past four decades, no dramatic breakthrough has been made. Rising segregation levels are most pronounced for Latinos and Asians as their numbers and concentration increase in more places. The notion of a racially integrated America remains an idea and not a reality.[41]

Sociologist John Logan summarized the current state of housing affairs in the United States: "It's a mistake to talk about a breakthrough. The only evidence of [integration] comes from places where there are few minorities to incorporate. In the other America, where 80 to 90 percent of minorities live, there's been very small change, if any."[42]

In 2000, the average white American lived in a neighborhood that was 80 percent white, 8 percent Hispanic, 7 percent black, and 4 percent Asian. Similarly, the typical black lived in a neighborhood that was 51 percent black, 33 percent white, 12 percent Hispanic, and 3 percent Asian.[43] In the major metropolitan areas where most African Americans, Latinos, and Asians live, segregation levels changed little between 1990 and 2000.

America's metropolitan world is more complex than the black-white race-relations paradigm. New ethnic immigrant enclaves now dot the urban and suburban landscapes. A new wave of ethnic segregation dominates many large central-city neighborhoods, first-ring suburbs, deep suburbs, and some rural communities in metropolitan regions that attract low-wage laborers.

Schools are a powerful perpetrator of metropolitan polarization.[44] The drift toward racially segmented metropolitan areas is most pronounced in public education. A 2002 Harvard Civil Rights Project study, *Race in American Public Schools*, reports that the nation's school districts are becoming more diverse and more segregated.[45]

In 2000, over 70 percent of black students attended schools where students of color were in the majority; 40 percent of black students attended schools that were 90 to 100 percent black. Black-white school segregation is most pronounced in districts with either no desegregation or where the courts rejected a city-suburban desegregation. Latino student segregation has been steadily rising since the 1960s. Today, Latino students are the most segregated ethnic minority in the country. The Latino share of the nation's students almost tripled since 1968. The black student enrollment increased by 30 percent and the white student enrollment decreased by 17 percent over the same period. Over 37 percent of Latino students attend schools where 90 to 100 percent of the students are students of color. The average Latino student is enrolled in a school that is less than 30 percent white.

Generally, over 80 percent of white students attend schools where more than 80 percent of the students are white.[46] Gary Orfield and Susan E. Eaton, two leading authors on schools desegregation, write:

Segregation is so deeply sewn into America's social fabric that the media rarely see it. And policy-makers, thinkers, pundits and "education reformers" steer around the gross fact [of] segregation as if it were heaven ordained, without insidious causes or acceptable cure.[47]

The rapid growth of mega-schools on undeveloped land is replacing the traditional small, walkable, community-centered schools. But, again it is new construction that has the incentives—building codes often support new construction, which in turn undermines upgrading existing historic neighborhood schools. Schools built in recent years take up more land and are farther from the city. These large schools outside of the city promote sprawl and destroy the sense of community of those neighborhoods that have to bus their students to these schools. Suburban school sprawl also drives up the price of transporting students to and from the mega-schools. When buses are used, many are one-third to one-half empty most of the time because parents drive their children to school or students drive themselves— adding to traffic gridlock and air pollution. It is not uncommon to see traffic jams and police directing traffic out of the parking lots of sprawl-driven mega-schools.

Urban and suburban schools reflect the same vast inequities of their transportation systems. Huge disparities exist between the educational quality and funding of suburbs versus inner-city schools, illustrated by the highest-spending and lowest-spending school districts within a given state. In California, the gap ranges from $16,343 per pupil at Indian Springs Elementary to $2,713 at Pacific Union Elementary. In New Jersey, Union County Regional spends $18,116 per pupil while Prospect Park Borough spends $5,144. It would be foolish to talk about smart growth without talking about strategies to "fix" public schools and other urban-suburban disparities.

Students of color comprise a majority of the students enrolled in fifteen of the sixteen "most sprawl-threatened" large cities. These cities include Washington, DC (96.0 percent), Detroit (95.1 percent), Atlanta (93.4 percent), Dallas (89.9 percent), Chicago (89.7 percent), Baltimore (87.2 percent), St. Louis (82.2 percent), Kansas City (81.9 percent), Cleveland (79.7 percent), Denver (74.7 percent), Cincinnati (71.0 percent), Minneapolis (67.9 percent), St. Paul (60.6 percent), Seattle (59.0 percent), Ft. Lauderdale (54.0 percent), and Tampa (44.7 percent).[48]

Walking: Health, Safety, and Sprawl

Sprawl is a major reason for the decline in walking. The most dramatic impact is seen in the decline of school children walking or riding their bikes to school. In its report, *Historic Neighborhood Schools in the Age of Sprawl*, the National Trust for Historic Preservation reports that fewer than one in eight students walk or bike to school.[49] Twenty-five percent of the trips on the road in the morning are parents taking their children to school. The typical parent spends 72 minutes a day in a car chauffeuring children to school, soccer games, birthday parties, and other activities.

Not walking is contributing to obesity, and ultimately ill health.[50] Obesity among American adults has increased 60 percent over the past decade. Today, one in five American adults is defined as obese. One quarter of American children aged six through seventeen are overweight. Changes in our lifestyles and communities have played the greatest role in the decline of physical activity among Americans.[51]

From 1975 to 1995, there was a 42 percent decline in walking by American adults, according to the U.S. Department of Transportation.[52] There are many reasons why people choose not to walk. Lack of structures or facilities (such as sidewalks and parks) and safety are the two main reasons. Some places are not safe for pedestrians. Highway sprawl results in increased accidents, delays, traffic gridlocks, and pedestrian injuries.

STPP reports in *Mean Streets* that walking is thirty-six times more dangerous than driving.[53] The most dangerous metropolitan areas for pedestrians were Tampa, Atlanta, Miami, Orlando, and Jacksonville. Poor planning affects safety. On average, states spend just 55 cents per person of their federal transportation funds on pedestrian projects, less than one percent of their total federal transportation dollars. Average spending on highways came to $72 per person.

Public Health and Public Transit

As a rule, sprawl development is not pedestrian-, bicycle-, or transit-friendly. Infrastructure enhancements and service improvements are needed to get people out of their homes and cars. Walking and biking are two major travel modes that produce zero pollution. In addition, sidewalks, bike lanes, and jogging paths all encourage physical activity, enhance public health, and promote social interaction and a sense of community.

Since the pedestrian fatality rate is highest among people of color, regional transportation agencies need to focus on neighborhood safety issues, particularly pedestrian safety. They should also ensure that a reasonable amount of transportation safety funds are spent on pedestrian-related projects such as sidewalks, lighting, crosswalks, and traffic calming in low-income and people of color communities.

Metropolitan Planning Organizations (MPOs) should incorporate social equity and environmental justice into air-quality conformity requirements at all stages of the transportation planning process.

They should also encourage the spending of congestion mitigation investments to benefit low-income communities and communities of color, especially if these areas exhibit disproportionately high levels of criteria pollutants. The US DOT should work closely with the federal EPA and the Centers for Disease Control and Prevention to monitor air quality levels in nonattainment regions with large concentrations of low-income and people of color residents.

Sprawl and Employment

Where highways are built and where public transport systems extend are not unrelated. Similarly, spatial mobility and social mobility are interrelated. New job growth and economic activity centers are concentrated on the fringe of the metropolitan areas and often beyond the reach of public transportation. Over 80 percent of the country's future growth (if current trends hold) is expected to occur in "edge cities" and other suburbs.[54]

In an analysis of office space in thirteen of the nation's largest metropolitan commercial real estate markets, a 2000 Brookings Institution study found that central cities' share of office space dropped from 74 percent in 1979 to 58 percent in 1999.[55] Nearly an equal share of office space is found in traditional downtowns (38 percent) and "edgeless" cities that often extend over hundreds of square miles. The latter are generally not mixed-use, pedestrian friendly, or accessible by transit.

The Brookings study also found that Detroit had the highest percentage (69.5 percent) of office space outside the city. Atlanta was second, with almost two-thirds of its 132 million square feet of space outside the city. This is a dramatic shift from two decades ago, when over 43 percent of Atlanta's office space was in the city. Other metropolitan areas with office sprawl included Washington, DC (57.7 percent), Miami (57.4 percent), and Philadelphia (55.2 percent).[56] People of color comprise the majority population in all five of the most office-sprawled cities.

The exodus of low-skilled jobs to the suburbs disproportionately affects central-city residents, particularly people of color, who often face a more limited choice of housing location and transportation in growing areas. Between 1990 and 1997, jobs on the fringe of metropolitan areas grew by 19 percent versus 4 percent job growth in core areas. While metropolitan regions expanded into the suburbs, many of America's central cities became forgotten places.[57]

Americans who have the economic means continue to leave central cities. Higher income households are leading this flight. Although affluent households (persons making $60,000 and over) make up only 24 percent of households in the nation's larger cities, they account for over 40 percent of the 1.2 million outmigrants. A 2000 study by Harvard University's Joint Center for Housing Studies reports that between 1990 and 1997, new construction in outlying counties in metropolitan areas grew by 15 percent, compared with only 5 percent housing growth in counties closer to central cities.[58]

Improving Access to Jobs

Sprawl-driven development diverts funds away from central cities. Improving low-income residents' mobility, particularly for those making the transition from welfare to work, may be the difference between employment and unemployment, and between self-sufficiency and dependency. Public transportation improvements go hand in hand with expanding job opportunities. Innovative programs are needed to improve transportation efficiency; reduce the impacts of transportation on the environment; reduce the need for infrastructure investment; provide efficient access; examine development patterns; and involve the community in such efforts.

The regional transportation planning process needs to include a thorough and comprehensive assessment of current and future travel needs. This assessment should incorporate transportation options such as transit, walking, and bicycling based on the location and demographics of forecasted population and employment trends. The assessment will also need to quantify the various infrastructure changes which may be needed: for example, miles of new roads, sidewalks, and bicycle lanes; public transit and vanpool service expansion; congestion pricing; and parking management.

All Roads Lead to Transit-Oriented Development

Transit stations can become more than places that commuters pass through on their way to somewhere else. One measure to combat sprawl and its inherent inequities is through transit-oriented development (TOD). Through TOD, transportation planners can shape land uses and development so that they are amenable to walking, bicycling, and transit use. When done right, TOD can promote more dense, mixed land uses. Furthermore, TODs can be combined with location-efficient mortgages (LEM). In LEMs, money saved from lower transportation costs (thus boosting disposable income) could be used to qualify a greater number of lower and moderate-income households for home mortgages. The spillover effect is increased home ownership in inner-city neighborhoods.

Conclusion

People of color communities are not waiting for government, business, or mainstream environmental groups to come up with a "silver-bullet" solution to address the transportation racism that fuels suburban sprawl and uneven development. Some communities and groups are taking action. Whether central city, suburb, or rural, it will take a coordinated effort among the divergent interests to fix the nation's transportation problems. Transportation racism and suburban sprawl act in concert to suck the life out of central cities. Employing smart growth strategies to address both problems would go a long way towards bringing economic vitality back to many declining urban communities.

It will also take time and resources to arrest suburban sprawl and the negative impacts it has had on central cities. Clearly, people of color organizations that have long track records in civil rights have a ready-made issue in transportation equity and smart growth. They need only seize the issue as their own. Without transportation equity, many of our nation's neighborhood revitalization efforts, brownfields redevelopment, location-efficient mortgages, transit-oriented development, and related smart growth initiatives will be difficult, if not impossible, to implement.

Building a Transportation Equity-Smart Growth Movement

Race still matters in the United States, and running from it solves nothing. Addressing social equity and improving race relations need to be explicit priorities in transportation equity and smart growth initiatives. Racial polarization is impeding community and economic development in almost every metropolitan region that has large concentrations of people of color. Dismantling racial barriers and institutional racism would go a long way towards boosting financial incentives and reinvestment in central-city neighborhoods. It makes little sense to have only white men and women in suits talking to each other about solving regional air pollution, transportation, sprawl, and overall quality of life problems.

Transportation planning is too important to be left solely in the hands of urban planners, many of whom drive cars, seldom use public transit, and have few real world experiences with poor people and people of color. Having transit riders on the local or regional transit provider's board and metropolitan planning organizations is a good first step in broadening stakeholder input into decision-making. However, serving on boards or sitting at the table is not sufficient. There must be some real power-sharing with poor people and people of color and other underrepresented groups before real change and real solutions are possible. There must be a national strategy to develop and disseminate transportation equity and smart growth messages to everybody involved in the equitable transportation movement to make sure our voices are heard loud and clear.

The transportation equity and smart growth issue has the potential for bringing together diverse community-based organizations, homeowners associations, civic clubs, academic institutions, activists, and government agencies to form broad coalitions and alliances. Working together, neighborhood groups in central cities, suburbs, and surrounding rural areas can band together to arrest sprawl. Special efforts need to be undertaken for outreach to include low-income people and people of color and to provide space for these groups to speak for themselves. Until African Americans and other people of color take ownership of the transportation equity and smart growth messages, they will remain marginalized and on the periphery of the smart growth debate. If they do not do it, it is unlikely to get done.

notes

1. Marlon Boarnet and Andrew Haughwout, *Do Highways Matter? Evidence and Policy Implications of Highways' Influence on Metropolitan Development* (Washinton, DC: Brookings Institution Center for Urban Metropolitan Policy, 2000), http://http://www.brookingsinstitution.org/dybdocroot/es/urban/boarnetexsum.htm.

2. "DOT Needs New Focus," *Atlanta Journal-Constitution*, September 20, 1999, A8.

3. David Firestone, "Suburban Comforts Thwart Atlanta's Plans to Limit Sprawl," *The New York Times*, November 21, 1999, 30.

4. Daniel Patrick Moynihan, "New Roads and Urban Chaos," *The Reporter* 22, no. 8 (April 14, 1960).

5. Haya El Nasser, "Urban Experts Pick Top Factors Influencing Future," *USA Today,* September 27, 1999, A4.

6. Scott Bowles, "National Gridlock: 167 Worst Bottlenecks," *USA Today*, November 23, 1999, 1A–2A.

7. Davis L. Schrank and Timothy J. Lomax, *The 2002 Urban Mobility Report* (College Station, TX: Texas Transportation Institute, Texas A&M University, 2002), http://www.mobility.tamu.org.

8. Scott Bowles, "National Gridlock: 167 Worst Bottlenecks," 2A.

9. Charles W. Schmidt, "The Specter of Sprawl," *Environmental Health Perspectives* 106 (June 1998): 275.

10. Ibid.

11. Barbara McCann, et al., *Driven to Spend: The Impact of Sprawl on Household Transportation Expenses* (Washington, DC: Surface Transportation Policy Project and the Center for Neighborhood Technology, 2000), http://www.transact.org/PDFs/DriventoSpend.pdf.

12. Richard J. Jackson and Chris Kochtitzky, *Creating a Healthy Environment: The Impact of the Built Environment on Public Health* (Atlanta: Centers for Disease Control, 2001), 3.

13. David Bollier, *How Smart Growth Can Stop Sprawl: A Briefing Guide for Funders* (Washington, DC: Essential Books, 1998).

14. Centers for Disease Control, "Asthma: United States, 1982–1992," *Morbidity and Mortality Weekly Report* 43 (1995): 952-955.

15. Centers for Disease Control, *Death Rates from 72 Selected Causes by Year, Age Groups, Race, and Sex: United States 1979-98* (Hyattsville, MD: National Center for Health Statistics, 2000).

16. The 1996 "Just Transportation" video examines transportation issues in major US. cities, including Atlanta, New York (Harlem), Chicago, Washington, DC, Los Angeles, and San Francisco.

17. President's Council on Sustainable Development, *Sustainable America: A New Consensus for Prosperity, Opportunity, and a Healthy Environment for the Future* (Washington, DC: Government Printing Office, 1996).

18. American Planning Association, *Policy Guide on Smart Growth* (2002), adopted by Chapter Delegate Assembly, Chicago, IL, April 14, 2002.

19. Ibid.

20. Robert D. Bullard, Glenn S. Johnson, and Angel Torres, *Sprawl City: Race, Politics, and Planning in Atlanta* (Washington, DC: Island Press, 2000).

21. Ibid.

22. C. Anthony, "Suburbs are Making Us Sick: Health Implications of Suburban Sprawl and Inner City Abandonment on Communities of Color" in *Environmental Justice Health Research Needs Report Series* (Atlanta: Environmental Justice Resource Center, 1998).

23. Myron Orfield, *Metropolitics: A Regional Agenda for Community and Stability* (Washington, DC: Brookings Institution Press, 1997).

24. Robert D. Bullard and Glenn S. Johnson, eds., *Just Transportation: Dismantling Race and Class Barriers to Mobility* (Gabriola Island, British Columbia: New Society Publishers, 1997); Conservation Law Foundation, *City Routes, City Rights: Building Livable Neighborhoods and Environmental Justice by Fixing Transportation* (Boston: Conservation Law Foundation, 1998).

25. C. W. Schmidt, "The Specter of Sprawl," *Environmental Health Perspective* 106, (June 1998): 274.

26. Robert D. Bullard, Glenn S. Johnson and Angel O. Torres, "Atlanta: Megasprawl," *Forum for Applied Research and Public Policy* 14, no. 3 (Fall 1999): 17-23.

27. Urban Land Institute, *Smart Growth: Myth and Fact* (Washington, DC: Urban Land Institute, 1999).

28. US Bureau of the Census, *Demographic Trends in the 20th Century* (Washington, DC: US Department of Commerce, November 2002), 71-114.

29. US Bureau of the Census, *The Black Population: 2000 Census Brief* (Washington, DC: US Department of Commerce, August 2001), 7.

30. Ibid.

31. William H. Frey, *Census Shows Large Black Return to the South, Reinforcing the Region's "White-Black" Demographic Profile Report No. 01-473* (Ann Arbor: Population Studies Center, Institute for Social Research, University of Michigan, May 2001).

32. US Bureau of the Census, *The Hispanic Population in the United States: Population Characteristics* (Washington, DC: US Department of Commerce, March 2001), 2.

33. William H. Frey, *Census Shows Large Black Return to the South.*

34. "The Top Ten Cities for African Americans to Live, Work, and Play," *Black Enterprise*, July 2001.

35. Valerie Menard, "Top 10 Cities for Latinos," *Hispanic Magazine*, July/August, 2000.

36. "Ten Best Places to Live in America: Money Picks Cities That are Economic and Cultural Magnets," *Money*, November 19, 2002.

37. Ibid.

38. Robert D. Bullard, J. Eugene Grigsby, and Charles Lee, eds., *Residential Apartheid: The American Legacy* (Los Angeles: UCLA Center for African American Studies, 1994).

39. Sierra Club, *The Dark Side of the American Dream: The Cost and Consequences of Suburban Sprawl* (College Park, MD: Sierra Club, August, 1998), 3.

40. Ibid.

41. Bullard, Grigsby, and Lee, eds., *Residential Apartheid.*

42. Robin Fields, "Integration Progress Unclear: Same Census Numbers Used to Say it Has Climbed, Stalled," *Dallas Morning News*, June 25, 2001 (quoting John Logan).

43. John R. Logan, "Separate and Unequal: The Neighborhood Gap of Blacks and Latinos in Metropolitan America," *Mumford Monthly* (October 13, 2002), http://comm-org.utoledo.edu/pipermail/colist/2003-May/002803.html.

44. Erica Frankenberg and Chungmei Lee, *Race in American Public Schools: Rapidly Resegregating School Districts* (Cambridge: Harvard Civil Rights Project, August 2002).

45. Ibid., 2.

46. Gary Orfield and Susan E. Eaton, "Back to Segregation," *The Nation*, March 3, 2003.

47. Ibid.

48. US Department of Education, National Center for Education Statistics, "Characteristics of the 100 Largest Public and Secondary School Districts in the United States: 1997-1998," (July 1999), http://nces.ed.gov/pubsearch/pubs info.asp?pubid=1999318; US Department of Education, Office of Educational Research and Improvement "Racial and Ethnic Distribution of Elementary and Secondary Students*," Indicator of the Month, NCES 2000-005* (February 2000); US Department of Education, Office of Education Research and Improvement "Revenues and Expenditures for Public Elementary and Secondary Education: School Year 1997-98" *Statistics in Brief, NCES 2000-348* (May 2000).

49. National Trust for Historic Preservation, *Historic Neighborhood Schools in the Age of Sprawl: Why Johnny Can't Walk to School* (Washington, DC: National Trust, 2000).

50. Richard Jackson and Chris Kochtitzky, *Creating a Healthy Environment: The Impact of the Built Environment on Public Health* (Atlanta: Centers for Disease Control, 2001).

51. US Department of Health and Human Services, *Physical Activity and Health: A Report of the Surgeon General* (Washington, DC: Government Printing Office, 1996).

52. U.S. Department of Transportation, *Federal Highway Administration. 1995 Nationwide Personal Transportation Survey* (October 2001), http://www_cta.ornl.gov/npts/1995/Doc/databook95/contents.pdf

53. Michelle Ernst and Barbara McCann, *Mean Streets 2002: Pedestrian Safety, Health and Federal Transportation Spending* (Washington, DC: Surface Transportation Policy Project, 2002), http://www.transact.org/PDFs/ms2002/MeanStreets2002.pdf.

54. H. Diamond, L. Diamond, & P. F. Noonan, *Land Use in America* (Washington, DC: Island Press, 1996).

55. Robert E. Lang, *Office Sprawl: The Evolving Geography of Business* (Washington, DC: The Brookings Institution, 2000).

56. Ibid.

57. Robert D. Bullard, Glenn S. Johnson, and Angel. O. Torres, *Sprawl City: Race, Politics, and Planning in Atlanta* (Washington, DC: Island Press, 2000), 1-19.

58. Joint Center for Housing Studies, *The State of the Nation's Housing: 2000* Executive Summary. (Cambridge: Harvard University, 2000).

Appendix of Acronymns

ABAG	Association of Bay Area Governments
ACTA	Alameda County Transportation Agency
ADA	Americans with Disabilities Act
AHA	Atlanta Housing Authority
APA	American Planning Association
ATEP	Atlanta Transportation Equity Project
BART	Bay Area Rapid Transit
BOSS	Building Opportunities for Self-Sufficiency
BRTB	Baltimore Regional Transportation Board
BRTP	Baltimore Regional Transportation Plan
BRU	Bus Riders Union
CCT	Cobb Community Transit
CMAQ	Congestion Mitigation and Air Quality
CNG	Compressed Natural Gas
CNT	Center for Neighborhood Technology
CPHA	Citizens Planning and Housing Association
CTA	Chicago Transit Authority
DOT	Department of Transportation
EA	Environmental Assessment
EIS	Environmental Impact Statement or Environmental Impact Study
EJAG	Environmental Justice Advisory Group
EJRC	Environmental Justice Resource Center
FHWA	Federal Highway Administration
FTA	Federal Transit Administration
GECC	Gowanus Expressway Community Coalition
GRTA	Georgia Regional Transportation Authority
ISTEA	Intermodal Surface Transportation Efficiency Act
JARC	Job Access and Reverse Commute

KIWA	Korean Immigrant Workers' Advocates
LACTC	Los Angeles County Transportation Commission
LCSC	Labor/Community Strategy Center
LEM	Location-Efficient Mortgages
LIF	Latino Issues Forum
LOTS	Locally Operated Transit Systems
LRT	Light Rail Transit
LRV	Light Rail Vehicle
MARTA	Metropolitan Atlanta Rapid Transit Authority
MATEC	Metropolitan Atlanta Transportation Equity Coalition
MFT	Mon/Fayette Toll Road
MLK-EB	Martin Luther King, Jr.-East Busway
MPO	Metropolitan Planning Organization
MTA	Metropolitan Transportation Authority or Maryland Transit Administration
MTC	Metropolitan Transportation Commission
NEPA	National Environmental Policy Act of 1969
NYCEJA	New York City Environmental Justice Alliance
NYMTC	New York Metropolitan Transportation Council
NYS DOT	New York State Department of Transportation
PAT	Port Authority of Allegheny County
PCBs	Polychlorinated Biphenyls
PTC	Pennsylvania Turnpike Commission
PTEP	Pittsburgh Transportation Equity Project
RIVER	Reaching and Including Youth Voices for Environmental Rights
RPA	Regional Plan Association
RTD	Rapid Transit District
RTP	Regional Transportation Plan
SBRWA	Southern Bronx River Watershed Alliance
SCLC	Southern Christian Leadership Conference
STIP	Statewide Transportation Improvement Program
STPP	Surface Transportation Policy Project
TALC	Transportation and Land Use Coalition
TANF	Temporary Assistance for Needy Families
TCSP	Transportation and Community and System Preservation
TEA-21	Transportation Equity Act for the 21st Century
TIP	Transportation Improvement Plan
TMA	Transportation Management Area
TOD	Transit-Oriented Development

TSC	Transportation Steering Committee
UDL	United Defense League
UPROSE	United Puerto Rican Organization of Sunset Park
US DOT	United States Department of Transportation
VTA	Santa Clara Valley Transportation Authority

Glossary of Terms

above-grade. Above street level.

adverse effects. Includes effects that go against human health, the environment, or a group's social and economic wellbeing.

air pollution. When air contains one or more substances such as sulfur dioxide that may cause harm to plants, animals, or the physical environment.

Americans with Disabilities Act of 1990. Provides that no qualified individual with a disability shall, by reason of such disability, be excluded from the participation in, be denied the benefits of, or be subjected to discrimination by a department, agency, special purpose district, or other instrumentality of a state or a local government. The act provides enforceable standards to address discrimination against individuals with disabilities.

at-grade. At street level.

attainment area. An area with air quality that meets or exceeds the US Environmental Protection Agency's (EPA) health standards as stated in the Clean Air Act. An area may be an attainment area for one pollutant and a nonattainment area for others.

brownfields. Typically refers to urban industrial or commercial facilities that are abandoned or underutilized due to environmental contamination or fear of contamination.

bus depots. Large facilities commonly utilized for the storage and sometime maintenance of transit buses. Bus depots are known for generating pollution, noise, vibration, and stormwater runoff.

busway. A special roadway designed for exclusive bus use. It may be constructed at above or below grade and may be located in separate rights-of-way or within highway corridors.

carbon monoxide (CO). A colorless, odorless, tasteless gas that impedes the oxygenation of blood. It is formed in large part by incomplete combustion of fuel.

carbon dioxide (CO_2). One of the gases in our atmosphere that is uniformly distributed over the earth's surface. The gas is colorless, odorless, and nonflammable at room temperature. Activities such as the combustion of fossil fuels have drastically increased the concentration of CO_2 in the atmosphere and contributed to global warming.

civil rights. Rights of personal liberty that are granted to American citizens through the Thirteenth and Fourteenth Amendments to the Constitution of the United States and other laws and regulations.

class action suit. A legal action taken on behalf of all members of a group identically affected by a case.

Clean Air Act (CAA). The federal law designed to make sure all Americans have air that is safe to breathe. Public health protection is the primary goal, though the law also seeks to protect our environment from damage caused by air pollution.

Clean Air Act Amendments (CAAA). The Clean Air Act Amendments of 1990 specifically target vehicle fleets. The amendments mandate a broad range of new requirements aimed at improving air quality. The goal is for air quality in all metropolitan areas in the country to eventually meet federal standards, which are based on human health concerns. The standards will list maximum acceptable levels (in a specified time period) of nitrogen oxides (NO_x), carbon monoxide (CO), hydrocarbons, sulfur oxides (SO_x), ozone, and suspended particulates.

Compressed Natural Gas (CNG). CNG-powered vehicles use natural gas—the same fuel that is used by stoves, water heaters, and clothes dryers—stored in cylinders under high pressure. Compressed natural gas is used in light-duty passenger vehicles and pickup trucks, medium-duty delivery trucks, and in transit and school buses.

Congestion Mitigation and Air Quality improvement program (CMAQ). A categorical federal-aid funding program created with ISTEA, CMAQ directs funding to projects that contribute to meeting national air-quality standards. CMAQ provides guidance to help states implement transportation/air quality plans. Eligible projects include: transit improvements, shared-ride services, traffic flow improvements, demand management strategies, and bicycle programs.

criteria pollutants. A list of air pollutants identified in the 1970 Clean Air Act Amendments deemed to be critical to controlling air pollution and for which National Ambient Air Quality Standards (NAAQS) were established. Criteria pollutants include sulfur dioxide (SO_2), nitrogen dioxide (NO_2), Volatile Organic Compounds (VOCs), particulate matter (PM), carbon monoxide (CO), and lead (Pb).

density. Having enough residents within walking distance of transit stations to generate high ridership.

diesel fuel. Fuel for diesel engines obtained from the distillation of petroleum. Its volatility is similar to that of gas oil. Diesel exhaust contains more than forty chemicals that are listed by the EPA as toxic air contaminants, probable carcinogens, reproductive toxins, or endocrine disrupters.

Draft Environmental Impact Statement (Draft EIS). The first document produced, which discusses the impact of each transit alternative on humans and the natural environment and how serious the impacts are. The draft is circulated to all involved parties, interested individuals and organizations, and is available to the public at libraries and other public offices.

emission standard. The maximum amount of pollutants that are permitted by law or regulation to be released into the environment.

Environmental Impact Statement (EIS). A document that describes the effects a proposed action is likely to have on the environment. The EIS is now required by law before many projects can be initiated.

environmental justice (EJ). The pursuit of equal justice and equal protection under the law for all environmental statutes and regulations without discrimination based on race, ethnicity, and/or socioeconomic status.

environmental justice movement (EJM). The catalyst for the environmental justice movement had its beginnings in a small, predominately African American community in the South. While there had always been an awareness of the disproportionate burden borne by minorities and low-income communities, events did not give rise to a "movement" until 1982 in Warren County, North Carolina.

Environmental Protection Agency (EPA). The Federal regulatory agency responsible for administering and enforcing federal environmental laws including the Clean Air Act, the Clean Water Act, and others.

Federal Highway Administration (FHWA). A branch of the US Department of Transportation that administers the federal-aid Highway Program, providing financial assistance to states to construct and improve highways, urban and rural roads, and bridges.

Federal Transit Administration (FTA). A branch of the US Department of Transportation that is the principal source of federal financial assistance to communities for planning, development, and improvement of public or mass transportation systems.

fair share housing. In California, municipalities are required by law to plan for their fair share of affordable housing. All cities and counties in California must have a plan that includes a housing plan. The general plan serves as the local constitution for land use and development. Once adopted, it becomes law and a local government cannot legally act inconsistently with its general plan. Plans must be certified by the state, which can require changes if they do not comply with state mandates.

farebox recovery ratio. Measure of the proportion of operating expenses covered by passenger fares; found by dividing fare box revenue by total operating expenses for each mode and/or systemwide.

farebox revenue. Value of cash, tickets, tokens, and pass receipts given by passengers as payment for rides; excludes charter revenue.

fare elasticity. The extent to which ridership responds to increases or decreases in the price of fare.

fare structure. The system set up to determine how much money is to be paid by various passengers using a transit vehicle at any given time.

Federal Highway Administration (FHWA). An agency of the US Department of Transportation that funds highway planning and programs.

Federal Transit Administration (FTA). An agency of the US Department of Transportation that funds transit planning and programs. Formerly known as the Urban Mass Transportation Administration (UMTA).

Final Environmental Impact Statement (FEIS). The resulting document after all comments on the draft EIS have been addressed.

fixed guideway system. A system of vehicles that can operate only on its own guideway constructed for that purpose (for example, rapid rail or light rail). Federal usage in funding legislation also includes exclusive right-of-way bus operations, trolley coaches, and ferryboats as fixed guideway transit.

fixed route. Service provided on a repetitive, fixed-schedule basis along a specific route with vehicles stopping to pick up and deliver passengers to specific locations; each fixed-route trip serves the same origins and destinations, unlike demand-responsive service.

flexible funds. Federal funds which can be used for highway, transit, or other transportation projects, as decided by regional metropolitan planning organizations (MPOs) and state governments. Examples of federal funds are the Surface Transportation Program (STP) and the Congestion Mitigation and Air Quality (CMAQ) fund.

formula funds. Funds distributed or apportioned to qualifying recipients on the basis of formulas described in law; for example, funds in the Section 18 program for Small Urban and Rural Transit Assistance, which are distributed to each state based on the state's percentage of national rural population.

gentrification. The restoration of deteriorated urban property.

Highway Trust Fund. The federal trust fund established by the Highway Revenue Act of 1956; this fund has two accounts—the Highway Account and the Mass Transit Account. Trust fund revenues are derived from federal highway-user taxes and fees such as motor fuel taxes; trust fund uses and expenditures are determined by law.

high-occupancy vehicle (HOV). A vehicle that carries two or more occupants.

infill housing. Housing built on vacant or underutilized lots within urbanized areas.

intermodal. The ability to connect, and connections between, modes of transportation. Those issues or activities that involve or affect more than one mode of transportation, including transportation connections, choices, cooperation and coordination of various modes. See also multimodal.

ISTEA. Intermodal Surface Transportation Efficiency Act (1991) was a six-year act that was reauthorized in 1998 as TEA-21. In September 2003, TEA-21 was extended for five months through February 2004.

land use. Manner in which portions of land or the structures on them are used for commercial, residential, retail, or industrial activity.

locally unwanted land uses (LULUs). Facilities in communities that cause tension and conflict. For example, hazardous waste management facilities, airports, and prisons.

long-term transportation planning. Generally refers to a time span of twenty years. The transportation plans for metropolitan areas and for states should include projections for land use, population, and employment for the twenty-year period.

low-income housing. Residential facilities that are designed and built for families whose income is less than a standard that is set by the government.

low-income population. Any readily identifiable group of low-income persons who live in geographic proximity, and, if circumstances warrant, geographically dispersed or transient persons.

maglev. A magnetic levitation rail transportation system with exclusive right-of-way, which is propelled along a fixed guideway system by the attraction or repulsion of magnets on the rails and under the rail cars.

mass transit account. The federal account, established by the Surface Transportation Assistance Act of 1982, into which a designated portion of the Federal Highway Trust Fund revenue from motor fuel taxes is placed (1.5 cents in 1994). This account is used for federal mass transportation assistance.

Metropolitan Planning Organization (MPO). An ISTEA-required regional policy body for urbanized areas with populations over 50,000 that are designated by local officials and the governor of a state. MPOs are responsible, in cooperation with the state and other transportation providers, for carrying out the metropolitan transportation planning requirements of federal highway and transit legislation in ways that weigh the social and economic effects of transportation decisions. Ideally, they encourage the expansion and enhancement of transit services and other transportation alternatives.

minority population. Any readily identifiable groups of minority persons who live in geographic proximity, and if circumstances warrant, geographically dispersed or transient persons who will be similarly affected by a proposed FHWA program, policy, or activity.

mobility. The ability to move or be moved from place to place.

mode. A form of transportation, such as automobile, transit, bicycling, and walking.

multimodal. The availability of transportation options within a system or corridor.

National Ambient Air Quality Standards (NAAQS). Federal standards that set allowable concentrations and exposure limits for various pollutants. The EPA developed the standards in response to a requirement of the CAA.

National Environmental Policy Act (NEPA). A comprehensive federal law requiring analysis of the environmental impacts of federal actions, such as the approval of grants. It also requires preparation of an Environmental Impact Statement (EIS) for every major federal action significantly affecting the quality of the human environment.

National Highway System (NHS). The nation-wide system of approximately 155,00 miles of major roads that provides principal arterial routes, which serve major population centers, major transportation facilities, and major travel destinations.

National Transportation System (NTS). An intermodal system consisting of all forms of transportation in a unified, interconnected manner to reduce energy consumption and air pollution while promoting economic development and supporting the nation's preeminent position in international commerce. The NTS includes the National Highway System (NHS), public transportation, and access to ports and airports.

nitrogen oxide (NO_x). The sum of nitric oxide and nitrogen dioxide. The primary nitrogen pollutant emitted from the combustion process.

nonattainment area. An area considered not to have met federal standards for designated pollutants. An area may be an attainment area for one pollutant and a nonattainment area for others.

ozone (O_3). A colorless gas with a sweet odor. Ozone is not a direct emission from transportation sources. It is a secondary pollutant formed when hydrocarbons (HC) and nitrogen oxides (NO_x) combine in the presence of sunlight. It is associated with smog or haze conditions.

paratransit. Comparable transportation service required by the Americans with Disabilities Act (ADA) of 1990 for individuals with disabilities who are unable to use fixed-route transportation systems. Examples include, dial-a-ride, vanpool, and subscription service.

park and ride. Parking facilities mostly located near transit stations, bus stops, or highway exit ramps, usually in suburban areas. The facilities are used to facilitate the use of transit and carpooling. Parking is generally free or significantly less expensive than in urban centers.

particulate matter (PM). Any material that exists as solid or liquid in the atmosphere that are less than ten microns (a micron is one-millionth of a meter). Particulate matter is too small to be filtered by the nose and lungs. Particulate matter may be in the form of fly ash, soot, dust, fog, or fumes.

people of color. Individuals whose skin pigmentation may be other than white (brown, black, or yellow), and whose culture is different from that of white Americans of European descent. African Americans, Hispanic Americans, Native Americans,

Asian Americans, and Pacific Island Americans are usually regarded as being people of color.

protected low-income and minority population. Defined as a group of persons within geographic proximity of each other or a group that is dispersed but would be similarly affected by a proposal.

public comment. The second major opportunity for public involvement in the EIS process. Stakeholders or members of the general public can voice concerns with the technical analyses, the elimination or inclusion of specific alternatives, mitigation strategies, or anything else addressed in the Draft EIS.

public involvement. Providing significant input to assist in defining a project's study area, substantiating the project's purpose, and supplying information for developing project alternatives to address specific needs of the project.

public transit system. An organization that provides transportation services owned, operated, or subsidized by any municipality, county, regional authority, state, or other governmental agency, including those operated or managed by a private management firm under contract to the government agency owner.

public transportation. Transportation by bus, rail, or other conveyance, either publicly or privately owned, which provides to the public general or special service on a regular and continuing basis. Also known as mass transportation, mass transit, public transit, and transit.

rail, commuter. Local railroad and regional passenger train operations between a central city, its suburbs, and/or another central city. It may be either locomotive-hauled or self-propelled, and is characterized by multitrip tickets, specific station-to-station fares, railroad employment practices, and usually only one or two stations in the central business district. Also known as suburban rail.

rail, heavy. An electric railway with the capacity for a heavy volume of traffic and characterized by exclusive rights-of-way, multicar trains, high speed and rapid acceleration, sophisticated signaling, and high platform loading. Also known as rapid rail, subway (underground), elevated railway, or metropolitan railway (metro).

rail, high speed. A rail transportation system with exclusive right-of-way which serves densely traveled corridors at speeds of 124 miles per hour and greater.

rail, light. An electric railway with a light volume traffic capacity, as compared to heavy rail. Light rail may use shared or exclusive rights-of-way, high or low platform loading and multicar trains or single cars. Also known as streetcar, trolley car, and tramway.

rail modernization. Federal funding granted under Section 3(h) of the Federal Transit Act (formerly known as the Urban Mass Transportation Act). These discretionary funds are distributed by a formula and made available to transit systems for improvements on fixed guideway systems that have been in service for at least seven years. Also known as fixed guideway modernization.

rapid transit. Rail or motorbus transit service operating completely separate from all other modes of transportation on an exclusive right-of-way.

regional transportation plan (RTP). The plan required by state and federal law to guide a region's transportation development over a twenty-year period. This plan is updated every three years to reflect changing conditions and new planning priorities based on travel demands, projections of growth, and financial assumptions.

response to comments. All comments on a Draft EIS must be addressed either by modifying an alternative, developing and evaluating additional alternatives, improving the analysis, making corrections, or documenting why no action was taken.

reverse commuting. Movement in a direction opposite the main flow of traffic, such as from the central city to a suburb during the morning peak period.

scoping. The first step when an agency must file an EIS and the first opportunity for public input into the EIS. The lead agency invites representatives from all government agencies that might be involved, the project's supporters, and interested members of the public to a meeting to identify all of the issues involved with the project that could have a significant impact.

single-occupancy vehicles (SOV). An automobile that is used to get just one person to a destination.

smart growth. Urban development strategies that are economically sound, environmentally responsible, and socially just. The emphasis of smart growth is on partnerships among local governments, developers, businesses, farmers, social justice advocates, and environmentalists.

spatial mismatch. The effects of physical isolation on the economic wellbeing of the inner-city poor.

sprawl. Random unplanned growth characterized by inadequate accessibility to essential land uses such as housing, jobs, and public services like schools, hospitals, and mass transit.

Standard Metropolitan Statistical Area (SMSA). As defined by the US Census Bureau, an urban area having a central city or pair of cities and suburban area with a population of more than 50,000 residents and an average population of at least 1,000 persons per square mile.

state implementation plan (SIP). Air-quality planning documents that must be prepared by states and submitted to the EPA for approval. SIPs identify actions and programs to show how the various nonattainment areas of the state will attain and maintain air-quality standards.

subway. An electric underground railway or an underground tunnel or passage enabling pedestrians to cross a road or railway.

sulfur dioxide (SO_2). Sulfur dioxide belongs to the family of sulfur oxide gases. These gases are formed when fuel containing sulfur (mainly coal and oil) is burned during metal smelting and other industrial processes. High concentrations of SO_2 can result in temporary breathing impairment for asthmatic children and adults who are active outdoors.

Surface Transportation Program. The STP provides flexible funding that may be used by states and localities for projects on any federal-aid highway, including the NHS, bridge projects on any public road, transit capital projects, and intracity and intercity bus terminals and facilities. A portion of funds reserved for rural areas may be spent on rural minor collectors. STP was a federal program established under ISTEA and overseen by the Federal Highway Administration.

Surface Transportation Policy Project (STPP). The goal of the Surface Transportation Policy Project is to ensure that transportation policy and investments help conserve energy, protect environmental and aesthetic quality, strengthen the economy, promote social equity, and make communities more livable. Emphasis is on the needs of people, rather than vehicles, in assuring access to jobs, services, and recreational opportunities.

sustainability. Meeting the needs of the present without compromising the ability of future generations to meet their own needs.

TEA-3. A reauthorization of TEA-21, it is the third iteration of ISTEA.

TEA-21. Renewed ISTEA in 1998 as the Transportation Equity Act for the 21st Century. TEA-21 authorized the federal surface transportation programs for highways, highway safety, and transit for the 6-year period 1998-2003.

Title VI of the 1964 Civil Rights Act (Title VI). Section 601 provides that no person in the United States shall, on the ground of race, color, or national origin, be excluded from participation in, be denied the benefits of, or be subjected to discrimination under any program or activity receiving federal financial assistance.

transportation improvement program (TIP). A program of intermodal transportation projects, to be implemented over several years, growing out of the regional transportation planning process and designed to improve transportation in a community. A comprehensive listing of all the regional transportation projects that receive federal funds or that are subject to a federal required action, such as a review for impacts on air quality. The MPO prepares and adopts the TIP every two years. By law the TIP must cover at least a three-year period and contain a priority list of projects grouped by year. This program is required as a condition of a locality receiving federal transit and highway grants.

transportation management area (TMA). The metropolitan planning organizations of areas with a population greater than 200,000.

transit. Generally refers here to passenger service provided to the general public along established routes with fixed or variable schedules at published fares. Does not usually refer to automobile transportation. Related terms include: rapid transit, public transit, mass transit, public transportation, urban transit, and paratransit.

transit-oriented development (TOD). The residential and commercial areas that are designed to maximize access by transit and nonmotorized transportation, and with other features to encourage transit ridership.

transit system. An organization (public or private) providing local or regional multioccupancy-vehicle passenger service. Organizations that provide service under contract to another agency are generally not counted as separate systems.

transportation equity. Where concerns extend to disparate outcomes in planning, maintenance, and infrastructure development. Transportation is a key component in addressing poverty, unemployment, equal opportunity goals, and ensuring equal access to education, employment, and other public services.

transportation plan. The MPO-adopted long-range plan that identifies facilities that should function as an integrated transportation system and developed pursuant to Title 23 of the United States Code and the Federal Transit Act. It gives emphasis to those facilities that serve important national and regional transportation functions, and includes a financial plan that demonstrates how the long-range plan can be implemented. Transportation plans serve as the initial step and framework in developing a regionally based network of transportation facilities and services that meet travel needs in the most efficient and effective manner possible.

Uniform Relocation Assistance and Real Property Acquisition Policies Act. Adopted in 1970, this act ensures the fair and equitable treatment of persons whose real property is acquired or who are displaced as a result of a federal or federally assisted project. Government-wide regulations provide procedural and other requirements (such as appraisals, payment of fair market value, and notice to owners) in the acquisition of real property and provides for payments and advisory assistance in the relocation of persons and businesses.

US Department of Transportation (US DOT). The principal direct federal-funding agency for transportation facilities and programs includes the Federal Highway Administration

(FHWA), the Federal Transit Administration (FTA), the Federal Railroad Administration (FRA), and others.

urbanized area. A term used by the US Census Bureau to designate urban areas. These areas generally contain population densities of at least 1,000 persons per square mile in a continuously built-up area of at least 50,000 persons; factors such as commercial and industrial development, and other types and forms of urban activity centers are also considered.

Unified Work Program (UWP). The MPO's program of work activities noting planning priorities, assigned staffs, work products, budgets, and funding sources.

vehicle miles of travel (VMT). A standard areawide measure of travel activity. The most conventional VMT calculation is to multiply the average length of trips by the total number of trips.

volatile organic compounds (VOCs). The compounds from vehicle exhaust, paint thinners, solvents, and other petroleum-based products. A number of exhaust VOCs are also toxic, with the potential to cause cancer.

zoning. A method of setting aside certain tracts of land for specified purposes.

Principles of Environmental Justice

W E, THE PEOPLE OF COLOR, gathered together at this multinational People of Color Environmental Leadership Summit, to begin to build a national and international movement of all peoples of color to fight the destruction and taking of our lands and communities, do hereby re-establish our spiritual interdependence to the sacredness of our Mother Earth; to respect and celebrate each of our cultures, languages and beliefs about the natural world and our roles in healing ourselves; to insure environmental justice; to promote economic alternatives which would contribute to the development of environmentally safe livelihoods; and, to secure our political, economic, and cultural liberation that has been denied for over 500 years of colonization and oppression, resulting in the poisoning of our communities and land and the genocide of our peoples, do affirm and adopt these Principles of Environmental Justice:

1.   **Environmental justice** affirms the sacredness of Mother Earth, ecological unity, and the interdependence of all species, and the right to be free from ecological destruction.

2.   **Environmental justice** demands that public policy be based on mutual respect and justice for all peoples, free from any form of discrimination or bias.

3.   **Environmental justice** mandates the right to ethical, balanced, and responsible uses of land and renewable resources in the interest of a sustainable planet for humans and other living things.

4.   **Environmental justice** calls for universal protection from nuclear testing, extraction, production and disposal of toxic and

hazardous wastes and poisons, and nuclear testing that threaten the fundamental right to clean air, land, water, and food.

5.   **Environmental justice** affirms the fundamental right to political, economic, cultural, and environmental self-determination of all peoples.

6.   **Environmental justice** demands the cessation of the production of all toxins, hazardous wastes, and radioactive materials, and that all past and current producers be held strictly accountable to the people for detoxification and the containment at the point of production.

7.   **Environmental justice** demands the right to participate as equal partners at every level of decision-making including needs assessment, planning, implementation, enforcement, and evaluation.

8.   **Environmental justice** affirms the right of all workers to a safe and healthy work environment, without being forced to choose between an unsafe livelihood and unemployment. It also affirms the right of those who work at home to be free from environmental hazards.

9.   **Environmental justice** protects the right of victims of environmental injustice to receive full compensation and reparations for damages as well as quality health care.

10. **Environmental justice** considers governmental acts of environmental injustice a violation of international law, the Universal Declaration on Human Rights, and the United Nations Convention on Genocide.

11. **Environmental justice** must recognize a special legal and natural relationship of Native Peoples to the US government through treaties, agreements, compacts, and covenants affirming sovereignty and self-determination.

12. **Environmental justice** affirms the need for urban and rural ecological policies to clean up and rebuild our cities and rural areas in balance with nature, honoring the cultural integrity of all our communities, and providing fair access for all to the full range of resources.

13. **Environmental justice** calls for the strict enforcement of principles of informed consent, and a halt to the testing

of experimental reproductive and medical procedures and vaccinations on people of color.

14. **Environmental justice** opposes the destructive operations of multinational corporations.

15. **Environmental justice** opposes military occupation, repression, and exploitation of lands, peoples, and cultures, and other life forms.

16. **Environmental justice** calls for the education of present and future generations which emphasizes social and environmental issues, based on our experience and an appreciation of our diverse cultural perspectives.

17. **Environmental justice** requires that we, as individuals, make personal and consumer choices to consume as little of Mother Earth's resources and to produce as little waste as possible; and make the conscious decision to challenge and reprioritize our lifestyles to insure the health of the natural world for present and future generations.

—Adopted October 27, 1991, in Washington, DC.

Selected Bibliography

Alvord, Katharine T., Katie Alvord, and Stephanie Mills. *Divorce Your Car! Ending the Love Affair with the Automobile*. Gabriola Island, British Columbia: New Society Publishers, 2000.

Barnett, Jonathan. *Planning for a New Century: The Regional Agenda*. Washington, DC: Island Press, 2001.

Benfield, F. Kaid, Jutka Terris, and Nancy Vorsanger. *Solving Sprawl: Modes of Smart Growth in Communities Across America*. Washington, DC: Island Press, 2002.

Benfield, F. Kaid, Matthew D. Rami, and Donald D. T. Chen. *Once There Were Greenfields: How Urban Sprawl is Undermining America's Environment, Economy, and Social Fabric*. Washington, DC: Natural Resources Defense Council and Surface Transportation Project, 1999.

Bernick, Michael, and Robert Cervero. *Transit Villages in the 21st Century*. New York: McGraw-Hill, 1997.

Boarnet, Marlon G., and Randall Crane. *Travel by Design*. New York: Oxford University Press, 2001.

Bollier, David. *How Smart Growth Can Stop Sprawl: A Briefing Guide for Funders*. Washington, DC: Essential Books, 1998.

Borgren, Scott. "A Tale of Two Transit Networks: Separate but Not Equal." *CT Magazine,* September/October 1990.

Boyer, Kenneth D. *Principles of Transportation Economics*. New York: Addison-Wesley, 1998.

The Brookings Institution Center on Urban and Metropolitan Policy. *Moving Beyond Sprawl: The Challenge for Metropolitan Atlanta*. Washington, DC, 2000.

Bullard, Robert D. "Taken for a Ride in Metro Atlanta." *Orion Afield,* Fall 2000, 28–29.

Bullard, Robert D., J. Eugene Grigsby, and Charles Lee. *Residential Apartheid: The American Legacy*. Los Angeles: UCLA Center for African Studies, 1994.

Bullard, Robert D., and Glenn S. Johnson. *Just Transportation: Dismantling Race and Class Barriers to Mobility.* Gabriola Island, British Columbia: New Society Publishers, 1997.

Bullard, Robert D., Glenn S. Johnson, and Angel O. Torres. "Atlanta: Megasprawl." *Forum for Applied Research and Public Policy* 14, no. 3 (Fall 1999): 17–23.

_____. *Race, Equity, and Smart Growth: Why People of Color Must Speak for Themselves.* Atlanta: Environmental Justice Resource Center, 2000.

_____. "The Routes of American Apartheid." *Forum for Applied Research and Public Policy* 15, no. 3 (Fall 2000): 66–74.

_____. *Sprawl City: Race, Politics, and Planning in Atlanta.* Washington, DC: Island Press, 2000.

Burden, Dan. *Streets and Sidewalks, People and Cars: The Citizens' Guide to Traffic Calming.* Sacramento: Local Government Commission, 2000.

Burrington, Stephen H., and Veronika Thiebach. *Take Back Your Streets.* Boston: Conservation Law Foundation, 1998.

Calthorpe, Peter, and William Fulton. *The Regional City: Planning for the End of Sprawl.* Washington, DC: Island Press, 2001.

Carlson, Daniel, and Don Billen. *Transportation Corridor Management.* Seattle: Institute for Public Policy and Management, 1996.

Center for Community Change. *Getting to Work: An Organizer's Guide to Transportation Equity.* Washington, DC, August 1998.

Cervero, Robert. *The Transit Metropolis: A Global Inquiry.* Washington, DC: Island Press, 1998.

Conservation Law Foundation. *City Routes, City Rights: Building Livable Neighborhoods and Environmental Justice by Fixing Transportation.* Boston, June 1998.

Downs, Anthony. *Stuck in Traffic: Coping with the Peak-Hour Traffic Congestion.* Washington DC: The Brookings Institution and the Lincoln Institute of Land Policy, 1992.

Durning, Alan Thein. *The Car and the City: 24 Steps to Safe Streets and Healthy Communities.* Seattle: Northwest Environment Watch, 1996.

Edwards, John D., Jr. *Transportation Planning Handbook.* Washington, DC: Institute of Transportation Engineers, 1999.

Environmental Justice Resource Center. *Environmental Justice and Transportation: Building Model Partnerships Conference Proceedings.* Atlanta: Clark Atlanta University, 1996.

Florida Department of Transportation, Public Transit Office and National Center for Transit Research. *Community Impact Assessment and Environmental Justice for Transit Agencies: A Reference.* Tampa, FL: National Center for Transit Research, University of South Florida, 2002.

Forkenbrock, David J., and Lisa A. Schweitzer. *Environmental Justice and Transportation Investment Policy.* Public Policy Center, University of Iowa, 1997.

Gillham, Oliver. *The Limitless City: A Primer on the Urban Sprawl Debate.* Washington, DC: Island Press, 2002.

Gomez-Ibanez, Jose A., William R. Tyre, and Clifford Winston. *Essays in Transportation Economics and Policy: A Handbook in Honor of John R. Meyer.* Washington, DC: Brookings Institution Press, 1999.

Kay, J. H. *Asphalt Nation: How the Automobile Took Over America and How We Can Take It Back.* New York: Crown Publishers, Inc., 1997.

Litman, Todd. *Evaluating Transportation Equity.* Victoria, British Columbia: Victoria Transport Policy Institute, December 1997.

Mann, Eric. *A New Vision for Urban Transportation: The Bus Riders Union Makes History at the Intersection of Mass Transit, Civil Rights, and the Environment.* Los Angeles: Labor/Community Strategy Center, 1996.

Moe, Richard, and Carter Wilkie. *Changing Places: Rebuilding Community in the Age of Sprawl.* New York: Henry Holt and Company, 1997.

National Governors' Association. *How Smart Growth Can Address Environmental Justice Issues.* Washington, DC: Natural Resources Policy Studies, Division of the NGA Center for Best Practices, 2001.

Newman, Peter, and Jeffrey Kenworthy. *Sustainability and Cities: Overcoming Automobile Dependence.* Washington, DC: Island Press, 1999.

Oliver, M. L., and T. Shapiro. *Black Wealth/White Wealth: A New Perspective on Racial Inequality.* New York: Routledge, 1996.

O'Neill, David. *The Smart Growth Tool Kit: Community Profiles and Case Studies to Help Advance Smart Growth Initiatives.* Washington, DC: ULI-Urban Land Institute, 2000.

Orfield, Myron. *Metropolitics: A Regional Agenda for Community and Stability.* Washington, DC: Brookings Institution Press, 1997.

powell, john a. "Race, Poverty and Urban Sprawl: Access to Opportunities Through Regional Strategies." *Forum for Social Economics* 28, no. 2 (1999): 1–20.

Research Atlanta, Inc. *The Impact of MARTA on Station Area Development,* Atlanta: School of Policy Studies, Georgia State University, 1997.

Schmidt, Charles, W. "The Specter of Sprawl." *Environmental Health Perspectives* 106 (June 1998): 275.

Schrank, Davis, L., and Timothy J. Lomax. *Urban Mobility Report 2002.* College Station, TX: Texas Transportation Institute, Texas A&M University, 2002.

Sierra Club. *The Dark Side of the American Dream: The Cost and Consequences of Suburban Sprawl.* College Park, Maryland: Sierra Club (August 1998).

Surface Transportation Policy Project. "Mean Streets 2000: Pedestrian Safety, Health and Federal Transportation Spending." *Progress*, June/July 2000, 2.

US Department of Transportation. *Community Impact Assessment: A Quick Reference for Transportation*. Washington, DC: Federal Highway Administration, 1996.

US Department of Transportation Federal Highway Administration. Draft. *Environmental Justice and National Environmental Policy Act Process for Federal Highway Administration: A Quick Reference for Transportation*. May 1999.

————. *Transportation and Environmental Justice: Case Studies*. 2000

White, M. C., R. Etzel, W. D. Wilcox, and C. Lloyd. "Exacerbations of Childhood Asthma and Ozone Pollution in Atlanta." *Environmental Research* 65 (1994): 56–68.

Winston, Clifford and Chad Shirley. *Alternate Route: Toward Efficient Urban Transportation*. Washington, DC: Brookings Institution Press, 1998.

Resource Organizations

Alternatives for Community and Environment (ACE)
2343 Washington Street, 2nd Floor
Roxbury, MA 02119
Telephone: (617) 442-3343
Fax: (617) 442-2425
info@ace-ej.org
http://www.ace-ej.org/

Bethel New Life
Bethel New Life, Incorporated
4950 West Thomas
Chicago, IL 60651
Telephone: (773) 473-7870
Fax: (773) 473-7871
agordon@bethelnewlife.org
http://www.bethelnewlife.org/

The Brookings Institution Center on Urban and Metropolitan Policy
The Brookings Institution
1775 Massachusetts Avenue, NW
Washington, DC 20036
Telephone: (202) 797-6000
Fax: (202) 797-6004
brookinfo@brook.edu
http://www.brook.edu/dybdocroot/es/urban/urban.htm

Building Opportunities for Self-Sufficiency (BOSS)
2065 Kittredge Street, Suite E
Berkeley, CA 94704
Telephone: (510) 649-1930
Fax: (510) 649-0627
bossmail@self-sufficiency.org
http://www.self-sufficiency.org/

The Bus Riders Union (BRU)
3780 Wilshire Boulevard, Suite 1200
Los Angeles, CA 90010
Telephone: (213) 387-2800
Fax: (213) 387-3500
busridersunion@mindspring.com
http://www.busridersunion.org

Center for Community Change (CCC)
1000 Wisconsin Avenue, NW
Washington, DC 20007
Telephone: (202) 342-0567
Fax: (202) 333-5462
info@communitychange.org
http://www.communitychange.org/default.asp

Center for Neighborhood Technology (CNT)
2125 W. North Avenue
Chicago, IL 60647
Telephone: (773) 278-4800
Fax: (773) 278-3840
info@cnt.org.
http://www.cnt.org/

Civil Rights Project
Harvard University
125 Mount Auburn Street, 3rd Floor
Cambridge, MA 02138
Telephone: (617) 496-6367
Fax: (617) 495-5210
crp@harvard.edu
http://www.civilrightsproject.harvard.edu

Conservation Law Foundation (CLF)
62 Summer Street
Boston, MA 02110-1016
Telephone: (617) 350-0990
Fax: (617) 350-4030
issues@clf.org
http://www.clf.org/

Deep South Center for Environmental Justice (DSCEJ)
Xavier University of Louisiana
1 Drexel Drive 45b
New Orleans, LA 70125
Telephone: (504) 304-3324
Fax: (504) 304-3329
dscej@aol.com
http://www.xula.edu/dscej/

Detroiters Working for Environmental Justice (DWEJ)
12101 Mack Service Drive
Detroit, MI 48215
Telephone: (313) 821-1064
Fax: (313) 821-1072
http://www.members.aol.com/dwdwej/

Environmental Justice Resource Center (EJRC)
Clark Atlanta University
223 James P. Brawley Drive, SW
Atlanta, Georgia 30314
Telephone: (404) 880-6911
Fax: (404) 880-6909
ejrc@cau.edu
http://www.ejrc.cau.edu

Institute of Transportation Studies (ITS)
University of California Berkeley
109 McLaughlin Hall
Berkeley, CA 94720-1720
Telephone: (510) 642-3585
Fax: (510) 642-1246
its@its.berkeley.edu
http://www.its.berkeley.edu/index.html

Labor/Community Strategy Center (LCSC)
3780 Wilshire Boulevard, Suite 1200
Los Angeles, CA 90010
Telephone: (213) 387-2800
Fax: (213) 387-3500
laborctr@igc.org
http://www.thestrategycenter.org

The Latino Issues Forum (LIF)
785 Market Street, 3rd Floor
San Francisco, CA 94103
Telephone: (415) 284-7220
Fax: (415) 284-7222
lifcentral@lif.org
http://www.lif.org/

Metropolitan Atlanta Transportation Equity Coalition (MATEC)
PO Box 42350
Atlanta, GA 30311
Telephone: (404) 755-2294
Fax: (404) 755-0575
matecatlanta@yahoo.com

Montgomery Transportation Coalition (MTC)
600 S. Court Street, Room 200
Montgomery, AL 36105
Phone: (334) 717-5464
Fax: (334) 244-3718
reclaimingthedream@envirocitizen.com
http://www.motranco.org

National Neighborhood Coalition (NNC)
1030 15th Street, NW, Suite 325
Washington, DC 20005
Telephone: (202) 408-8553
Fax: (202) 408-8551
nncnnc@erols.com
http://www.neighborhoodcoalition.org/

New York Environmental Justice Alliance (NYCEJA)
115 West 30th Street, Suite 709
New York, NY 10001
Telephone: (212) 239-8882
Fax: (212) 239-2838
info.nyceja@nyceja.org
http://www.nyceja.org/

People Organizing to Demand Environmental Rights (PODER!)
474 Valencia Street, Suite 125
San Francisco, CA 94103
Telephone: (415) 431-4210
Fax: (415) 431-8525
poder@igc.org

People United for a Better Oakland (PUEBLO)
1920 Park Boulevard
Oakland, CA 94606
Telephone: (510) 452-2010
Fax: (510) 452-2017
info@peopleunited.org
http://www.peopleunited.org/

Rutgers Voorhees Transportation Institute
Rutgers, State University of New Jersey
33 Livingston Avenue, 5th Floor
New Brunswick, NJ 08901
Telephone: (732) 932-6812, ext. 700
Fax: (732) 932-3714
cdanku@rci.rutgers.edu
http://www.policy.rutgers.edu/tpi/

Save Our Valley (SOV)
5218 Rainier Avenue South
Seattle, WA 98118
Telephone: (206) 721-9898
info@saveourvalley.org
http://www.saveourvalley.org

Sierra Club
85 Second Street, 2nd Floor
San Francisco, CA 94105-3441
Phone: (415) 977-5500
Fax: (415) 977-5799
information@sierraclub.org
http://www.sierraclub.org/

Smart Growth America (SGA)
1100 17th Street NW, 10th Floor
Washington, DC 20036
Telephone: (202) 715-2035
Fax: (202) 466-2247
sga@smartgrowthamerica.org
http://www.smartgrowthamerica.org

Southern Resource Center
Federal Highway Administration (FHWA)
61 Forsyth Street, SW, Suite 17T26
Atlanta, GA 30303
Telephone: (404) 562-3574
Fax: (404) 562-3700
hrcso.fhwa@fhwa.dot.gov
http://www.fhwa.dot.gov/resourcecenters/southern/

Sprawl Watch Clearinghouse
1400 16th Street, NW, Suite 225
Washington, DC 20036
Telephone: (202) 332-7000
Fax: (202) 265-0182
allison@sprawlwatch.org
http://www.sprawlwatch.org/

Surface Transportation Policy Project (STPP)
1100 17th Street, NW, 10th Floor
Washington, DC 20036
Telephone: (202) 466-2636
Fax: (202) 466-2247
stpp@transact.org
http://www.transact.org/

Transit Riders League of Metropolitan Baltimore (TRLMB)
A Project of Citizens Planning and Housing Association
218 W. Saratoga, 5th Floor
Baltimore, MD 21201
Telephone: (410) 539-1369 x244
Fax: (410) 625-7895
carolineh@cphabaltimore.org
http://www.transitriders.org/

Transportation and Land Use Coalition (TALC, formerly BATLUC)
414 13th Street, 5th Floor
Oakland, CA 94612
Telephone: (510) 740-3150
Fax: (510) 740-3131
info@transcoalition.org
http://www.transcoalition.org/

Urban Habitat Program (UHP)
436 14th Street, Suite 1205
Oakland, CA 94612-2723
Telephone: (510) 839-9510
Fax: (510) 839-9610
info@urbanhabitat.org
http://www.urbanhabitat.org/

Victoria Transportation Policy Institute (VTPI)
1250 Rudlin Street
Victoria, BC, V8V 3R7, Canada
Telephone and Fax (250) 360-1560
info@vtpi.org
http://www.vtpi.org

West Harlem Environmental Action (WHE ACT)
271 W. 125th Street, Suite 308
New York, NY 10027-4424
Telephone: (212) 961-1000
Fax: (212) 961-1015
Berlinda@weact.org
http://www.weact.org/

Video Resources

Bus Riders Union Film

86 min. The Labor/Community Strategy Center (2000).

A new documentary by Academy Award-winning cinematographer Haskell Wexler that traces three years in the life of the Los Angeles Bus Riders Union as it forges a powerful multiracial movement to fight transit racism, clean up LA's lethal auto pollution, and win billion-dollar victories for real mass transit for the masses.

The Labor/Community Strategy Center
3780 Wilshire Boulevard, Suite 1200
Los Angeles, CA 90010
Telephone: (213) 387-2800
Fax: (213) 387-3500
laborctr@igc.org
http://www.thestrategycenter.org/

Divided City: The Route to Racism

22 min. Films for the Humanities and Science (2000).

An excerpt from the ABC News *Nightline* show, in which where the death of Cynthia Wiggins from Buffalo, New York, is discussed. Ms. Wiggins was killed by a dumptruck while crossing a seven-lane highway to get to her job at the Walden Galleria Mall. The mall's operators and planners were charged with racism because the bus route that served inner-city residents was prevented from stopping at the shopping mall.

Films for the Humanities & Sciences
PO Box 2053
Princeton, NJ 08543-2053
Telephone: (800) 257-5126 or (609) 275-1400
Fax: (609) 275-3767
custserv@films.com
http://www.films.com

Divided Highways

85 min. Films for the Humanities and Sciences (1997).

About the interstate highway system, and combines archival material, newsreels, and interviews to describe the impact of what has been called the world's largest public works project. The video shows how the interstate affects our community, culture, regionalism, and freedom. The highway system has altered our sense of space, fueled our megaeconomy, knifed into the hearts of thriving city neighborhoods, and changed the lives of millions of people over the forty years it took to build.

Films for the Humanities & Sciences
PO Box 2053
Princeton, NJ 08543-2053
Telephone: (800) 257-5126 or (609) 275-1400
Fax: (609) 275-3767
custserv@films.com
http://www.films.com

Fat of the Land

60 min. Great Lakes Television Consortium (2001).

The second hour of the *Sprawling of America* video (see below). This video examines the economics behind suburban sprawl, studies the quality of life in today's American suburbs, and searches the country for innovative solutions to the loss of farmland and reckless third-ring suburban development.

Great Lakes Television Consortium
5000 LSA Building
500 South State Street
Ann Arbor, MI 48109
Telephone: (734) 764-9210
Fax: (734) 647-3488
gltv@michiganradio.org.

Just Transportation

45 min. Clark Atlanta University: EJRC-CAU Television (1996).

Includes highlights from the 1995 Atlanta, Georgia conference entitled "Environmental Justice and Transportation: Building Model Partnerships Conference." The Atlanta conference brought together grassroots organizers, civil rights activists, local, state, tribal, and federal transportation planners, public officials, legal experts, and academics to discuss strategies for building livable and just communities. Transportation issues in people of color communities are explored and shot on location in Atlanta, Chicago, Los Angeles, San Francisco, Harlem (New York City), and Washington, DC.

Environmental Justice Resource Center
Clark Atlanta University
Atlanta, GA 30314
Telephone: (404) 880-6911
Fax: (404) 880-6909
ejrc@cau.edu
http://www.ejrc.cau.edu.

Paving the American Dream: Southern Cities Shores & Sprawl

55 min. University of North Carolina, Wilmington, NC (2001).

A documentary of what led to the explosive growth along the southeastern seaboard. In 1960, 8 million people lived along the coast. That number is expected to reach nearly 23 million by the year 2015—a staggering 188 percent increase. Inland areas also suffer from unmanaged growth. Issues such as traffic congestion, air and water pollution, disappearing farms, forests, and coastline all lead to a declining quality of life and environment.

UNCW Division of University Advancement
601 South College Road
Wilmington, NC 28403
Telephone: (910) 962-2650
cowanb@uncwil.edu
http://www.uncwil.edu/smartgrowth.

Sprawl: Inner Cities and Outer Suburbs

60 min. Films for the Humanities and Sciences (2001).

To at least one resident of the fictional city of Metropolis, a new outer suburb being planned for pristine farmland sounds like the American Dream come true. His brother, also a Metropolite but an advocate of smart growth, sees it as a nightmare. Moderated by Harvard Law School's Arthur Miller, this Fred Friendly seminar seeks to understand the housing situation facing the United States—a burgeoning nation that creates more than 1.5 million new households per year.

Films for the Humanities & Sciences
PO Box 2053
Princeton, NJ 08543-2053
Telephone: (800) 257-5126 or (609) 275-1400
Fax: (609) 275-3767
custserv@films.com
http://www.films.com

The Sprawling of America

60 min. Great Lakes Television Consortium (2001).

Provides a comprehensive examination of the devastating social, economic, and environmental impacts of sprawl on urban and rural communities. This video documents how America grew from cities to suburbs, how the movement changed society, and how suburban communities are now reevaluating their quality of life.

Great Lakes Television Consortium

5000 LSA Building
500 South State Street
Ann Arbor, MI 48109
Telephone: (734) 764-9210
Fax: (734) 647-3488
gltv@michiganradio.org.

Taken for a Ride.
52 min. New Day Films (1997).
Jim Klein and Martha Olson provide an overview of the tragic story of a secret auto/oil industry campaign, led by General Motors, to buy and dismantle America's streetcars. Across the nation, tracks were torn up and buses took their place. The highway lobby then pushed through Congress an urban freeway system, which increased auto dependence and elicited opposition. Seventeen city freeways were stopped by citizens who would become the leading edge of a new environmental movement. This video provides a revealing history of our cities in the twentieth century that is also a meditation on corporate power, citizen protest, and the social and environmental implications of transportation.

New Day Films
22 D Hollywood Avenue
Hohokus, NJ 07423
Telephone: (888)-367-9154
Fax: (201) 652-1973
orders@newday.com.

Tango 73: A Bus Rider's Diary
28 min. New Day Films (1998).
A documentary film by Gabriela Quiros that illustrates the importance of public transportation. The documentary uncovers the social rituals of bus riders who travel the number 73 busline along the east shore of the San Francisco Bay Area.

New Day Films
22 D Hollywood Avenue
Hohokus, NJ 07423
Telephone: (888)-367-9154
Fax: (201) 652-1973
orders@newday.com.

Transportation: A History
53 min. Films for the Humanities and Sciences (1999).
Over thousands of years, we have traveled by foot, horseback, carriage, and sailing ship. The advent of steamships, trains, automobiles, and airplanes has changed the way we get around in society. In this video, historians, researchers, and transportation officials examine the revolutionary impact of modern transportation on society and on the environment, where pollution is effecting all of us.

Films for the Humanities & Sciences
PO Box 2053
Princeton, NJ 08543-2053
Telephone: (800) 257-5126 or (609) 275-1400
Fax: (609) 275-3767
custserv@films.com
http://www.films.com

Understanding Urban Sprawl

47 min. Films for the Humanities and Sciences (1998).

Dr. David Suzuki examines the social, economic, and environmental implications of "sprawl," and low-density development that spreads out from the edges of cities and towns. For decades, suburban housing has carried the promise of paradise, but the need for continuous infrastructure development and the intensification of sprawl-related ecological issues, which are eroding health and quality of life, are making the true impact of suburbia painfully clear in the areas surrounding Los Angeles, Mexico City, and Vancouver, British Columbia. However, Portland, Oregon, has become a model of what can be accomplished when administrators, businesses, and residents commit themselves to slowing sprawl and reestablishing the amenities that make for a happy and healthy community.

Films for the Humanities & Sciences
PO Box 2053
Princeton, NJ 08543-2053
Telephone: (800) 257-5126 or (609) 275-1400
Fax: (609) 275-3767
custserv@films.com
http://www.films.com

About the Editors and Contributors

Robert D. Bullard is the Ware Professor of Sociology and director of the Environmental Justice Resource Center at Clark Atlanta University (CAU). As an environmental sociologist, he has conducted research and written extensively on environmental justice, urban land use, transportation, urban sprawl, smart growth, community development, minority health, training, industrial facility siting, environmental quality, and housing issues for over two decades. Prior to joining the CAU faculty in 1994, he was a professor of sociology at the University of California at Riverside, and visiting professor in the Center for African American Studies at UCLA. He is the co-editor with Glenn S. Johnson of *Just Transportation: Dismantling Race and Class Barriers to Mobility* (New Society Publishers, 1997). He is co-editor with Glenn S. Johnson and Angel O. Torres of *Sprawl City: Race, Politics, and Planning in Atlanta* (Island Press, 2000). He is co-editor with Julian Agyeman and Bob Evans of *Just Sustainabilities: Development in an Unequal World* (Earthscan/MIT Press, 2003).

Stuart Cohen is executive director of the Transportation and Land Use Coalition (TALC). Founded in 1997, TALC has become a major player in Bay Area transportation and growth issues by complementing strong grassroots campaigns with high quality policy analysis and strategic media efforts. Previously, Cohen worked with the International Council for Local Environmental Initiatives, researching and promoting alternative fuel and transportation-demand strategies for municipalities in the United States. Cohen has authored eight reports on transportation and regional planning. He received a master's degree in public policy from the University of California at Berkeley.

Michelle Ernst is the senior analyst for the Surface Transportation Policy Project (STPP) in Washington, DC. Since joining STPP in 1998, she has authored many reports on transportation and its impact on family budgets, air pollution and traffic safety, including *Clearing the Air: Public Health Threats from Cars and Heavy Duty Vehicles—Why We Need to Protect Federal Clean Air Laws*; *Mean Streets 2002: Pedestrian Safety, Health and Federal Transportation Spending*; and *Measuring Up: The Trend Toward Voter*

Approved Transportation Funding. Ernst also convenes STPP's Energy and Environment Issue Team, a network of national and regional environmental organizations committed to transportation reform. She holds a master's degree in environmental policy from Yale University.

Omar Freilla is the program director for Sustainable South Bronx, a newly founded organization that seeks to make environmental justice alternatives a reality. Currently, he is the Chairperson of the Board of Directors for the New York City Environmental Justice Alliance. He is the former transportation coordinator for the New York City Environmental Justice Alliance, a coalition of community-based organizations in New York City working for environmental justice. He is also a resident of the Hunts Point neighborhood in the South Bronx.

Caroline Harmon is a rider of the number 36 bus line in Baltimore, and is the current organizer for the Transit Riders League. Her work has been in anti-poverty and anti-homelessness advocacy, mediation, and direct service to survivors of domestic violence. A graduate of the University of California at Berkeley, she is currently completing the Community Organizing program at the University of Maryland School of Social Work.

Jeff Hobson is policy director at the Transportation and Land Use Coalition (TALC). He helped found the Access to Opportunities project in November 1998 to focus on the transportation needs of low-income communities. He authored *Clearing the Road to Work: Developing a Transportation Lifeline for Low-Income Residents in Alameda County.* He has also provided policy analysis for TALC's Transportation Justice Working Group, which brings together representatives of low-income communities and social justice groups to coordinate and increase public participation in transportation decisions. Hobson began chairing TALC's East Bay Chapter at its inception in 1999, where he spent the next two years as a major force behind Measure B, Alameda County's successful $1.4 billion transportation initiative. Hobson has experience as a policy analyst and an advocate on environmental justice issues regarding transportation and industrial pollution, and has worked in nonprofit organizations, a government agency, and the private sector. Hobson holds a master's degree from the Energy and Resources Group at the University of California at Berkeley and a bachelor's degree in physics from Harvard University.

Nancy Jakowitsch is the director of policy development for the Surface Transportation Policy Project (STPP) in Washington, DC. She has also introduced transportation justice, affordable housing, community development, and civil rights partners to social justice opportunities in TEA-21 reauthorization, and managed the organization's effort to educate over sixty transportation decision-makers in the US to European approaches to transportation, land use, and quality of life issues. Prior to joining STPP in 1998, Jakowitsch worked as a consultant to National Center for Economic and Security Alternatives. Jakowitsch holds a bachelor's degree in environmental policy from the American University.

Glenn S. Johnson is a research associate in the Environmental Justice Resource Center and associate professor in the Department of Sociology and Criminal Justice at Clark Atlanta University. He coordinates several major research activities including transportation, urban sprawl, smart growth, public involvement, facility siting, and toxics. He has worked on environmental policy issues for nine years and assisted Robert D. Bullard in the research for the third edition of *Dumping in Dixie: Race, Class, and Environmental Quality* (Westview Press, 2000). He is co-editor of the book *Just Transportation: Dismantling Race and Class Barriers to Mobility* (New Society Publishers, 1997). He also co-edited with Robert D. Bullard and Angel O. Torres *Sprawl City: Race, Politics, and Planning in Atlanta* (Island Press, 2000).

Ayanna King is a native of Pittsburgh. She has a master's degree in urban planning from the University of Pittsburgh. King has over twelve years of experience in community development, project management, and organizational development. She served as the community consultant for the Pittsburgh Transportation Equity Project (PTEP) during its formation. Currently, King serves as the Project Director for the PTEP and serves on the following boards: New Horizon Theater, Sustainable Pittsburgh's Advisory Board (co-chair for the Diversity and Civic Engagement Committee), Point Park Alumni Association, Pittsburgh Family Development, and Carlow Hill College Entrepreneur Advisory Board.

John Lewis is a long-time civil rights activist and US Congressman from Georgia's Fifth District. He is currently serving his eighth term in Congress. Lewis has been profiled in numerous national publications and network television and radio broadcasts, including a profile in a *Time Magazine* article entitled "Saints Among Us" (December 29, 1975); and profiles in the *New Yorker* (October 4, 1993); *Parade Magazine* (February 4, 1996); and the *New Republic* (July 1, 1996). Lewis, with writer Michael D'Orso, authored *Walking with the Wind: A Memoir of the Movement* (June 1998). The book is a first-hand account of this nation's civil rights movement.

Eric Mann is executive director of the Los Angeles-based Labor/Community Strategy Center. He has been a civil rights, anti-Vietnam war, labor, and environmental organizer for thirty years, and has worked with the Congress of Racial Equality, Students for a Democratic Society, and the United Auto Workers, including eight years on auto assembly lines. His books include *Comrade George: An Investigation Into the Life, Political Thought, and Assassination of George Jackson* (Harper and Row, 1974), and *Taking on General Motors: Labor Insurgency in a UAW Local* (UCLA Institute of Industrial Relations, 1987). He also published *Dispatches from Durban* (Frontline Press, 2002).

Amy Menzer has been active on campaigns for environmental justice in Chester, Pennsylvania, unionization in Philadelphia, and living wages for workers at Johns Hopkins Institutions in Baltimore, and was the first chair of the Transit Riders League. After serving as the League's organizer, she is now director of housing at Citizens Planning and Housing Association, and is completing her Ph.D. in human geography at Johns Hopkins. Her dissertation is entitled "Smart Growth and the Scaling of Community Interest: Examining the Relationships Between Growth Management, Social Equity, and Community Revitalization in Baltimore County, Maryland."

Brian Nogrady is the coordinator for the East Light Rail Transit Main Line Park Coalition. He has worked as an advocate for innovative transportation planning and equity in transit investments and policies in Pittsburgh, Pennsylvania, since 1996. He has developed extensive plans to integrate bike trails, greenways, and park space with the transit system to improve the livability, sustainability, and economic future of Pittsburgh's eastern communities. Nogrady has given numerous presentations in the Pittsburgh metropolitan area on the economic benefits of bike trails and greenways. He holds a bachelor's degree from Carnegie Mellon University. He would like to acknowledge Jonathan Hill and David Rodes for their contributions and thank his parents Al and Norma Nogrady and sister Lorraine Nogrady for their endless support.

Angel O. Torres is a geographic information systems training specialist (GIS) with the Environmental Justice Resource Center at Clark Atlanta University. He has a master's degree in city planning from Georgia Institute of Technology, with a concentration in GIS. He has expertise in several mapping programs including Landview III, Atlas-GIS, ARC-Info, and ArcView. Torres previously worked for the Corporation for Olympic Development of Atlanta and the Atlanta Project, where he was the GIS specialist on several neighborhood and housing redevelopment plans. He co-edited with Robert D. Bullard and Glenn S. Johnson *Sprawl City: Race, Politics, and Planning in Atlanta* (Island Press, 2000).

Index

A

ABAG (Association of Bay Area Governments), 111, 112
AC Transit, 102, 104
ACTA (Alameda County Transportation Agency), 105, 106
ADA (Americans with Disabilities Act), 59, 62–63, 67
ADA (Atlanta Development Authority), 56
air quality, 5, 6, 26, 59, 85, 100, 132, 163–64, 167–68, 182, 191
Alabama Christian Movement for Human Rights, 18
Alameda County, 103–4
Alexander v. Sandoval, 33, 44, 45, 172
Allegheny County, 123
American cities, 18–19
APA (American Planning Association), 183, 184
Arteaga, Luis, 107
Assembly Transportation Committee, 37
ATEP (Atlanta Transportation Equity Project), 58
Atlanta, 49–69
Atlanta Housing Authority, 54
automobiles, 3–4, 166, 181, 182

B

Baltimore, 145–57
Baltimore Regional Rail Plan, 153
BART (Bay Area Rapid Transit), 108–10

Baton Rouge, 16
Bay Area RTP, 100–116
bicycle safety, 107–8
Billions for Buses campaign, 36
Black Brotherhood of Sleeping Car Porters Union, 16
Black Metropolis, 19
Bliss, Donald, 43
BOSS (Building Opportunities for Self-Sufficiency), 101–105, 113
Bronx, 79–80, 85–91
Brooklyn, 77–79, 81–85
Brown, Henry, 15
Brown v. Board of Education, 1, 16, 18
BRTB (Baltimore Regional Transportation Board), 146, 147
BRU (Bus Riders Union), 2, 33, 39–46, 59
Bullard, Robert D., 1, 9, 10, 15, 49, 179
Bus Riders Union documentary, 59
bus shelters, 64
bus stations, 133–34
bus versus rail, 34–36
buses (diesel), 5, 7–8, 28, 63, 68, 87, 121–123, 125–126, 128, 131–135, 179

C

C-TRAN, 57
California Highway Patrol, 107
Caro, Robert, 79, 87
Carter Administration, 87
Carter, Majora, 94
Cayton, Horace R., 19

CCT (Cobb Community Transit), 57
Center for Disease Control, 182
Chicago's South Side ghetto, 19
Civil Rights Act, Title VI, 23, 33, 44–45, 46, 59, 63–65, 67, 170–172, 175
Clark, Kenneth, 19
Clean Air Act Amendments of 1990, 7, 164–165, 170
Clean Air Act of 1970, 167
Clinton Administration, 23
CMAQ (Congestion Mitigation and Air Quality), 164, 165
CNG (Compressed Natural Gas), 55, 60, 63–64, 68
CNT (Center for Neighborhood Technology), 182
Cohen, Stuart, 10, 99
Confronting Environmental Racism, 21
CORE (Congress for Racial Equality), 18
Corless, James, 107
CPHA (Citizens Planning and Housing Association), 145–57

D

Daley, Mike, 106
Davis, Mike, 108
Dexter Avenue Baptist Church, 16
disability discrimination, 62, 150
Disability Law and Policy Center of Georgia, 62
discrimination, 1, 5, 8, 19, 20, 28, 34, 36, 40, 44–45, 52, 59, 62, 122, 129, 137, 138
DOT (Department of Transportation), 6, 24, 28, 66, 162, 170, 172, 179
Drake, St. Claire, 19
Driven to Spend, 182
Du Bois, W.E.B., 1
Dumping in Dixie: Race, Class and Environmental Quality, 21

E

EA (The Environmental Assessment), 129
East Louisiana Railroad, 15
economic development policies, 181
EIS (Environmental Impact Statement), 132

environmental justice, 2, 10, 20–21, 23–25, 28, 58, 66, 81, 85–87, 90, 92–93, 106, 114–115, 138–139, 161–163, 168–175
EJRC (Environmental Justice Resource Center), 58, 138
Ellison, Ralph, 18
employment, 169–70, 191–92
Environmental Defense, 105
environmental issues, 100, 103, 104, 111–15, 131–33, 161
EPA (Environmental Protection Agency), 103, 21, 132, 191
Ernst, Michelle, 10, 161
Executive Order on Environmental Justice (EO 12898), 23–24, 170, 172, 175
Ezzard, Martha, 64

F

Fair Share Housing, 111
farebox recovery requirement, 154–55
Federal Aid Highway Act of 1970, 23
Federal Highway Trust Fund, 173
federal transportation laws, 174
FHWA (Federal Highway Administration), 81, 83, 162, 170, 181
First National People of Color Environmental Leadership Summit, 22–23
Ford, Nathaniel, 59, 68
Freedom Riders, 1, 2, 17–18
Freilla, Omar, 10, 75
Frey, William H., 186
FTA (Federal Transit Authority), 170

G

GAO (General Accounting Office), 21
gasoline consumption, 3
GECC (Gowanus Expressway Community Coalition), 83, 84
gentrification, 91–92, 94
geographic inequity, 27
Georgia Department of Transportation, 180
Giuliani Administration, 76
grassroots groups, 27–28, 76
Greenbelt Alliance, 111
gridlock, 181

growth, 183–85
GRTA (Georgia Regional Transportation Agency), 57–58
Gwinnett County Transit, 57

H

Hahn, James K., 44
Harmon, Caroline, 10, 145–57
Hartsfield, William, 51
Hatter, Terry, 39, 43
health, 167–68, 189, 190
Highway Statistics, 181
highways, 4, 179, 180
Hobson, Jeff, 10, 99
horizontal equity, 26
housing, 111–12, 187–88
Hunt, James, 20
Hunt's Dump, 20

I

inner-city transit, 5
Invisible Man, 18
ISTEA (Intermodal Surface Transportation Efficiency), 6, 163–65, 170, 174, 180

J

Jakowitsch, Nancy, 10, 161
JARC (Job Access and Reverse Commute), 164, 165
Jim Crow laws, 8, 16
Johnson, Glenn S., 9, 10, 49, 179
Just Transportation: Dismantling Race and Class Barriers to Mobility, 8, 9, 21

K

Katz, Richard, 37
Kerner Commission, 19
King, Ayanna, 10, 121
King, Martin Luther, Jr., 16, 17
Korean Immigrant Workers Advocates, 40, 45

L

Labor/Community Strategy Center, Bus Riders Union, et al. v. Los Angeles County MTA, 40, 61
LACTC (Los Angeles County Transportation Commission), 34, 36, 37
Latino Issues Forum, 101

LCSC (Labor/Community Strategy Center), 33, 36–46, 58
LEM (location-efficient mortgages), 192
Lewis, John, 2, 17
LIF (Latino Issues Forum), 107, 108
Loftin, Daniel, 94
Logan, John, 187
Los Angeles, 33–46, 58
LOTS (Locally Operated Transit Systems), 147
Louisiana, 15–18
LRT (light rail transit), 55, 121–41
LRV (light rail vehicles), 131, 132, 134

M

Maglev Project (Pennsylvania High Speed Maglev), 135–36
Mann, Eric, 9, 33, 59
MARC, 147, 150
Marcus, Sherrill, 59
MARTA (Metropolitan Atlanta Rapid Transit Authority), 52–69
MATEC (Metropolitan Atlanta Transportation Equity), 58–61, 64–68
Mean Streets, 190
Measure A, 109, 110, 115
Measure B, 104, 106, 107, 113, 115
Melrose Commons Plan, 92
Menzer, Amy, 10, 145–57
MFT (Mon/Fayette Toll Road), 136–37
MIA (Montgomery Improvement Association), 16, 17
Milwaukee, 91
MLK-EB (Martin Luther King, Jr. East Busway), 121–41
Montgomery, 16–18
Montgomery Bus Boycott, 1, 2, 16–17
Moses, Robert, 10, 75–94
Moving Art, 64
Moynihan, Daniel Patrick, 163, 180
MPO (Metropolitan Planning Organization), 6, 7, 28, 163, 170, 174, 190
MPPACT (MARTA Police Proactively Attacking Crime Trends), 68
MTA (Los Angeles County Metropolitan Transportation Authority), 33–46

MTA (Maryland Transit Administration), 145–57
MTC (Metropolitan Transportation Commission), 100–116

N

NAACP (National Association for the Advancement of Colored People), 18
NAACP Legal Defense and Educational Fund, 40, 44
National Advisory Commission on Civil Disorders, 19
National Trust for Historic Preservation, 189
NCLC (Nashville Christian Leadership Conference), 18
NEPA (National Environmental Policy Act), 23, 24, 165, 170
New Roads to Chaos, 180
New York City, 75–94
Nixon, E. D., 16
No Justice, No Tax, 109
Nogrady, Brian, 10, 121
Non-Profit Housing Association of Northern California, 112
North Carolina, 20–21
Nos Quedamos/We Stay, 85, 92
NYCEJA (New York City Environmental Justice Alliance), 85–91
NYMTC (New York Metropolitan Transportation Council), 84
NYS DOT (New York State Department of Transportation), 81–90, 94

O

obesity, 190
Office of Environmental Justice, 25
office space, 191
Olympic Games 1996, 55
Order on Environmental Justice, 24

P

Parks, Rosa, 1, 2, 16
Pasadena Blue Line Rail, 37
Pascal, Bob, 149
PAT (The Port Authority of Allegheny County), 121–41
PCB (polychlorinated biphenyl), 20–21

pedestrian safety, 107–8, 168–69, 190
Perry Homes public housing development, 53
Peterson, Rachel, 103
Phillips, Dawn, 101, 106
Pittsburgh, 121–41
Plessy, Homer, 15
Plessy v. Ferguson, 1, 15
Policy Guide on Smart Growth, 183
Portland, 91, 130
Power Broker, The, 79, 87
Pratt Institute Center for Community and Environmental Development, 86
Principles of Environmental Justice, 22–23
procedural inequity, 27
Proposition A, 35
Proposition C, 35, 36
PTC (Pennsylvania Turnpike Commission), 136
PTEP (Pittsburgh Transportation Equity Project), 138–41
public transit, 4

R

race in America, 185–87
Race in American Public Schools, 188
racism, 18–19, 193–94
regional control, 173–74
Rehabilitation Act, Section 504, 62
Rockefeller, Nelson, 79–80
RPA (Regional Plan Association), 83
RTD (Southern California Rapid Transit District), 34, 36, 37
RTP (regional transportation plan), 7, 100, 151
Rubin, Thomas A., 61

S

Safe Routes to School bill, 108
San Francisco, 91, 99–116
Sanford, Mary, 53
SBRWA (Southern Bronx River Watershed Alliance), 87–91
Schaeffer, Donald, 150
schools, 188–89
SCLC (Southern Christian Leadership Conference), 18, 40, 45
Second National People of Color

Environmental Leadership Summit, 22–23
segregation, 187–89
separate but equal, 1, 15
Separate Car Act, 15
Shelton, Stacy, 64
Sierra Club, 104–106
Silicon Valley, 109
Sjoquist, David, 51
slum clearance, 76
SMART Team program, 68
SNCC (Student Nonviolent Coordinating Committee), 18
social inequity, 27
social justice, 100, 103, 115
Soto, Nell, 108
Souls of Black Folks, The, 1
sprawl, 182, 184, 187–92
STPP (Surface Transportation Policy Project), 6, 100, 108, 163, 182, 190
suburban America, 179–81, 184
suburban commuter transit, 5
Sustainable America, 183

T

TALC (Transportation and Land Use Coalition), 99–116
TANF (Temporary Assistance for Needy Families), 164
TCSP (Transportation and Community and System Preservation, 164, 165
TE (Transportation Enhancements program), 164, 165
TEA-21 (Transportation Efficiency Act of the 21st century), 6, 7, 163, 164, 170, 174, 175
Texas Transportation Institute, 181
The Point CDC, 85, 86
Thirteenth Amendment, 15
TIP (transportation improvement program), 7
TMA (transportation management areas), 6
TOD (transit-oriented development), 56, 164, 192
Toronto, 91
Torres, Angel O., 9, 10, 49, 179
Torres-Flemming, Alexie, 86
toxic waste sites, 21

Transit Riders League of Baltimore, 145–57
transit stations, 133–34
transportation
costs, 2, 110, 166
discrimination, 166
equity, 25–27
investment, 164
justice, 161–75
planning, 19–20, 162, 193–94
Transportation Injustice, 110
Tri-State Transportation Campaign, 86, 89

U

UCC (United Church of Christ Commission for Racial Justice), 21
UDL (United Defense League), 16
UPROSE (United Puerto Rican Organization of Sunset Park), 81–85
Urban Ecology, 111
Urban Habitat, 101
Urban Mobility Study of 2002, 181
urban renewal, 76
US Commission on Civil Rights, 172

V

vertical equity, 26
VTA (Santa Clara Valley Transportation Authority), 109, 110

W

walking, 189
Warren County, 20–21
Washington, DC, 153–54
Washington Metropolitan Area Transit Authority, 153
We Stay/Nos Quedamos, 85, 92
Wexler, Haskell, 59
World Class Transit for the Bay Area, 108

Y

Yeampierre, Elizabeth, 81
Youth Ministries for Peace and Justice, 86
Youth Ministries RIVER team, 86, 89

Z

Zukas, Hale, 102

About South End Press

South End Press is a nonprofit, collectively run book publisher with more than 200 titles in print. Since our founding in 1977, we have tried to meet the needs of readers who are exploring, or are already committed to, the politics of radical social change. Our goal is to publish books that encourage critical thinking and constructive action on the key political, cultural, social, economic, and ecological issues shaping life in the United States and in the world. In this way, we hope to give expression to a wide diversity of democratic social movements and to provide an alternative to the products of corporate publishing.

Through the Institute for Social and Cultural Change, South End Press works with other political media projects—Alternative Radio; Speakout, a speakers' bureau; and *Z Magazine*—to expand access to information and critical analysis.

To order books, please send a check or money order to: South End Press, 7 Brookline Street, #1, Cambridge, MA 02139-4146. To order by credit card, call 1-800-533-8478. Please include $3.50 for postage and handling for the first book and 50 cents for each additional book.

Write or e-mail southend@southendpress.org for a free catalog, or visit our web site at http://www.southendpress.org.